Contemporary Studies
in Philosophical Idealism

Contemporary Studies
in Philosophical Idealism

Edited by

John Howie

and

Thomas O. Buford

CLAUDE STARK & CO.
CAPE COD, MASSACHUSETTS 02670

FIRST PRINTING

Printed in the United States of America

Library of Congress Cataloging in Publication Data

Contemporary studies in philosophical idealism.

    Essays published in honor of P. A. Bertocci.
    Includes index.
    CONTENTS: Reck, A. J. Idealism in American philosophy since 1900.–Rouner, L. S. The surveyor as hero.–Hocking, R. The personal dialectic of the impersonal [etc.]
    1. Idealism–Addresses, essays, lectures. 2. Religion–Philosophy–Addresses, essays, lectures. 3. Bertocci, Peter Anthony. 4. Bertocci, Peter Anthony–Bibliography. I. Howie, John. II. Buford, Thomas O., 1932- III. Bertocci, Peter Anthony.

B823.C66   141   74-29474

ISBN 0-89007-601-4

Contents

Preface

FOR MORE THAN A century idealism has been a major current in both British and American philosophy. It is a perspective that continues to affect any discussion of the main philosophical problems, and its contemporary spokesmen have an influence that is far-reaching. It has shown itself adaptable by appropriating insights from phenomenology and by responding constructively to criticisms offered by linguistic analysts, behaviorists and others. It has explored and continues to probe the nature of the self, including its identity, will, and power; the role of the teacher in education; the status of nature and the warrant for scientific knowledge; the function and meaning of mystical experience; and the possibility of survival. Such perennial problems often appear and reappear in intelligent conversations and, whether implicitly or explicitly, are never far from the center of philosophical discussion. The editors are proud to make available in this volume some of the best contemporary American and British thinking on these crucially important topics.

To the disciplined search for a meaningful understanding of these topics, together with their attendant problems, Professor Peter A. Bertocci has devoted the greater portion of his life as a teacher and scholar. It is therefore with distinct pleasure that these essays are published to honor him upon his retirement from Boston University as Borden Parker Bowne Professor of Philosophy.

In the preparation of this book the editors have had the support and encouragement of Furman University, Greenville, South Carolina, and Southern Illinois University, Carbondale, Illinois. Special thanks is due Claude Stark who has been unreserved in his generosity and unwavering in his interest.

John Howie

Thomas O. Buford

Contributors

ROBERT NELSON BECK, the founder and Editor of *Idealistic Studies*, is Professor of Philosophy and Chairman of the Department at Clark University. He received the A.B. degree from Clark and the A.M. and Ph.D. degrees from Boston University. He is the author of *Introduction to Philosophy* (with Edgar Sheffield Brightman), *Ethical Choice* (with J. B. Orr), and editor of *Perspectives in Philosophy* and *Ideas in America: Source Readings in the Intellectual History of the United States* (with G. N. Grob).

THOMAS O. BUFORD is Professor and Chairman of the Department of Philosophy at Furman University. He received the B.A. from North Texas State University, the B.D. from Southwest Baptist Theological Seminary, and the Ph.D. from Boston University. Subsequently he taught at Kentucky Southern College. He is the editor of *We Pass This Way But Once*, *Essays on Other Minds*, *Toward a Philosophy of Education*, and the author of articles in professional journals.

JOHN NIEMEYER FINDLAY is University Professor at Boston University. Previously he was Clark Professor of Moral Philosophy and Metaphysics at Yale University (1967-1972). He was Professor of Philosophy at the University of London, King's College, and held several university chairs in his native South Africa and in New Zealand. His publications include *Meinong's Theory of Objects and Values*; *Hegel, A Re-*

Examination; *Values and Intentions*; *Language, Mind and Value*; *The Discipline of the Cave*; *The Transcendence of the Cave*; *Logical Investigations* (translation of Husserl's work); *Axiological Ethics*; and *Ascent to the Absolute.*

ERROL EUSTACE HARRIS is Professor of Philosophy at Northwestern University. He received the B.A. and M.A. from Rhodes College, the Litt.B. from Oxford University and the Litt.D. from Witwatersrand University. He is the author of *The Survival of Political Man*; *Nature, Mind and Modern Science*; *Revelation through Reason*; *Foundations of Metaphysics in Science*; *Fundamentals of Philosophy*; and *Hypothesis and Perception.*

CHARLES HARTSHORNE is Professor of Philosophy at the University of Texas, Austin. He received the A.B., A.M. and Ph.D. degrees from Harvard University. He taught at the University of Chicago (1928-1955) and at Emory University for several years before assuming his present position. Among his many books and articles are *The Philosophy and Psychology of Sensation*, *Beyond Humanism*, *Man's Vision of God*, *The Divine Relativity*, *Reality as Social Process*, *The Logic of Perfection*, *Anselm's Discovery*, *A Natural Theology for Our Time*, and *Creative Synthesis and Philosophic Method.*

RICHARD BOYLE O'REILLY HOCKING is Professor Emeritus and former Chairman of the Department of Philosophy at Emory University. He received the B.S. and M.A. degrees from Harvard and the Ph.D. degree from Yale University. He taught at the University of Minnesota, Williams College, University of California (Los Angeles), and the University of Chicago before taking the position at Emory. He is joint author (with W. E. Hocking) of *Types of Philosophy*, and his other writings include "The Influence of Mathematics on Royce's Metaphysics," "Fanfare for Augustine," "Degrees of Historical Consciousness in Eastern Religious Thought," and "Event, Act and Presence."

JOHN HOWIE is Associate Professor and Assistant Director of Graduate Studies in the Philosophy Department, Southern Illinois University, Carbondale. He received the B.A. from Vanderbilt, the B.D. and M.A. degrees from Emory University, and the Ph.D. degree from Boston University. He has also studied at Cambridge University. His writings include "Is Violence Always Wrong?" "What Can Philosophy Contribute to the New Morality?" and "Metaphysical Elements of Creativity in the Philosophy of W. E. Hocking."

JOHN HILLMAN LAVELY is Professor of Philosophy and Chairman-Elect of the Department of Philosophy at Boston University. He has served previously as Chairman of the Department (1962-1967), Director of Graduate Studies in Philosophy (1967-1969), Editor of the *Philosophical Forum* (1955-1967), and Director of Undergraduate Studies (1970-1972). He taught at Albion College (1947-1951) earlier. He is the author of "Santayana's Thought as an Interpretation of History," "A Definition of Philosophy of History," "The Plight and Prospects of Metaphysics in an Age of Science," and two articles, "Personalism" and "Edgar Sheffield Brightman" in *The Encyclopedia of Philosophy* (Paul Edwards, Editor).

HYWEL DAVID LEWIS is Professor and Head of the Department of the History and Philosophy of Religion, King's College, University of London. He has served as Dean of the Faculty of Theology (1964-1968, 1970-1972) and Dean of the Faculty of Arts, King's College (1966-1968). He is Editor of The Muirhead Library of Philosophy and of *Religious Studies*. Among his many books are *Morals and the New Theology*, *Morals and Revelation*, *Contemporary British Philosophy*, Vol. III (editor), *Our Experience of God*, *Freedom and History*, *Clarity Is Not Enough* (editor), *Teach Yourself the Philosophy of Religion*, *World Religion* (with R. L. Slater), *Dreaming and Experience*, and *The Elusive Mind*.

RICHARD MARLON MILLARD is Director of Higher Education Services for the Education Commission of the States. Before assuming his present position he taught at Hofstra College, served as Chairman of the Department of Philosophy, and was Dean of the College of Liberal Arts of Boston University. He received the A.B. from DePauw University, and the M.A. and Ph.D. degrees from Boston University. He is co-author (with Peter A. Bertocci) of *Personality and the Good: Psychological and Ethical Perspectives* and author of "Value and Good in Aristotle's Metaphysics," "The Ghost of Eternalism in Whitehead's Theory of Value," "Space, Time, and Space-Time," "The Realistic Predicament," and other articles.

WALTER GEORGE MUELDER is Dean Emeritus of Boston University

School of Theology. He received the B.S. from Knox College and the
S.T.B. and Ph.D. degrees from Boston University. He has also taught
at Berea College and the University of Southern California. He is the
author of *Historical Outline of the Bible* (with E. S. Brightman),
Religion and Economic Responsibility, *In Every Place a Voice*, *Foundations of the Responsible Society*, *Methodism and Society in the
Twentieth Century*, and *Moral Law in Christian Social Ethics*. He is
co-editor of *Institutionalism and Church Unity* and *Development of
American Philosophy*.

WILLIAM NORMAN PITTENGER is Lecturer, King's College, Divinity
Faculty, Cambridge University. He received the S.T.B. degree from
General Theological Seminary (New York) and the S.T.M. and S.T.D.
from Berkeley Divinity School. Before assuming his present position
he served as instructor and Professor of Christian Apologetics at General
Theological Seminary (1945-1966). He is the author of many books
including *The Historic Faith and a Changing World*, *Man's Frustration
and Christian Conviction*, *The Faith of the Church* (with James A. Pike),
Christian Sacrifice, *The Principles and Practice of the Christian Faith*,
Christian View of Sexual Behavior, *Christian Affirmations*, *Theology
and Reality*, *Rethinking the Christian Message*, *The Christian Understanding of Human Nature*, *God in Process*, *Process Thought and
Christian Faith*, and *God's Way with Man*.

ANDREW JOSEPH RECK is Professor and Chairman of the Department
of Philosophy, Tulane University. He received the B.A. and M.A.
degrees from Tulane and the Ph.D. from Yale University. He has also
studied at the University of Paris and at the University of St. Andrews,
Scotland. He is the author of numerous articles and several books
including *Recent American Philosophy*, *The New American Philosophers:
An Exploration of Thought Since World War II*, *Introduction to William
James: An Essay and Selected Texts*, *Speculative Philosophy*, and
editor of the *Selected Writings of George H. Mead*.

LEROY S. ROUNER is Professor of Philosophical Theology, Boston
University School of Theology. He earned his undergraduate degree at
Harvard College, the B.D. at Union Theological Seminary, and the
Ph.D. in philosophy of religion at Columbia University. He also taught
for several years at the United Theological College in Bangalore, South
India. He is the author of *Within Human Experience: The Philosophy*

of *William Ernest Hocking*, and the editor of *Philosophy, Religion, and The Coming World Civilization.* He is a founding member of the Association for Asian and Comparative Philosophy and a frequent contributor to journals both in India and the United States.

JOHN EDWIN SMITH is Professor of Philosophy at Yale University, and has served as Chairman of the Philosophy Department at Yale. He completed his undergraduate work at Columbia University; he received the B.D. degree from Union Theological Seminary and the Ph.D. degree from Columbia. He taught for several years at Vassar and Barnard Colleges before going to Yale (1952). He is the author of *Experience and God, Philosophy of Religion, Reason and God: Encounters of Philosophy with Religion, Religion and Empiricism, Royce's Social Infinite: The Community of Interpretation, The Spirit of American Philosophy, Themes in American Philosophy,* and the editor of *Contemporary American Philosophy* and Jonathan Edwards' *Treatise Concerning Religious Affections.* He has translated R. Kroner's *Kant's Weltanschauung.*

Introduction

A ROUGH-HEWN CLASSIFICATION suggests that there are three major contemporary varieties of idealism: *Absolute idealism*, *panpsychistic idealism*, and *personalistic idealism*. This grouping is rough-hewn since the varieties overlap, and differences between them are often simply a matter of emphasis rather than doctrine. The varieties do, however, provide a key to understanding the different perspectives.

All three of these varieties of idealism stand in contrast to materialism, naturalism, existentialism, and logical positivism. What is distinctive of idealism, however, is its central focus and not primarily its differences from these other philosophical perspectives. All varieties of idealism acknowledge that mind and the contents of mind are in some sense ultimately real. Differences arise from diverse emphases concerning the nature of mind and its contents and the correlated implications of these divergences in terms of the knowing process and reality.

Absolute idealism is distinguished from its near relatives by its identification of reality with what is called the Absolute. The Absolute is usually conceived as a "whole," "totality," or "system" that is mental or spiritual in nature. The Absolute is one in the respect that all real objects, whether objects of cognition or valuation, fall within its system. Differences among Absolute idealists generally hinge on different views of the Absolute (for example, for Bradley, "sentience"; for Royce, "Self"). For present purposes these differences may be safely ignored. Two essays in the present volume reflect this general perspective: John E. Smith's essay, "Creativity in Royce's Philosophical Idealism," and Leroy Rouner's critical appraisal of Ernest Hocking's view of nature.

A second variety, panpsychistic idealism, is also represented in this volume. It holds that all things consist of "souls," "spirits," or "minds," or units of experiencing, with their relations and qualifications and communities or groupings. Differences within panpsychistic idealism usually arise because of divergent conceptions of the various kinds of subjects or "souls" and the relationships thought to obtain between them. Generally speaking, the Leibnizian monadology is considered the paradigm panpsychist theory. It is for this reason that Hartshorne's essay in the present volume comparing Leibniz and Whitehead, a prominent twentieth-century panpsychist, is especially interesting. In another essay Pittenger offers a fusion of a Whiteheadean view of the self with a basically Christian theological and ethical perspective.

The third major variety of idealism is personalistic idealism. It holds that the "person" is the basic explanatory concept because the person is ontologically ultimate. Reality is generally conceived in pluralistic and personal terms. Differences among personalistic idealists may arise because of different views of the person or the knowing process.

These three types of idealism provide a clue to understanding the historical development of this philosophical viewpoint in America and a broad framework for the perennial problems of the status of nature, the self, and knowledge with which it has been primarily concerned.

As Andrew Reck unfolds the story of American idealism, he considers the philosophies of individual American idealists and of those who have embraced idealist principles even though they have avoided the name. Warrant for this approach is derived from the insight that this philosophy, in virtually all its varieties, is a "reflective refinement" of man's experiences of nature, his fellow men and women, and himself. Among those significantly influenced by the Absolute idealism of Royce are Mary Whiton Calkins, John Elof Boodin, DeWitt H. Parker, Wilbur H. Urban, and, more recently, William Ernest Hocking and Brand Blanshard.

In the early twentieth century one of the most influential philosophers, strongly influenced by Absolute idealism, was James Edwin Creighton. He established the Sage School of Philosophy at Cornell University and assembled an able faculty of idealists including Frank Thilly, Ernest Albee, Elijah Jordan, and later, G. Watts Cunningham and Edwin S. Burtt. While head of the school, Creighton founded *The*

Philosophical Review, served as its editor until his death, and helped to organize the American Philosophical Association of which he was elected the first president, all of which contributed to the school's widespread influence.

From its outset personalistic idealism, which originated in Europe, has emphasized that the finite individual is the key to reality and has focused its attention on the value areas of human experience, especially the philosophy of religion. The most influential center of personalistic idealism or personalism was Boston University. Borden Parker Bowne, who served as professor of philosophy there for thirty-four years, taught that God, a Creator-Person, and the finite persons he created constitute reality. Two of Bowne's students did much to develop and spread personalism. Ralph Tyler Flewelling, who was educated at Boston University, joined the faculty of the University of Southern California. There he founded and directed the School of Philosophy and started the interdisciplinary journal, *The Personalist*, of which he served as editor until recent times. The other student of Bowne, who set forth a theistic personalism in more than a dozen books and more than one hundred fifty articles and essays, was Edgar Sheffield Brightman. To him personalism owes much of its recent development. He insisted that nature was one facet of God's experience: it is God expressing his will in action, controlling "the Given," and communicating with other selves or persons. A unique development in personalism by Brightman is the doctrine of a finite God. The finiteness of God is the passive element or "the Given" in his nature that does not respond fully to his deliberate choice.

In recent years personalistic idealism has been developed, amplified, and applied by Peter A. Bertocci, a student of Brightman and his successor in the Borden Parker Bowne chair of philosophy at Boston University.

Taking note of the growth in scientific knowledge, Leroy Rouner, a colleague of Dr. Bertocci, explores and develops Ernest Hocking's view of nature. Hocking, as Rouner indicates, was not convinced that Royce had solved the problem of solipsism, and he felt that his teacher's dialectic of interpretation made the lines of connection between persons always indirect. For Hocking, it is nature, properly conceived, that serves as the common coin of our communication with other selves. As what we think about, the objects of nature comprise the content of mind, and the objectivity of nature is grounded in the fact of our neighbor's common perception of those objects. Solipsism is overcome by the insight that the world of natural objects is the content of the common mind that the individual shares with his neighbor. The world of natural objects or nature is essentially an objective causal network of events, external to us, purposeless in its operations and without meaning.

To this view of nature Rouner raises serious objections. Man does not in fact experience nature as purposeless, but rather as having what may be called a contrary "natural purpose." Moreover, recent modifications of efficient causality broadly hint that Hocking's Newtonian, mechanistic view of nature is not adequate. Nor would recognition of some natural process in the physical world prevent us, as Hocking claims, from using the objects and forces of nature for our own ends. Rather, Rouner argues, such recognition would simply require a responsiveness to that natural purpose and an exercise of responsibility in integrating that purpose into our own human purposes.

Taking his cue from Emerson and following a broadly conceived historical approach, Richard Hocking rejects the Newtonian, mechanical view of nature and insists that nature is an embodiment of spirit, not inimical to essential human interests and development.

Through the centuries the term "nature" has had a progressively shrinking denotation. In its most inclusive meaning the term refers to "all that generates," including all things, persons, and God. Scholasticism reduced its scope to "all that receives existence," including all things and persons but not God. The scientific revolution of the seventeenth century reduced further the scope of its denotation to "all that is mechanical" (with the exception of human artifacts). This shrunken "nature" includes all things but not persons or God.

"The Romantic turn" (as Hocking appropriately labels Emerson's approach) involves the recognition that this apparently impersonal and amoral thing-world is the required opposite for the progressive moral expression and embodiment of freedom of persons. As the material field for the exercise of human will the impersonal thing-world is taken by persons as having a personal dialectic. From the other side, Hocking hints, "nature's creative process presents itself in the new light of a varied ascent to higher forms having progressively closer analogies to the free existence of persons." Ample evidence for this ascent is found in contemporary animal ecology and sociology. Granted the apparent goal of this progressive development of nature, its dialectic can be appropriately called personal.

The Romantic turn in this dialectic of the impersonal receives its completion from existential philosophy. That philosophy insists upon the twofold insight that being a person means being situated in the world and being in the presence of others. To be in the presence of others is to be incarnate, or to have a body in nature. Understood reflectively, nature's impersonal or neutral developments are rather "the testimony of an infinite presence making itself felt to the community of finite persons."

Errol Harris is also concerned about our philosophical view of nature. Instead of taking a comprehensive view of nature, he calls our attention to the specific problem of the status of nature taken as the object of study for science. He defends the objectivity of scientific knowledge against its recent detractors, notably Karl Popper, Husserl, Heidegger, Kuhn, and Feyerabend.

These philosophers have called into question both former supports of the reliability of scientific knowledge: its mathematical reasoning and the empirical character of its data. The upshot of the criticisms is that discovery is explained psychologically and science itself is a subjective, albeit sometimes conventional phenomenon. For changes in scientific views and progress in science, generally, no rational justification can be given. The effect of these doctrines is to relativize and subjectivize science.

Feyerabend, carrying the critical thrust to its completion, holds that scientific theories are simply products of the creative imagination. If this is true, there is no reasonable basis for the adoption of any theory over any other. Criteria of acceptance or rejection become simply a matter of taste just as in literature and art.

Such a viewpoint, Harris notes critically, involves a thoroughgoing skepticism that undercuts its own foundation. If all scientific knowledge is theory-laden and subjective, there can be no standards for truth and falsehood. Unless we acknowledge some objective and defensible conception of truth, no statement can be meaningfully made.

But there is no need to yield to relativism and subjectivism since a viable account of objectivity can be given. Science is, after all, simply a further developed systematization of the organization of experience, beginning in perception and developing in commonsense practice. When theories come into collision with each other, either adjustments are made within the system or the entire system may need to be reorganized. Comprehensive coherence, in any case, is the criterion for a satisfactory theory. The elements or relevant aspects are integrated without mutual conflict or inconsistency so that they fit with the background knowledge which gives them contextual meaning. Such coherence is "the final touchstone of objectivity" and the foundation for any notion of scientific progress.

Charles Hartshorne in his essay gives a comparison and critical appraisal of two panpsychistic idealists, Whitehead and Leibniz. Without ignoring their differences, he lists and explains in considerable detail the metaphysical beliefs that were common to both of these philosophers. Among these common beliefs are the insistence that neither being or becoming are "unreal" or "mere appearance," that definite unit-realities are subjects in the psychical, logical, and ontological respects, "that God exists and is incomparably exalted above all other individuals, being alone cosmic, primordial, and everlasting in influence, incorruptible, ideally wise and beneficent, and the 'ground of order,'" and that, in different ways, actuality is numerically infinite. Such common beliefs, he suggests, may be indicative "of truths neutral to the advances of knowledge and insight" that occurred in the two hundred fifty years that separate the two thinkers.

Although the changes Whitehead makes in the Leibnizian system are generally "in the direction of good sense and greater intelligibility," there are two aspects in which Leibniz has the advantage over Whitehead: recognition of the importance of the *a priori* and, correlatively, the limitations of the empirical, and insight into the methodological difficulty of applying to physics, psychology, and physiology the metaphysical truth that ultimate explanations must be psychical.

The most impressive results of the comparison are the similarities between the two philosophers and the "striking fact" that Whitehead and Leibniz (and Peirce) agree that only mind can be intelligible to itself and be the source of existence. This insight opens the possibility for an in-depth understanding of the world.

A topic of long-standing interest to most of those with idealist sympathies is religious knowledge: its meaning and importance for the religious life and development of the individual. While acknowledging that Bertocci has stimulated his reflections on religious experience, John Lavely argues that religious experience has evidential import even though it is not as such cognitive. What is there about such experience that enables us to speak of it as factual or evidential? Lavely suggests that a "subtle decoding" of those features of religious experience described as ineffable, unique, and immediate will disclose its evidential warrant.

"Ineffability" refers to an intrinsic religious dimension that can be neither derived from something else nor translated without remainder into anything else. "Ineffable" suggests that the experience is unutterable as an inexpressible love requiring expression. It may be that the experience is ineffable because of its uniqueness. The uniqueness of the experience refers to its "supremely normative character," or "wholeness as the measure of fulfillment" together with the implicit acknowledgment that such fulfillment is intelligible only as a function of a transaction with reality. The immediacy of religious experience attests to something at the time given and to its reception by the experient.

The terms "ineffable," "unique," and "immediate," almost invariably used to describe religious experience, suggest that religious experience is evidential even though it is not an independent and indubitable source of religious knowledge.

Carrying the reasoning forward another step, John Findlay boldly contends that "dynamic mysticism" is not only intelligible but deeply rational since it helps us account for present instances of self-transcendence, explains the rationality of our admittedly rational enterprises, and hints that life after death may carry further "decorporealization and departicularization."

Findlay cautions that from the standpoint of human experience, the mystical must not be conceived as a concept resulting from the exercise of philosophical imagination or from an expression of technical jargon which attempts to fuse traits that we do not ordinarily observe as belonging together. Rather, the mystical is a phenomenon that is vividly expressed in certain forms of human speech, behavior and experience. Occurring again and again, it possesses a uniformity that puts its forms, regardless of geography, history, and culture, into a few salient types. The various traits of mysticism fit together with a natural-ness that seems to suggest an inherent coherence. "Mysticism," Findlay explains, "is an intellectual-affective state characterized [although not described] by the suggested fusion or vanishing of the diverse things we ordinarily acknowledge." This unity is often spoken of as a deep identity and oneness with all things in such a manner that the contours of separateness are temporarily obliterated. The affective atmosphere of such experience is a sense of indescribable blessedness or ecstasy.

The contrast between the mystical state of consciousness and ordi-nary conscious awareness is both odd and stark. For the man of under-standing it gives to mystical utterances the appearance of logical contradiction. The use of self-contradictory language by the mystic, however, may simply reflect his inability to meet the novel demands of some radically transformed situation.

Mystical views are usually accompanied by a schema of steps or stages leading from the extreme separation and disconnection of normal experiences to a "point of convergence," unity, and interpenetration. There is a pattern or an *a priori* structure in the "ascent" to this mystical state and in the "descent" to the diversified world of ordinary experience. The "transitional spectrum" of ascent and descent may offer insight about the state of men and women and the world in which they live.

Many commonplace matters, Findlay indicates, suggest that the unity insistently affirmed by the mystic is meaningful. First, there is a unity and continuity of the two great media, space and time. These media, in addition to fostering gulfs and setting limits, link all things in an unbroken fashion with each other. Their continuity is discerned in the fact that they have to be accepted as totalities rather than aggregates of disparate parts. Points, instants, lines, and surfaces are convenient (often even conventional) fictions employed operationally upon the media. Moreover, the great media require the integrative action of universals that we label the "natures" of the enduring entities and "species." Organisms and minds also provide support for the mystic's theme of unity and interconnectedness since organisms have no invariant functions and may modify themselves to suit the environment.

The most remarkable instances of self-transcendence are those in which we understand the experiences and hopes of others and subordinate our own interests and those of other particular beings to the interests of conscious beings in general.

The rationality of mysticism seems (so Findlay argues) to require and draw support from a belief in life after death. A life after the death of the body would be simply an extrapolation or projection of the varied facets of the mind's present self-transcendence. It would carry further "the process of decorporealization and departicularization." Mysticism is rational, moreover, because it brings to clear consciousness our obscure insights into the nature of things and persons and because "it explains why our admittedly rational enterprises are rational." It serves as a coordinating point for our rational thought and life.

In "The Belief in Life After Death," Hywel Lewis bases his position on two primary allegiances: a profound admiration for Plato as a philosophical thinker and a commitment to Christ. He notes at the outset that there are two main ways in which a belief may be held: we may adhere to it even though the evidence for it is not overwhelming and perhaps not even very strong, or we may affirm it with only "one side of our minds." Holding a belief in the second manner, one may fervently affirm it at one time and reject or disregard it with equal intensity at another.

The deeper truth seems to be that beliefs need to be cultivated. Not at all an exercise in wishful thinking, this cultivation requires intellectual effort to dispel doubt, to discover new bases of evidence, and to renew belief. It also requires a certain disposition and a period of living with the evidence which can nourish spiritual awareness and discernment. Meditation has its requirements and discipline. In the fullness of meditation, involving both thought and practice, faith may be renewed.

True religion offers a valuable corrective to Plato's view of the immortality of the soul. It provides an emphasis upon the particular and specific, while Plato's view stressed the eternal and impersonal aspects of things. Religion accomplishes this emphasis through revelation in which the transcendent discloses itself through a particular involvement in a concrete situation. Revelation bestows immeasurable worth on particular things and persons. The worth so bestowed seems to put the elimination of any person out of the question. The Christian religion claims that God's love comes to a finality of fulfillment in the sacrifice of Christ; the celebration of this sacrifice in holy communion gives us some assurance that death is not ultimately final. It is an integral part of the Christian expectation (ultimately grounded in faith) that we shall continue to live with a transformed quality of life. This belief is tied to the work and person of Christ in their fullness.

While he acknowledges the contributions Bertocci has made to our understanding of the self, Norman Pittenger invites us to consider carefully what process philosophy of the Whiteheadean variety has to say about the self. The two admitted bases of Pittenger's perspective are a Whiteheadean philosophical approach and Christianity. He intends to fuse both into a coherent account of as many facts as possible. Neither base, however, is to be taken as fixed or unalterable. The stress in the Whiteheadean process view is upon the evolving and changing cosmos, the societal quality of that cosmos (manifest in "prehensions"), the composition of the universe as essentially foci of energy routed toward realizing potentialities, and the fundamental force of the universe conceived as "persuasion" or love. Christianity here joins with process metaphysics. It holds that "through genuine human loving to the point of self-giving death, cosmic love is believed to be actively at work."

In the Whiteheadean view each person is "a routing of events or occasions." We cannot say that a man or woman has a soul if it be conceived as something of a different order and separate from the series of routings or occasions. To do so (as Pittenger conceives the matter) is to open oneself to the charge made by Ryle of "the ghost in the machine." Rather, Pittenger suggests that we consider carefully what we mean by human identity. Human identity is the direction and continuity of the routing of the series. By "subjective aim" the future lures the entities in their routing. In this luring, the past, the present, and the future are held together by prehensions. The ability to know and to feel what takes place distinguishes human routings from all other finite routings in the cosmos. Man has a conscious sense of identity in the consecutive instances. It is in this respect that a human as a self is a distinctive emergent. And the self is both a mind and a body; it is psychosomatic in constitution.

The personhood of the self is a development that occurs in social relations. The social belonging of mankind is as integral to his being as his physiology.

The answer to the question "What is man's essential purpose?" is found, for Pittenger, in the Christian facet of his philosophy. From the Christian perspective, "to become human is to become a lover." Being a lover means "conscious giving-and-receiving, mutuality, sharing, participation, and union which does not destroy either partner but brings each to his finest reach of development." In other words, "man is being created, by his own creative activity in decision as he responds to the lure of cosmic Love, towards the image of God who is love."

In "The Riddles of Behaviorism" John Howie explores some of the problems inherent in B. F. Skinner's behavioristic view of consciousness. Behavioristic methodology is shown to be at odds with the principal aims of behaviorism. The behavioristic method is itself objectionable since it claims to be *the* approach, has purposes that are ethically indefensible, and is incompatible with the major conclusions endorsed by the behaviorists themselves.

Four riddles make the behavioristic view of consciousness philosophically untenable. First, there is the odd circumstance that no behaviorist actually behaves as though his own theory were true. Taking one by one the actual contents of consciousness from a behavioristic approach, the critic discovers that the behaviorist does not act in relation to sensations, feelings, ideas, and volitions in a manner that lends support to his theory. A second puzzle more completely confounds the behaviorist. His method of appealing to observation and experimental practices presupposes the reality of the consciousness which he repeatedly denies. Third, behaviorists (especially Skinner) are in the habit of appealing to "survival value" as "the only value." The paradox is that survival can have no value at all apart from the reality of a consciousness whose very existence is repudiated. A fourth riddle is the presumption of the behaviorist that the goals of "independence" and "creativity" for persons can be attained through the meticulous application of a technology of behavior. It is a deep irony that in their enthusiastic endorsement of such goals they espouse the very means that make their attainment unmistakably impossible.

In "Will" Robert Beck examines a key aspect of Bertocci's idealistic notion of self in the light shed by recent philosophical developments, especially the forthright criticisms of Gilbert Ryle. Ryle rejects the notion of will, claiming that it is grounded in false assumptions about the reality and causal efficacy of mental states and processes.

Noting that Ryle's objections to will carry little argumentative force, Beck hints that they may reflect a cruder behaviorism than even Ryle would acknowledge and a "meaning-is-use" doctrine that Findlay has clearly refuted. Ryle contends that people do not describe human behavior in terms of "willing" because there is no class of predicates through which to express the description. Findlay has argued success-fully that words may refer to first-personal and inner experiences (such as willing) as well as to third-personal and outer experiences. The reason that one does not ordinarily refer to acts of willing is simply that willing (unlike physical actions) enters as an essential ingredient into all actions. The Rylean notion of "meaning-is-use" blithely ignores this fact.

Leaving aside a fully adequate defense for the existence of mental acts and even acts of willing, Beck proposes to set forth a more adequate phenomenology of will by modifying Bertocci's view when necessary.

For convenience and brevity he explains Bertocci's understanding of will under four headings: will agency, will power, freedom, and obliga-tion. Will agency is the qualitatively unique experience of effort. The making of an effort cannot be reduced to the activity of wanting, desiring, or feeling. It is initiative put forth in relation to a specific approved goal or objective. Will power, as distinct from will agency, is the measure and extent of control exerted by the self in view of external (physical conditions and situations) and internal (habits, attitudes, and drives) limiting factors. Freedom, for Bertocci, is a correlative of the act of willing itself. It is discovered through a phenomenological examina-tion of experience in acts of choice. Obligation as an experience is qualitatively unique and irreducible. As experienced, "oughting" feels different from wanting, liking, or being compelled. Oughting enters an experience of willing only in a choice situation. And there is no conscious choice without an ought being involved.

Beck, in opposition to Bertocci, insists that willing needs to be conceived more broadly as expressive activity of the self rather than merely as effort or striving. Willing, unlike striving, always involves some immediate consciousness of self. This modified view of willing requires that choosing be distinguished from willing as a special subcase of it: and this means that there may literally be instances of willing where there is no choosing. Such a conception of willing, Beck explains, also involves modifications in Bertocci's views of freedom and obligation and in the relation of thought to willing.

In "Creativity in Royce's Philosophical Idealism" John E. Smith claims that Royce's Absolute idealism is a voluntarism that allows for expressions of individual will and purpose. Creativity, in contrast to reaction, is to be understood as "a constructive response" which involves appraisal, understanding, and judgment. Unlike bare repetition and chaotic novelty, it means to realize significant novelty as bearing on a projected aim or goal.

Smith discusses creativity in relation to three topics found in Royce's philosophy: a willful action that transcends the model it imitates, the metaphysical concept of the individual who has a creative will, and the logic of interpretation that expresses itself in the willful activity of establishing understanding for the mediation of socially detrimental conflicts. All three topics are essentially connected to Royce's notion of will. By "will" Royce means the life-plan, together with the purposes and series of acts which realize subservient aims within the scope of that life-plan, and the "*nisus*" toward self-realization of a free individual. The will is the whole inner life including the longing, desiring, feeling, and striving of the individual.

Imitation involves the recognition that the acts to be emulated belong to another and the discovery as one imitates these acts that their control lies within oneself. It acquaints us with our own will. The will is created through its expression of the powers, talents, and capabilities of the individual. Every act of imitation is a kind of experimental endeavor since it involves the construction of an act that stands between the individual's previous acts and the acts of the model. Through imitation as an exploratory activity the self creates by augmenting its own growth. In thus adding to the repertoire of its own will it adds to its own reality.

From an ethical perspective the being of the self is a task to be performed, a purpose to be fulfilled. From the metaphysical perspective this same realizing of being is an expression of the divine will in human form. The ethical task is to be an individual and unique self, and in being individual and unique the will of the individual is fulfilling the purpose of the finite self and the divine intent for that individual.

Interpretation, a triadic relationship, is a creative endeavor since it attempts to get the individual outside the circle of his own ideas and experience and, through understanding, into the thought and experience of another person. When it is successful, a community of understanding, grounded in a relationship to the same third term, comes into being.

Traditionally idealists have not been reluctant to apply their philosophical perspective to man's crucial problems. Three essays in this volume are applications of idealistic insights to the newly developing nations, to the nature of education, and to the pivotal role of the teacher in education.

Walter Muelder gives a critical appraisal of our understanding of third world ideologies of development in terms of personal and cultural autonomy. He indicates sharp contrasts and raises basic issues concerning the way development in the new nations is perceived and studied in Western countries and concerning the way developing nations view self and self-determination.

As a frame of reference for the discussion Muelder accepts Sigmund's definition of ideology as a belief that evokes a commitment by leaders and followers issuing into action that will bring about a new society conforming to goals. It functions to enable a people to develop through a period of modernization. The ideologies of the developing nations cluster around the goals of "modernizing nationalism."

"Modernizing nationalism" at its best is a fusion of ancient goals and values with modern aspirations. Focusing on national identity, it calls for a unity of meaning and value that can reshape the nation through a common spirit and that implies national pluralism. Troeltsch's view of personality is relevant to "modernizing nationalism" if it is understood in a dynamic way as self-consciousness leading to a "new" man. Its relevance is not discounted even if nationalism be conceived in terms of revolution rather than evolution.

Cultural autonomy has an important function in the ideologies of emerging nations. As a fulcrum for rallying the spirit of independence, it provides the basis for further development through the awareness of a heritage of common values. It appeals to habits, customs, and historical traditions to create a national identity.

Conflicts between cultural autonomy and the goals of modernizing nationalism may create a severe crisis for the newly emerging nation. This conflict is perhaps nowhere more apparent than in the economic sphere. The attempt to transplant Western economic theory with its general concepts of consumption, saving, production, unemployment, investment, output, etc., may be entirely misguided. To transfer technology, with the apparent aim of modernization, may be more a projection of the economic needs of the givers than a response to the needs of the receivers.

"Modernization which is specifically human calls for and requires a cultural transformation whereby the people develop and with that development transform the total social process." In such modernization the notion of cultural autonomy and the person (including human dignity) are indispensable aspects.

Another pressing problem is how teachers should think of themselves and the comprehensive goal of education. The two essays by Buford and Millard probe these difficult issues.

Holding that the current attack on the humanities in the university curriculum is nothing less than an attack on teaching itself, Thomas Buford takes issue with Arrowsmith's claim that what the crisis requires is "Socratic teachers." Such teachers would presumably be those who emulated the Socratic model of the teacher.

Careful examination of two Platonic dialogues, the *Laches* and *Symposium*, will clarify the meaning of the Socratic model. The gist of the model is that the teacher is to embody in life that which he teaches. The Socratic teacher is the one whose "words fit his deeds," and who, above all men, is worthy of emulation. Two Socratic paradoxes, virtue is knowledge, and no man intentionally does evil, shed additional light on the meaning of the deeds-words criterion.

Buford argues that the "Socratic teacher-model" is not the standard by which to distinguish a good teacher from a bad one. If the deeds-words criterion depends upon acceptance of the paradoxes, one could criticize the criterion by showing that the paradoxes do not actually hold. The paradox that virtue is knowledge flies in the face of the fact that frequently people do know what is best and yet do not act virtuously. The paradox that no man intentionally does evil overlooks the fact of our moral experience that some evil is a result of a failure of will not traceable to ignorance.

Even if it be granted that the deeds-words criterion does not depend upon acceptance of the paradoxes, Arrowsmith's remedy is still subject to telling criticism. Is being a good man a necessary or sufficient condition for being a good teacher? It is not a necessary condition since a man may be virtuous and yet not have mastered his discipline and therefore be unable to teach effectively. Conversely, a man may have mastered his discipline and be able to teach well without being virtuous.

Suppose that it is necessary for a good teacher of a discipline to be a virtuous man. Even on this supposition, difficulties would arise. At least two troublesome questions with undesirable implications must be answered. How does one decide which ethical ideal to adopt and apply? And how does one determine the competence of the teacher by reference to that ideal? In view of present quandaries in philosophical discussion, the first question does not admit a definitive answer. But even if an answer to the first question were found, any answer to the second question would involve intolerable restrictions on academic freedom and probably entail in the long run a degrading of the humanities.

Richard Millard contends in his essay that the goal of education needs to be conceived as an integration of mutually supplementary technical and liberal components. A newly modified conception of vocation would provide focus for this integration. A focus that transcends and combines these emphases would, as its essential function, enable the individual to acquire (in Whitehead's apt phrase) "the art of utilization of knowledge."

Millard believes that the evolution which higher education has undergone in the United States might fairly be said to be characterized by the tensions clustering around the emphases on technical and liberal education. Unfortunately the two emphases have often been conceived in mutually exclusive fashion.

Several crucial problems confronting higher education today are the reduced confidence in universities in the wake of the student unrest of the 1960s and early 1970s, unanswered fundamental questions concerning relevance, direction, and purposes of higher education, frequent and insistent demands for innovation and change, rising costs without correlated increased productivity, insistence by the state and federal governments upon greater financial and educational accountability, and the projected continual decline in college-age population (eighteen to twenty-one years of age) from the late 1970s through the turn of the century coupled with the increasingly apparent shift to enrollment in community colleges.

Consider one problem confronting higher education today. Apparently, there is an increasing interest among adults in some form of continuing education. This situation may provide an opportunity for institutions, alert to the challenge, to continue to serve effectively the educational needs of the population. It could also foster, when coupled with tight budgets and decreasing enrollments of traditional college age students, a kind of bitter interinstitutional competition which would further erode public confidence and homogenize educational institutions.

Facing problems of this sort, the question of the goal of higher education assumes magnified importance. Millard states that we must recognize that the central goal of education is vocation. By vocation, he explains, is meant "an involvement in and preparation for life work, life plan, life style." It means taking seriously Whitehead's emphasis on "the art of utilization of knowledge," and Plato's recognition that education must be adapted to a variety of needs and abilities and that it can serve as the process through which individuals discover what their interests, needs, and abilities actually are. Millard explains that taking vocation in this broad sense as the focus for education "provides a continuing yet flexible context for what Dr. Bertocci calls orchestrating the symphony of values, and through the society of vocations and their mutual yet shifting complementation provides the social context for harmonizing the principles of individualism and altruism."

With vocation as central, lifelong learning becomes an essential characteristic of higher education. Moreover, invidious comparisons between institutions and programs are seen to be expressions of a perverse demand for homogeneity oblivious to the diversity of vocations, of human interests, needs, and societal requirements. Only a healthy pluralism of complementary higher educational institutions with vocation as their major aim can meet the egalitarian and utilitarian needs of postsecondary education in this country in the years ahead.

These essays show that idealism is a lively and appealing approach to the perennial questions of man: Who am I? What ought I to do? What is my place in the nature of things? It is hoped that the reader will draw from them insights into present problems and find incentive for further reflection.

John Howie
Thomas O. Buford

Idealism in American Philosophy since 1900

Andrew J. Reck

INTRODUCTION

IDEALISM IS THAT TYPE of philosophy which affirms mind and its contents as ultimate reality. The phrase "mind and its contents" embraces a multitude of conceptions pertaining to spirit, consciousness, self, person, ideas, and values. Elsewhere I have distinguished idealism from three rival types of philosophy: realism, materialism, and process philosophy, each of which, I contended, is founded on a different conception or intuition of being.[1] In taking mind and its contents to be ultimately or really real, the idealist is inclined to esteem the values man cherishes not only as values which ought to be, but also as values metaphysically and cosmologically central in the universe. This is not to deny that idealists may, like Schopenhauer, be pessimistic. Indeed, perhaps only idealists are entitled to adopt optimism and pessimism as moods appropriate to the nature of the world. Nevertheless, idealists are characteristically optimistic; they are convinced that the world exhibits a teleology or design favorable to human values, that purposiveness pervades the cosmic process, that, in some fundamental way, mind guides the events and actions within the world toward the attainment of desirable ends. A rather inclusive, non-technical definition of idealism has been suggested by Maurice Mandelbaum, who described it as the belief that "within natural human experience one can find the clue to an understanding of the ultimate nature of reality, and this clue is revealed through those traits which distinguish man as a spiritual being."[2]

The history of idealism in America since 1900 may be construed negatively as the story of opposition and revolt. Twentieth-century American idealists have carried on the nineteenth-century idealist rejection of scientific naturalism in behalf of moral, aesthetic, and religious values. Meanwhile many—perhaps most—recent idealists have revolted against their heritage of Absolute idealism, viewing it as inimical to the being of finite human persons. Thus it is possible to interpret twentieth-century idealism as primarily defensive and divided. This interpretation, however, would miss the creative aspect of idealism from the turn of the century to the present.

Everywhere the influence of idealism on recent American philosophy is conspicuous. While among the so-called "classic six" American philosophers Josiah Royce alone avowed himself an idealist, four others have, at times, clearly moved within the fold. In his paper, "The Architecture of Theories" (1891), Charles Peirce declared: "The one intelligible theory of the universe is that of objective idealism, that matter is effete mind, inveterate habits becoming physical laws."[3] Even for a while William James succumbed to idealism when he yielded to the cogency of Royce's argument from error to the Absolute Mind.[4] John Dewey, America's leading exponent of pragmatic naturalism, began his career as a Hegelian; he consequently titled his intellectual autobiography "From Absolutism to Experimentalism" (1930).[5] And Alfred North Whitehead, although strictly classifiable as a process philosopher, displayed in his thought such affinities to idealism that he has been hailed as a "new idealist" by R. F. Alfred Hoernlé in the essay, "The Revival of Idealism in the United States," published in the cooperative volume, *Contemporary Idealism in America* (1932).[6] Only George Santayana might seem to have escaped the taint of idealism. Yet Santayana wrote his senior thesis at Harvard on Emerson and his doctoral dissertation on Lotze; throughout his life he grappled with transcendentalism; and the two most interesting volumes in his four-volume anthology are devoted to the realms of essence and of spirit.[7]

The plot of idealism in America in the twentieth century thickens and the cast of characters expands when attention is turned to those thinkers who have proudly styled themselves idealists or have emphatically allied themselves with idealist principles even when avoiding the name. The story of American idealism will be told by considering the philosophies of particular American idealists. There is a special propriety to tracing the development of idealism in terms of the contributions of individual thinkers, for idealism, more than its rival philosophical types, tends to esteem philosophy, as Hartley Burr Alexander has said,

> . . . to be, in the nature of things, ·necessarily more or less autobiographical: the reflective refinement out of the dross of a man's diurnal experience,—be it of nature, be it of men, be it of men's souls as portrayed in books,—of some form-giving character which is essential confession.[8]

ABSOLUTE IDEALISM AND ITS PROGENY

Idealism in the late nineteenth century focused on the Absolute, defined as an objective Mind which, though individual, embraces all other beings. The doctrine of the Absolute had originated earlier in the century, in the philosophies of Fichte, Schelling, and Hegel. It served to distinguish their idealism from those forms of idealism, such as Berkeley's, which were bound to the finite individual consciousness. In the last quarter of the nineteenth century Absolute idealism was transplanted from German to Anglo-American philosophy. Josiah Royce illustrates the problem which beset idealist philosophers at the end of the century—namely, the problem of relating the Absolute to finite personal minds. The challenges confronted by Royce's philosophy set the stage for American idealism in the twentieth century.

Josiah Royce (1855-1916)

Royce's adherence to Absolute idealism is unqualified in his early book, *The Religious Aspect of Philosophy* (1885). In this work Royce argued from the finitude of human experience to the existence of the Absolute. Although the book centers on moral and religious issues, discerning in the moral struggles of finite persons a universal will which is the Absolute in its moral guise, it is most remarkable for its epistemological argument for the Absolute. According to this argument, the fact of error indicates the existence of an Absolute Mind which compares every idea with the object it intends. The Absolute embraces the erroneous idea in the finite mind and also its intended object. As Royce said:

> All the many Beyonds, which single significant judgments seem vaguely and separately to postulate, are present as fully realized

intended objects to the unity of an all-inclusive, absolutely clear, universal, and conscious thought, of which all judgments, true or false, are but fragments, the whole being at once Absolute Truth and Absolute Knowledge.[9]

Royce's argument for Absolutism seemed so formidable that, as mentioned above, the inveterate pluralist, William James, momentarily yielded to it.

Nevertheless, other idealists raised serious criticisms and objections which compelled Royce to modify his position. The "Great Debate," as it was reported at the time, took place in the Philosophical Union of the University of California at Berkeley in 1895. Royce's Absolute—that is to say, his conception of God as an Absolute Experience which is related to our experience as an organic whole to its own fragments—was subjected to critique by Sidney E. Mezes, Joseph Le Conte, and George Holmes Howison. Presiding over the discussion, which he had arranged himself, Howison put the crucial questions to Royce and supplied answers which pointed the future direction of idealism in America. Howison asked:

> *Whose* omniscience is it that judges the ignorance to be real?—*whose* absolute experience pronounces the less organized experience to be really fallacious? [He answered:] Well,—whosoever it may be, it is certainly acting in and through my judgment, if I am the thinker of that argument; and in every case it is *I* who pronounce sentence on myself as really ignorant, or on my limited experience as fallacious . . . Is it not plain that *I* . . . am the sole authority?[10]

Howison raised the same kind of objection to Royce's monistic account of moral experience. He said:

> If the Infinite Self *includes* us all, and all our experiences,—sensations and sins, as well as the rest,—in the unity of one life, and includes us and them *directly*; if there is but one and the same final Self for us each and all; then, with a literalness indeed appalling, He is we, and we are He; nay, He is *I*, and *I* am He . . . If "He is I," is not He the sole real agent?[11]

Although Royce never explicitly conceded the cogency of Howison's arguments, his own philosophy took a turn which may be construed as an attempt to accommodate his monistic absolutism to the pluralistic requirements of finite individuals. In *The World and the Individual* (1899), Royce maintained that each finite individual is not merely a part of a greater system but is also a representation of the Absolute. For the Absolute is pictured as a self-representative system whose acts of iteration, each a finite individual with his own uniqueness and representational capacity, are infinite. Royce's final masterpiece, *The Problem of Christianity* (1913), pressed further his endeavor to reconcile pluralism and monism, to explain the relation of the many (finite individuals) and the one (the Absolute). Interpretation was the principle Royce employed, a principle he derived from Charles Sanders Peirce. The simple activity of interpreting a text illustrates a triadic relationship between the text, the interpreter, and those to whom the interpretation is addressed. The communication of meaning presupposes a community, at first simply a community of interpreters, but ultimately the Beloved Community in which every individual knows every other, all individuals are bound together by the love or loyalty that accompanies self-knowledge in the knowledge of others, and every one participates in the will to interpret, whose form is God or the Absolute.

James Edwin Creighton (1861-1924)

Despite Royce's pre-eminence at the beginning of the century as an American idealist, he never attained at Harvard University what Borden Parker Bowne at Boston University and James Edwin Creighton at Cornell University achieved—namely, the establishment of a school. In 1892 Creighton became head of the Sage School of Philosophy at Cornell, assembling a faculty of idealists such as Frank Thilly, William A. Hammond, Ernest Albee, and, later, G. Watts Cunningham and E. S. Burtt. Further, in 1892 he and Jacob Gould Sherman founded the *Philosophical Review*, and he served as its editor until his death. In 1902, through his initiative, the American Philosophical Association was formed, electing him its first president. In justifying the formation of the Association Creighton appealed to the idealist thesis that mind is social and the intellect in isolation is infertile.

Creighton sought to distinguish his type of idealism from mentalism. The idealistic claim of mentalism stems from its assertion that everything is "mental in character—of the content of mind, or of the substance of mind."[12] Yet mentalism fails to be genuinely idealistic, because it simply carries the outer order of things into the mind, employing the same existential categories as realism does, and even when it acknowledges the Absolute, it regards the Absolute as a magnified psychological consciousness. Following Bosanquet, Creighton termed his idealism "speculative." Speculative idealism, he said, is "the conscious effort to understand things as they are: to see things and their relations, reality in its concrete significance, without feeling the need of going behind this insight to explain, as it were, how reality is made."[13] While speculative idealism takes its stand within experience and does not try to go behind experience, it never reduces experience to self-enclosed independent centers, but rather deems experience to constitute a system. For Creighton, "the objective system of experience" is at once "my experience, the experience of my fellow men, and the nature of reality."[14] It is, moreover, "the order of the universe, or what is the same thing, the order of intelligence."[15]

Mary Whiton Calkins (1863-1930)

Mary Whiton Calkins was, in her own words, an "absolutistic personalist." Her philosophy owes as much to William James as to Josiah Royce. An idealist of the Berkeleyan stripe, she adhered to the mentalism which Creighton rejected. Calkins formulated her philosophical creed in four articles: (1) "The universe contains distinctively mental realities; it may or may not also contain non-mental entities, but in any case irreducibly mental entities exist."[16] (2) The directly observed mental phenomena are "not percepts, thoughts, emotions, and volitions in unending succession, but rather perceiving, thinking, feeling, and willing self or selves."[17] (3) "The universe is through and through mental in character, . . . all that is real is ultimately mental, and accordingly personal, in nature."[18] (4) "The universe literally is one all-including (and accordingly complete) self of which all the lesser selves are genuine and identical parts, or members."[19]

By "self" Calkins meant "a complex, unique, more-than-momentary (or persistent), yet changing entity, conscious of (and so related to) an environment."[20] By "all-including self" she meant an Absolute Self which includes everything, no matter how trivial, futile, and base, and which, being all-inclusive, is ultimately changeless. No simple aggregate of parts, the Absolute Self is a whole. It is also a conscious personal being.

John Elof Boodin (1869-1950)

John Elof Boodin elaborated a system of idealism based on modern science. "The only key we have to reality," he declared, "is what reality must be taken as in the progressive realization of the purposes of human nature."[21] At the same time he insisted that, to be vital, philosophy must keep in close touch with science.

A graduate of Harvard University, where he prepared his doctoral dissertation under Royce, Boodin early displayed his originality of thought. His first major publication, *Time and Reality* (1904), taking off from his doctoral dissertation, presented a remarkable theory of time as a negative factor in the cosmos. Time as dynamic nonbeing which "creeps in" is Boodin's counterpoint to his mentor's timeless Absolute.

Idealism is paramount in Boodin's cosmology. On empirical grounds and in consonance with the natural sciences, Boodin subscribed to the view that evolution pervades the cosmos. But he subordinated evolution to a cosmic structure; evolution occurs in a world structured by permanent coexistent levels of energy. Calling his position "cosmic idealism," Boodin maintained that in the flux of matter, form (Spirit or God) exercises control and direction, guaranteeing the preservation and triumph of the highest ideals to which man aspires. "The whole process of evolution," Boodin wrote, "is a process of spiritualization."[22]

Boodin also held an original theory of social mind. By "social mind" he meant "the synthesis of individual minds into wholes, with new properties."[23] And he contended that "there is a genuine unity distinguishable from what we call the unity of individual experience, and if not more real, at least more inclusive than this."[24]

Joseph Alexander Leighton (1870-1955)

Joseph Alexander Leighton imbibed his idealism at Cornell University, where the program of graduate study in philosophy centered on the history of philosophy and idealism. Though he cherished Creighton as his "friend and teacher," he could neither accept the timeless Absolute, nor the absolute idealists' "apparent indifference to the uniqueness and value of the *individual person*."[25]

> ... the universe ... is an organic whole, a living system. Its real constituents are active individual wholes, principles of organizing activity. It is a creative whole; at the highest known level it flowers in the creative life of personality-in-community. New values emerge by the transmutation of older values. It may be a growing universe, but if so, its growth is the empirical realization of individualities and values that are grounded in its eternally real possibilities.[26]

William Ernest Hocking (1873-1966)

After Josiah Royce's death William Ernest Hocking carried on the idealist tradition at Harvard University. Besides Royce, William James, with his pragmatism and empiricism, radically influenced his thought, for Hocking is one of the large number of early twentieth-century philosophers, including pragmatists, positivists, phenomenologists, and process metaphysicians, who appealed to experience in philosophy.

Hocking's first book, *The Meaning of God in Human Experience* (1912), is a lasting contribution to metaphysics and the philosophy of religion. It opens with Hocking's confession of dissatisfaction with philosophical idealism. The critics of idealism, he admitted, "do not find the Absolute of idealism to be identical with the God of religion; they cannot worship the Absolute."[27] To correct idealism it is necessary to discover "what, in terms of experience, its [religion's] God means and has meant to mankind."[28] As pragmatism demands, the categories of idealism are to be converted into the "hard cash" of experience. Religion does make differences to human experience, and these differences are the clues to its nature and truth. "God is to be known in experience if at all."[29] Nevertheless, the Absolute cannot be totally reduced to experience. As a category, it is an immutable universal which transcends experience; and this transcendence of experience is, in religion, also ascribed to God. So Hocking declared, "I do not say that the Absolute is equivalent to God; I say that God, whatever else he may be, must needs also be the Absolute."[30]

A "widened empiricism" is Hocking's phrase for his philosophical method; it focuses on the "I-thou" factors in experience. At heart his idealism contains a personalistic theory similar to Mary Whiton Calkins', except that its justification is more experiential than it is dialectical. Unlike Royce, Hocking brought the Absolute down to immediate experience, and so his idealism embraces mysticism. Hocking's writings cover a wide compass of philosophical and practical concerns. He offered a theory of man in *Human Nature and its Remaking* (1918) and a theory of politics in *Man and the State* (1926) and *The Spirit of World Politics* (1932). These writings reveal that the Absolute he inherited from Royce was not only remolded to yield itself in immediate experience, it was also pluralized and democratized more completely than Royce ever anticipated.

At the core of Hocking's philosophy is his conception of the human self as the will-to-power, and in its deepest expression, the will-to-power is the will to overcome death. This self, or soul, is capable "of feeling the natural bent of desire as invested with the omen of finitude" and yet "aware of, and seeking to control its metaphysical status."[31] Hence man has a dual nature, being at once (1) "the excursive self, which is (relatively) actual, finite, time-limited, time-discontinuous, created," and (2) "the reflective self, which is (relatively) potential, infinite, time-inclusive, time-continuous, creative."[32] While the excursive self is dated and vanishes at death, "the reflective self, having attained a measure of reality in that creative deed, is ready for another stage, not excluding the first, in knowing, and embodying the depth of being."[33]

Besides grounding the idea of immortality in human experience, Hocking's theory of man has a straightforward implication for politics, an implication which demolishes the common allegation that absolute idealism entails totalitarianism. The ideal society, Hocking insisted, must acknowledge what he called "the incompressible individual." The confluence of individual wills into the will-circuit of the state occurs rightly only on condition that "public purposes are prolongations of individual purposes, and derive their life therefrom. The individual thus remains mentally prior to the state."[34]

Wilbur Marshall Urban (1873-1952)

Wilbur M. Urban deemed the "value-centric predicament" to be inescapable in philosophy. And he accepted Josiah Royce's formulation of it: "The question, 'How ought I to conceive the real?' is logically prior to the question, 'What is the real itself?' . . . the ought is prior in nature to the real; or the proposition, I ought to think so, is prior to the proposition, this is so."[35] To Royce's statement Urban added:

> The very distinctions between truth and falsity, between appearance and reality themselves, depend upon certain ideals or norms of truth and reality. Every judgment that something exists presupposes the meaning of it as true. It is because meaning lies above all being, and because meaning is inseparable from value, that the value-centric predicament cannot be escaped.[36]

It is the persistent elaboration of the value-motif in all areas of philosophy which determines the unique quality and distinctive unity of Urban's thought. Urban intended first to formulate a general theory of value. His early book, *Valuation: Its Nature and Laws* (1909), is the first work in English in a field which he himself named "axiology." Although he later revised the value theory of *Valuation*, he persevered in his second intention—namely, to reinterpret all the major areas and problems of philosophy by means of axiology. As his numerous works make plain, his concern with values was practical as well as theoretical. When, after World War I, naturalism challenged the great tradition of philosophy, he responded with a defense of *philosophia perennis* in *The Intelligible World* (1929). During the same period, when the disputes between idealists and realists threatened to exhaust philosophy, he sought to transcend the conflict in *Beyond Realism and Idealism* (1949). When in the 1930s logical positivism and linguistic analysis first rose to impugn traditional philosophy and the objectivity of values, he replied with *Language and Reality* (1939). And after World War II, when existentialist theology and atheistic naturalism decried human reason and values, he grappled with the problems of natural theology in *Humanity and Deity* (1951).

More than any philosopher of his generation, Urban shifted the philosophical argument for idealism to the field of values. Just as philosophers were becoming aware that the criteria of meaningful discourse raise a major and significant philosophical problem, he insisted upon the intelligibility of the idealist program as regards values and upon the unintelligibility of the alternatives. He advocated an intimate connection between knowing and evaluating, and emphasized the primacy of evaluating. As Urban said: "We cannot detach meanings and values from mind without becoming unintelligible."[37]

Elijah Jordan (1875-1953)

Since the philosophy of Elijah Jordan has a primarily practical aim, its main contributions are in the fields of moral, political, social, and legal theory. Jordan was convinced that our civilization and its institutions rest upon metaphysical principles whose validity he passionately denied. He wrote:

> Either . . . there must be something wrong with the conceptions . . . upon which civilization appears to have rested, or the principles and agencies which dominate the practical life are metaphysically evil. Either those influences that lead to universal war and strife are wrong and false or else war and strife and hatred are right.[38]

Consequently, Jordan addressed himself to metaphysical questions in the formulation of a practical philosophy which was at once critical of existing institutions and visionary in regard to their reconstruction. The metaphysics he propounded, it seems, is a version of the speculative idealism which came to America from Bosanquet through Creighton and which prevailed at Cornell University when Jordan taught there for a few years after obtaining his Ph.D. from the University of Chicago.

Jordan attacked the doctrine of individualism with its emphasis on private interests. He argued that the erection of civilization on the principle of private interests was the cause of the social evils of the present era—economic depression, political corruption, wars. As he said, "Nothing will work in the world but the right and the true, and this bears no relation to interest."[39] Now the doctrine of interest stems from the extreme subjectivism of modern individualism. The proper metaphysics for the desired social order requires nothing less than the elimination of subjectivism and the establishment of a new objectivity which embraces both "overt objects" and "invert objects, or subjects." He wrote: "The modern *practical* problem is therefore how, and upon what principles, can the two modes of objectivity get integrated into a higher unity—that is, how can we find an effectual unity of the natural and the mental in the new objectivity?"[40] The solution, which Jordan offered in his book, *The Forms of Individuality* (1927), consists in "the discovery of the corporate character of cultural objects, the theory of corporation being the logical formulation of the new objectivity."[41] Because, according to this metaphysics, "the essence of individuality is corporeity,"[42] a new conception of individuality, differing from that of individualism, is advanced; the corporation emerges as a form of individuality higher than that of human individuals, which, indeed, may be understood to be functions of corporate institutions. Thus Jordan has been the first American non-Marxist philosopher to press philosophy hard in order to take account of contemporary corporations, such as General Motors, ITT, Exxon, and TVA. Of course he regarded the grounding of the corporation on the principle of private interest derived from an outmoded individualism to be the tragedy of modern civilization.[43]

G. Watts Cunningham (1881-1968)

G. Watts Cunningham, though less famous than Creighton, was the most creative philosopher in the idealist school at Cornell University. When he entered Cornell in 1905, the tradition was, as he has reported, "to conduct the student along the historical avenue of approach."[44] Plato, Kant, and Hegel were the subjects of the seminars he attended, and from Hegel and the Hegelian tradition he learned the most. Naturally Cunningham's first book was *Thought and Reality in Hegel's System* (1910).

Cunningham's career as a philosopher brilliantly illustrates the interplay between philosophical scholarship and creativity. His best known book is the scholarly work, *The Idealistic Argument in Recent British and American Philosophy* (1933). Yet, clearly, the quest for the solution of philosophical problems—what he called "a search for system"—was at the root of his scholarly investigations. Early difficulties with the timeless Absolute sent him in the direction of Bergson. The result was his book, *A Study in the Philosophy of Bergson* (1916). Here he advanced a theory of "creative finalism," which he thought to be in harmony with his tradition, but which "views reality as an organic process which is through and through teleological."[45] Having bent to the winds of temporalism, Cunningham's inherited idealism next faced the storm of pragmatist and realist theories of mind. In opposition to the rising tide of naturalism, Cunningham defended mind in a tough, analytic manner in his *Five Lectures on the Problem of Mind* (1925).

Cunningham selected for treatment the most difficult topics for idealism, such as the nature of mind and the theory of meaning. Yet his work always exhibited a clarity of style, a balance of argument, and a subtlety of conclusion which perpetuated the intellectual respectability of idealism in the changed atmosphere of philosophy in the second quarter of the twentieth century. His essay, "On the Meaning Situation" (1932), is exemplary. At a time when the "meaning of meaning" was captive to the pragmatists, the realists, and the positivists, he resurrected the Roycean distinction between internal and external meanings, but he expressed it in a more critical and hence more acceptable form than Royce's. Cunningham first distinguished the meaning situation into two components: "(1) that which means, and (2) that which is meant."[46] Next he distinguished "that which means" into "mind" and "content." Whatever the status of content, the object to which it refers lies beyond it and beyond mind. Cunningham urged that the relation between mind and content, on the one hand, and object, on the other hand,

> cannot be accurately read if abstracted from the mental reference of the content, and that consequently the 'object of knowledge' and the 'object *per se*' are systematically joined. The object is that which the mind intends, but the mind's intention is subject to the directive discipline which the object exerts. Just here, it may be noted parenthetically, is the fact which lies at the bottom of Royce's famous distinction between the 'internal' and the 'external' meaning of ideas, though the statement of the fact seems to involve an emphasis quite different from that which Royce himself placed upon it: the 'external' meaning controls, not the 'internal.'[47]

De Witt H. Parker (1885-1949)

De Witt H. Parker, longtime philosophy professor at the University of Michigan, presented a unique system of idealism centered on the philosophy of values and in particular on art and aesthetics. A student at Harvard when James, Royce, and Santayana graced her faculty, Parker assimilated his mentors' interests and principles in a distinctive way. His works in metaphysics, *The Self and Nature* (1917) and *Experience and Substance* (1941), present an idealism which appeals to experience in the Jamesian manner. His works on aesthetics and art, *The Principles of Aesthetics* (1920; 2d ed., 1946) and *The Analysis of Art* (1926), display a Santayanian concern with harmony. His originality, however, is most conspicuous in the field of values, where his works, *Human Values* (1931) and *The Philosophy of Value* (1957), begin on a naturalistic basis but move in the direction of more recent noncognitivism. Threading Parker's entire philosophical corpus is a Schopenhauerian theme of pessimism.[48]

Parker called his philosophy "empirical idealism."[49] Thus it is within the framework of an explicit metaphysics that he articulated his philosophy of values. Profoundly humanistic, this philosophy embraces a naturalist theory of values founded on a metaphysics of monadic idealism. Like the naturalists, Parker identified values with the satisfaction of desire. He traced the origin of values from basic organic needs and held that biological, moral, aesthetic, and religious values manifest a continuity which makes possible the formulation of a general theory of value with specifications in all these areas. Like the emotivists, who followed upon the heels of the naturalists, Parker held that value expressions are primarily non-cognitive, expressing private feelings and intending to excite corresponding feelings in others. Thus he doubted the efficacy of rational, scientific methods in the field of values. He did not, of course, disregard the normative component of value. On the contrary, he maintained that every satisfaction involves a normative dimension, determined by its position in and coherence with the basic system of desires defining the self. Accordingly, rational methods do not get to the heart of the matter of moral conflict and evil.

Parker conceived the world as a system of monadic selves, each willing its own satisfactions, so that the satisfactions of some are the frustrations of others. Good and evil are interlocked. Love may assuage the hurt by enabling the individual self to find value in the satisfactions of others. Love is man's main practical stay against the despair of the evil that undermines and overwhelms him. Philosophy is also an aid. Theoretical knowledge of the Omega system, interpreted as Divine Will underlying the physical universe, may guarantee the preponderance of good over evil. But despite his idealism, Parker never wavered in his conviction that the world contains ineradicable evil. Art in its highest moments makes it possible for man to face evil, and religion imbues men with faith in a victorious good despite the appearance of things. But in the final analysis the highest end of human life is a harmony which Parker described as tragic.[50]

Walter Terrence Stace (1886-1967)

Walter T. Stace has had a singular career; he has offered a curious philosophy, too. Paradox haunts his life and works. An Englishman who served in the British civil service in Ceylon from 1910 until his retirement in 1932, he then took a position teaching philosophy at Princeton University where he remained on the faculty until 1955. Rightly or wrongly, an early book, *The Philosophy of Hegel* (1924), won him the title "idealist." His famous 1934 article, "The Refutation of Realism," reconfirmed the title. Answering G. E. Moore's still more famous article, "The Refutation of Idealism" (1903), Stace proceeded in a manner which Berkeley would have applauded. Granting Moore's distinction between sense data and our awareness of them, Stace denied that there is any reason to hold that sense data exist independently of our awareness. He argued that we do not know that any single entity exists unexperienced, and that, even if such an entity exists, we cannot possibly know that it does. Finally, since we do not know and cannot know that unexperienced entities exist, we have no reason to believe such entities do exist.

In his own philosophy, however, Stace did acknowledge the possible non-mental character of sense data, so much so that he is alleged to have explained his 1934 article as primarily ironic, showing that "the simplest natural belief cannot be supported by strict logical proofs."[51] For Stace was, above all, a strict empiricist. Thus he deemed solipsism to be unassailable, and he regarded the external world and the objects it contains to be a construction from data privately given, or a fiction. He sought to analyze the steps whereby the external world is constructed, and though he conceded that the argument falls short of logical demonstration, he maintained that it satisfied the human demands for belief.

Blending together concepts and procedures drawn from Berkeley and from Leibniz, Stace has expounded a thoroughgoing phenomenalist metaphysics in his two major systematic works, *The Theory of Knowledge and Existence* (1932) and *The Nature of the World* (1940). Thus Stace wrote:

> The universe is fundamentally a colony of multitudes of minds. I hold back from saying that the ultimate stuff or reality of the universe is mind . . . Moreover, in addition to minds there are givens, floating colours and sounds, relations between these, mental states as themselves intuited and given. Each monadic mind possesses and dwells in its own self-enclosed world of givens.[52]

Stace refused to assert that mind is more fundamental than what is given, since empirical evidence was lacking to support such an assertion. Rather he upheld "the hypothesis that the universe is a plurality of cells, all cells being of the same fundamental structure, though apart from structure they vary indefinitely."[53] He continued: "The structure of every cell in the universe is correctly described if we say that it consists of two essential abstract elements, namely consciousness and datum."[54] Stace dissociated his position from Berkeley's on three points: 1) he declined to consider the objects of consciousness (data, givens) to be mental, 2) he did not suppose these objects to have been created by mind, and 3) he did not agree that there is a gap in the metaphysical system—the interperceptual levels—which necessitates the concept of God. For Stace, it is neither necessary for objects to exist when they are not perceived, nor necessary for them to be perceived when they do exist; and so God is "not a necessary concept of metaphysics," although He is "a legitimate contingent concept."[55]

Stace's later work focused on religious themes. While his metaphysics allowed only a contingent concept of God, he found God more securely when he abandoned rational for mystical approaches to experience. In Stace's final philosophy, British empiricism shares a place with Eastern mysticism. In *Time and Eternity* (1952), he declared: "Men have always found that, in their search for the Ultimate, contradiction and paradox lie all around them . . . Either God is a Mystery or He is nothing at all."[56]

Brand Blanshard (1892-   )

Brand Blanshard, the most distinguished living American philosopher, has presented a kind of philosophical idealism which has its roots in Hegel, Bradley, Bosanquet, and Royce, and which he absorbed in his studies at Oxford, where Joachim was his tutor. Blanshard, however, has preferred to call it rationalism. He has associated it with the work of a predecessor at Yale University, where he taught from 1945 to 1961, when he claimed that it is but one variation on the "ancient doctrine of 'the great tradition,' of what Professor Urban has been persuasively urging as *philosophia perpetua* or *perennis*, the doctrine of the autonomy and objectivity of reason, the doctrine that through different minds one intelligible world is in the course of construction or reconstruction."[57]

The affinity of Blanshard's rationalism for idealism is manifest in his book, *The Nature of Thought* (1939). The main ideas amplified in this work may be found in the Anglo-American Hegelian tradition. Take, for example, his theory of the idea. Admitting "that something very like it was the common property of metaphysicians of the Platonic turn of mind from the father of the great succession down to Bradley, Bosanquet, and Royce," Blanshard singles out Royce as the philosopher "whose agreement may be claimed more confidently and in more detail."[58] Accordingly, thought is "a half-way house on the road to reality . . . The idea can then be *both* the same as its object *and* different; the same because it *is* the object *in posse*; different because that object, which is its end, is as yet incompletely realized."[59] Thought, moreover, has an immanent end—namely, a logically coherent system of judgments. The immanent end of thought is matched by its transcendent end—namely, reality as a necessary system of internally related parts. Hence Blanshard unfolds the core concepts of Hegelian idealism—coherence as the nature and test of truth, the theory of the concrete universal, the doctrines of internal relations and of cosmic necessity.

As Blanshard transformed the idealism he inherited into rationalism, he has projected a trilogy on reason, in which he undertakes to defend reason by critically demolishing its contemporary detractors. The first volume, *Reason and Analysis* (1962), based on the Carus Lectures before the American Philosophical Association, is both critical and constructive. Besides taking logical positivists and linguistic analysts to task for undermining reason, Blanshard projects the ideal of a rational system of necessary knowledge representing the world as an intelligible whole of internally related parts. The second, *Reason and Goodness* (1961), based on the second series of Gifford Lectures delivered at St. Andrews University in Scotland, considers the role of reason in morality and is particularly critical of those recent movements in moral philosophy—such as subjectivism and emotivism—which have sought to minimize or deny that role. The third volume, *Reason and Belief*, now being printed, takes up topics considered in his first series of Gifford Lectures, wherein he sharply criticized the derogation of reason in recent theology of the neo-Thomist, neo-orthodox, and existentialist varieties.

In advancing a conception of the world as a rational system of logically necessary parts in which thought is satisfied, Blanshard differs from his Absolute idealist predecessors in one important respect. He does not contend, as they have done, that this world is also a system of value. On the contrary, breaking with the idealist tradition, Blanshard affirms, first, that "between the rational as the logically necessary and the rational as the morally right, there is an abyss of difference," and, second, that "to pass from 'everything is rational,' in the sense of necessity, to 'everything is rational,' in the sense of right, is to stultify one's moral perception."[60] In Blanshard's philosophy arguments drawn from metaphysics and philosophical logic reinstate the idealist conception of the world as a logical whole of necessary parts, but considerations of the principles of moral philosophy do not so far justify the attribution of supreme value to the world as a whole.[61]

Personalism

In the late nineteenth century Anglo-American idealism climaxed in the doctrine of the Absolute. Yet soon the Absolute was to undergo metamorphosis, assisted even by Josiah Royce, himself its leading spokesman on the American scene. During the early twentieth century, idealists like Creighton sought to save the Absolute by detaching idealism from mentalism and resurrecting it as speculation—as the search for a total, comprehensive, and coherent system of experience. Others, like Hocking, followed the suggestion of pragmatism and looked for the Absolute in human experience. Still others, like Leighton and Cunningham, confronted the claims of temporalism and realism, and modified the Absolute, while Stace, for empirical reasons, refuted realism but pluralized the cosmos. On the other hand, some, like Boodin, undertook to erect a system of idealism upon the foundations of modern science. During the first quarter of the twentieth century, furthermore, within the framework of absolutism, the argument for idealism began to shift from metaphysics and cosmology to value theory. As the diverse philosophies of Urban, Jordan and Parker testify, practical concerns about values motivated the shift. Yet even here absolutism was not consistent. Defending a version of absolutism, which he prefers to call rationalism, Blanshard today upholds a logico-metaphysical Absolute while refusing to ascribe values to it. The progeny of absolute idealism have engaged in quarrels which threaten to split up the family.

Among the numerous objections to the Absolute, the charge that it does not do justice to the finite individual person has been paramount. Of course many of the absolutists, M. W. Calkins most notably, have taken special pains to account for the finite person. Nevertheless, the alleged failure of absolutism in regard to the reality of the finite individual has been matched by the rise of another form of idealism—personalism. From the beginning, personalism as a type of philosophy has emphasized that the finite individual person is the key to reality, and has concentrated on the value areas of human experience, particularly the philosophy of religion. Indeed, at times, personalism has appeared to be an apologetic philosophy primarily, if not exclusively, intended to justify Christianity.

Personalism as a type of philosophical idealism originated in Europe, out it became a philosophical movement in America.[62] Schleiermacher first used the term *personalismus* in his *Discourses* (1799), in order to designate theism in contradistinction from pantheism. Used by such literary men as Goethe and Whitman in the nineteenth century, the term was not accepted in philosophy until the early twentieth century. Charles Renouvier was already long established as the proponent of neo-criticism in French philosophy when in 1903 he introduced the term in the title of a book, *Le personnalisme*, and adopted it as the true name for his own philosophy. In 1906 it appeared as the subtitle of the first volume of *Person und Sache* by William Stern. And in 1908, when Borden Parker Bowne published *Personalism*, it first occurred in English on the title page of a work. Soon, however, personalism was a term which numerous thinkers adopted to signify a common view of the world. As W. H. Werkmeister has reported, "It is . . . the basic program of a more or less definitely organized Movement."[63] Indeed,

at a meeting in Philadelphia on December 26, 1940, American personalists formulated a platform, containing a basic definition, two underlying premises, twenty-two principles, and two main propositions
dividing the varieties of personalism.[64]

Borden Parker Bowne (1847-1910)

Borden Parker Bowne, professor of philosophy at Boston University
from 1876 to 1910 and the first dean of its graduate school, advanced
a personalistic idealism which holds that God—a Creator-Person—and
the finite persons He created constitute reality. Bowne presented his
philosophy in an impressive series of books, the most significant of
which are *Metaphysics* (1882, rev. ed 1898), *Theory of Thought and
Knowledge* (1897), and *Personalism* (1908). Of Bowne's personalism
W. H. Werkmeister has remarked that it was "the first complete and
comprehensive system of philosophy developed in America which
has had lasting influence and which counts some of our outstanding
thinkers among its adherents."[65]

Bowne's philosophy is summed up in his book, *Personalism*. Thought,
Bowne maintained, originates in a personal world—"this living, aspiring,
hoping, fearing, loving, hating, human world, with its life and history
and hopes and fears and struggles and aspirations."[66] Starting out from
this personal world, thought becomes scientific when it discerns, by
means of observation and experiment, the uniformities of events, the
connections of things, and so provides a scientific knowledge which is
"of the utmost practical value for the guidance of our lives."[67] Science,
however, does not suffice, for we need to know not merely that things
exist and hang together in space and time, but more crucially "what
they mean, and what the cause is that underlies the cosmic process."[68]
Philosophy assumes the task.

Philosophical reflection on experience convinced Bowne that all
knowledge and all interpretation presuppose a permanent self. From the
inarticulate flux of impressions the mind reaches a permanent and
rational world by reacting to the flux with laws immanent in itself.
"The flitting and discontinuous impression is interpreted into a continuous and abiding world only by a permanent self with its outfit of
rational principles . . ."[69] Bowne's epistemological argument is Kantian
in form, without accepting the agnostic conclusion Kant drew. Rather
Bowne made a theistic assumption. The phenomenal world of things, he

held, "originated in thought and expressed thought," so that there is "no a priori reason why we should not know them."[70] In this sense, knowledge of things is tantamount to mutual understanding between persons.

The metaphysical principle of a permanent self is the key to Bowne's epistemology and metaphysics. It enabled him to reinterpret such basic categories as substantiality and causality. His discussion of causality, moving beyond the merely mechanical conception, stresses volitional causality which reveals "an abiding power which can form plans, foresee ends, and direct itself for their realization."[71] Such a power is just what a self is—"a living, conscious unity, which is one in its manifoldness and manifold in its oneness. . . . It is the living self in the midst of its experiences, possessing, directing, controlling both itself and them."[72]

"Personality" was Bowne's favorite term for selfhood. He amplified: "The essential meaning of personality is selfhood, self-consciousness, self-control, and the power to know. . . . Any being, finite or infinite, which has knowledge and self-consciousness and self-control, is personal; for the term has no other meaning."[73] Bowne's personalism led directly to theism. Although finite selves, with corporeal forms and other limitations, count as personalities, Bowne maintained, "that complete and perfect personality can be found only in the Infinite and Absolute Being, as only in Him can we find that complete and perfect selfhood and self-possession which are necessary to the fullness of personality."[74]

George Holmes Howison (1834-1916)

George Holmes Howison, professor of philosophy at the University of California at Berkeley at the turn of the century, had been in his early career a member of the St. Louis Philosophical Society, devoted to the study of Hegel and German idealism. Mention has already been made of the fact that he staged the Great Debate in 1895 and put questions to Royce which compelled modification of absolutism. In 1901 Howison published *The Limits of Evolution*. In this book he expounded a system of metaphysics which he called "personal idealism."

Condemning "historic idealism" for being "overwhelmingly impersonal,"[75] he proposed a thoroughly personal idealistic system. He wrote: "Instead of any monism, it puts forward a Pluralism, an eternal or metaphysical world of *many* minds, all alike possessing personal initiative, self-direction, instead of an all-predestinating single Mind that alone has real free-agency."[76] At the same time he was careful to reject the pluralism of William James for dissolving "reality into a radically distinct and wild 'multiverse' . . . instead of the universe of final harmony which is the ideal of our reason."[77]

Howison's system owes much to Kant and more to Leibniz, but it is unique nonetheless. Like Kant, Howison found the basis of knowledge and morality "in the native spontaneity of the human mind," although he discarded several cardinal Kantian principles, breaking down "the Kantian barrier between the 'practical' and the 'theoretical' consciousness, . . . to open a continuous *theoretical* highway for reason in both its scientific and its ethical uses."[78] In fact, Howison maintained not only that "the ethical first principle" is "an act of knowledge," but that it "is the principle of all knowledge."[79]

Like Leibniz, Howison was a pluralist, even confessing that his "scheme certainly does approach to the Leibnizian monadology more closely than to any other form of idealism that has preceded it."[80] Yet there are significant differences. Unlike the Leibnizian monadology Howison's personal idealism

> dislodges the self-enclosed isolation of the individual and finds a *social* consciousness, a tacit reference to others and a more or less developed recognition of them, to be inwrought in the very self-defining thought whereby each exists.[81]

Spontaneous rather than pre-established harmony characterizes Howison's system. He rejects the hierarchical principle with God as the Monad of monads, since this "amounts to a system of caste in the world of real individuals, annulling human freedom."[82] The world constitutes "the City of God," although, in Howison's metaphor, it is also an "Eternal Republic." He amplified:

> All the members have the equality belonging to their common aim of fulfilling their one Rational Ideal; and God, the fulfilled Type of every mind, the living Bond of their union, reigns in it, not by the exercise of power, but solely by light; not by authority, but by reason; not by efficient, but by final causation— that is simply by being the impersonated Ideal of every mind.[83]

Ralph Tyler Flewelling (1871-1960)

After receiving his education at Boston University, where he was influenced by Borden Parker Bowne, and after serving for several years as a minister in the East, Ralph Tyler Flewelling went West. In 1917 he joined the faculty of the University of Southern California, where he founded and directed the School of Philosophy. In 1920 he founded the interdisciplinary journal, *The Personalist*, of which he was editor until 1959. A teacher, a popularizer, an organizer, an editor, and, above all, a missionary for personalism, Flewelling authored a number of books in which he argued in behalf of his philosophy. His major work of systematic philosophizing is his book, *Creative Personality* (1926), and its subsequent revision, *The Person* (1952).

The problem Flewelling faced is the problem of reconciling science with moral and religious values. It is not merely a theoretical problem stemming from mutual misunderstandings, but rather an intensely practical problem. As Flewelling remarked: "Science daily places in the hands of society powers so great that all the gains of the past and even human existence itself must come to an end unless moral and spiritual gains shall equal the scientific."[84] For solution Flewelling looked to philosophy. He drew a distinction between knowledge and truth reminiscent of Augustine's distinction between science and wisdom. Restricted to the phenomenal order of material facts, knowledge is subsumed under truth, which comprehends the order of values beyond phenomena. Thus, as Flewelling put his point in *The Person*, science, philosophy, and religion are different windows on reality. "With science it is an absolute space-time world of universal law and predictability; with philosophy it is absolute truth, or logical coherence; with religion it is an absolute person or God."[85] The unity of the approaches to reality pivots on the person. Division or opposition betrays inner conflict in the human person. Hence humanism is a dominant characteristic of Flewelling's personalism.

Another noteworthy characteristic of Flewelling's philosophy is temporalism. For while he advocates the standard conceptions of personalism, stressing the central reality of the person, which he defined as "a self-conscious unique unity capable of reflection upon its conscious states, of self-direction and transcending time," and "as the self-identifying subject of experience, possessor of intrinsic values and creative powers,"[86] he also drew upon process philosophy and relativity physics to describe the person as "a continuum in a world of space-time events"[87] and as "a field of energy."[88] In particular, Flewelling was influenced by the flux philosophy of Bergson, which he assimilated to his personalistic picture of the cosmos with a creator God creating nature and creative finite personal beings. Evolution is not the product of a blind *élan vital*, but a process guided by a purposive Cosmic Intelligence, an immanent and transcendent being whose purpose was to create men. As Flewelling said:

> With the directive will of man came the great break in evolution. ... With the person emerges a new world of freedom and values. ...
>
> When we come to man we have passed a distinct frontier into a new field of relations not before existent. Here for the first time appears a conscious relationship between the Creative Purpose and the object which it creates, a relationship involving freedom. Along with the gift of purposive self-direction has emerged the capacity to bring into being new existences, new meanings, new values hitherto impossible. What has been behind the world order comes to consciousness within the process. In the exercise by man of creative powers is mirrored the deeper fact of how a Supreme Creator can at the same time be immanent and transcendent.[89]

Albert Cornelius Knudson (1873-1953)

A professor of theology and dean of the School of Boston University School of Theology, Albert C. Knudson carried on Bowne's tradition. His book, *The Philosophy of Personalism* (1927; reprinted 1949), is a vigorous statement of the fundamental ideas of personalism; it also furnishes a broad survey of the history of personalism and a critical exposition of alternative philosophies. Knudson defined personalism as

> that form of idealism which gives equal recognition to both the pluralistic and the monistic aspects of experience and which finds in the conscious unity, identity, and free activity of personality the key to the nature of reality and the solution of the ultimate problems of philosophy.[90]

Although Knudson as historian recognized different types of personalism, including the atheistic personalism of the British philosopher McTaggart, he adhered to the theistic personalism of Bowne. Further, he cultivated theistic personalism to entail what, in the first edition of his book, he called "occasionalism" and what, in the 1949 edition, he called, deeming the term more accurate, "panentheism." Whatever the name, the doctrine maintains that

> . . . nature has no independent forces resident in itself. It is 'nothing more than the orderly and continuous intervention of God,' a ceaseless product of the divine energizing. Things are not themselves 'real' causes. They simply furnish the 'occasions' on which God 'intervenes.' It is he who does everything. In him the world has its sole causal ground.[91]

Knudson's religious commitment was at the heart of his philosophy. Taking human personality to be the key to reality and interpreting nature to be the expression of a personal God, Knudson regarded his personalistic philosophy as essentially Christian. He declared:

> That the personality of God and the sacredness of human personality express the true genius of the Christian religion, whatever may be said of its theology, is hardly open to question; and that these beliefs have received their completest philosophical justification in modern personalistic metaphysics, would seem equally clear. Personalism is *par excellence* the Christian philosophy of our day.[92]

Edgar Sheffield Brightman (1884-1953)

A student at Boston University while Bowne was still active, Edgar Sheffield Brightman later advanced the case for personalism as Bowne Professor of Philosophy (1919-1951). He pressed for theistic personalism, the essential thesis of which is that "the whole universe is a society of intercommunicating selves or persons, of which God is the creative center,"[93] and he elaborated its implications in more than a dozen books and a cornucopia of articles. The posthumously published *Person and Reality* (1958) presents personalism as a systematic metaphysics.

Brightman defined metaphysics as "the mind's effort to view experience as a living whole."[94] Hence his metaphysics is empirical, rational, and synoptic. It approaches being (reality) by drawing a distinction between four realms: the realm of essences, the realm of nature, the realm of values, and the realm of persons. Of the four realms, that of persons is ontologically primary; for all realms are concretely grounded in personal experience. Brightman defined a person as "a unity of complex conscious changes, including all its experiences—its memories, its purposes, its values, its powers, its activities, and its experienced interactions with its environment."[95] Hence not only consciousness and experience, but change, value, activity characterize persons.

Brightman's elucidations of the other three realms of reality underscore the primacy of the person. Following Santayana, Brightman described essences as immediate qualitative contents considered in isolation. However, he construed essences personalistically. "For personalism," he wrote, "essences of all sorts are experiences of persons. They belong to the unity of consciousness and have no other existence or function of any sort, except as indicating that selves are interrelated with each other."[96] In similar fashion, liberating nature from materialistic interpretations, he regarded it, in the fashion of Flewelling and Knudson, to be the revelation of the divine Person. "Nature is one area of Divine experience, exhibiting God in action, God controlling the Given, and God communicating and interacting with other persons or selves."[97] When Brightman affirmed values as constituting a realm on a par with nature, he displayed the conviction shared by most twentieth century idealists that values are really real. Yet even their reality depends upon persons. "Without personality," he once insisted, "no other values exist. Unless personality is value, all else is devalued."[98]

The most striking feature of Brightman's philosophy is his doctrine of a finite God. He unveiled this doctrine in *The Problem of God* (1930). Here he defined God as "a Person supremely conscious, supremely creative, supremely valuable, yet limited by both the free choices of other persons and by restrictions within his own nature."[99] The finiteness of God stems not merely from the fact that other persons are free, nor from the existence of evil, nor even the wastefulness of the evolutionary process which is God's way in nature. All of these facts refer to what is external to God. Brightman, however, insisted that the finiteness of God is due to His own internal nature. He called this internal nature "the Given," and he described the Given as

... a passive element which enters into every one of his conscious states, as sensation, instinct, and impulse enter into ours, and constitutes a problem for him ... The evils of life and the delays in the attainment of value, in so far as they come from God and not from human freedom, are thus due to his nature, yet not wholly to his deliberate choice.[100]

In a later book, *The Finding of God* (1931), Brightman modified his conception of the Given in God; he acknowledged a rational element as well as an irrational one. But this modification did not eradicate altogether "a problematic resisting force that produces a tension and a drag within the divine nature."[101] As Brightman once put the point, "Jesus reveals a God who bears an eternal cross; and it is this cross which I have called the Given."[102]

W. H. Werkmeister (1901-   )

W. H. Werkmeister, whose contributions as a historian of American philosophy have been utilized throughout the present essay, is singular in his espousal of personalism. In the formative years of his career he was affiliated with none of the leaders of personalism. Rather, immersed in Kant and methodology, he arrived at his position independently at the University of Nebraska. In mid-career he was called to the University of Southern California, and from 1959 to 1966, he served as editor of *The Personalist*. He then transplanted personalism to the American South when he became professor of philosophy at Florida State University. Whereas personalism has conventionally focused on metaphysics and religion, Werkmeister's personalistic philosophy has been inspired by science and has centered on methodology and epistemology. His first book was *A Philosophy of Science* (1940).

Epistemology is the starting point of Werkmeister's thinking. In *The Basis and Structure of Knowledge* (1948) he expounded a theory of knowledge which is Kantian yet is consonant with the spirit of logical empiricism. It is, in brief, an epistemology akin to that of C. I. Lewis. In epistemology Werkmeister is a foundationalist—that is, he holds that knowledge is based on firm grounds. For him our first-person experience is the basis and anchorage of all we know. This view, with its emphasis on methodological solipsism, was shared by the logical positivists of a generation ago. However, Werkmeister's acknowledgment of the categorial structure of knowledge, a structure which the mind does not construct from data but which is itself *a priori* and hence requisite for any cognitional construction from data, is one major departure from positivism. Another is his thesis that value judgments and moral judgments are cognitive—that is, they are true or false.

Man and His Values (1967) is the most systematic statement of Werkmeister's personalism. Placing value judgments and moral judgments squarely on an experiential basis, Werkmeister contends that "the empirical subject cannot be eliminated as the agent who knows and values and does."[103] First-person experience, however, is not confined to the empirical subject, for Werkmeister did not reduce the person to a mere empirical subject. In terms which avowedly owe much to Kant, he describes the person as a free, rational, autonomous being.[104] Thus Werkmeister divides the field of values into two parts, a division which has its parallel in the philosophy of C. I. Lewis.

Value and value judgments are both rooted in value experience, which is an affective-conative experience. A value experience in this empirical sense is a transaction between a subject and an object, such that the subject has a feeling-state which the object induced and toward which the subject has an attitude. Cognitive in the same sense that other empirical judgments are, value judgments ultimately are verified or falsified in first-person experience.

In addition to the value-ought which is prudential and empirical, Werkmeister recognized another ought, the moral ought. The latter is in the nature of a commitment. An obligation, as in the case of a promise, is self-imposed; it is a right freely granted to another. Judgments of moral obligation, like prudential value judgments, refer back to first-person experience. But the experience in question is different. It is not empirical value experience, but rather rationally volitional experience. The test of a moral judgment, therefore, is its consistency with the ultimate commitment of the person, and that ultimate commitment is grounded freely on an act of will. As Werkmeister's argument unfolds, it becomes clear that he conceives the person to be as sensual as prudential value experience allows, and as willful (rational and volitional) as his commitments. Such a sensuous, profound, spiritual, concrete person, with all his valuations and aspirations, reveals the nature of reality, since, in Werkmeister's words, "reality can never be less than its highest manifestations."[105]

Peter A. Bertocci (1910-   )

A student of Brightman and his successor in the Borden Parker Bowne chair of philosophy at Boston University, Peter A. Bertocci is, in his own words, "a teleological personalistic idealist." The basic theses to which he adheres are: (1) "that everything that is depends ultimately upon a *self-existent Person*," (2) "that the Good, as Plato said, is the source of everything's being, and being known," and "that the ultimate aim of God . . . [is] to include the creative growth of persons in a responsive-responsible community," and (3) that "the qualitative structure of all being is psychic or mental as well as goal-directed."[106] Clearly Bertocci belongs to the line of theistic personalists who have flourished at Boston University, advancing the case for personalism in the philosophy of religion, moral philosophy, and metaphysics.

In the theory of the person Bertocci relies as much on recent psychology as on the personalist tradition he inherited. Here Gordon Allport has been most influential. In contrast with the dominant scientific psychologies, Allport has underscored the singularity of the individual. No matter how constant human nature is nor how universal human needs are, each individual manifests his own unique style in making his life. Thus the person is a pattern of becoming; his inward unity, which Allport called the *proprium*, consists in an interrelated web of attachments (of goals and values) which represent the significance the person's life has for himself. For Allport's psychological theory Bertocci has furnished the metaphysical foundations. A person is defined as "a unique, indivisible, but complex unity of sensing, feeling, desiring, remembering, imagining, thinking, (and willing and oughting)."[107] The person is also a continuant, self-identifying agent. Two metaphysical marks characterize the person: unity and continuity. From these marks it would be tempting to infer that the person is a substance which underlies and integrates its various states. However, Bertocci repudiates such an inference. The person, he insists, is a self-identifying agent; self-identification is a process of consciousness, and agency is a dynamic rather than a substantialist principle. Rejecting the substance concept in his theory of the person, Bertocci further offers a positive alternative. He urges that we identify a person not only with conscious-self-conscious activity but also with "*telic* or *purposive* activity. . . . In this sense, *conor, ergo sum* tells a more complete story of the human being than *cogito, ergo sum*."[108]

Since Bertocci considers telic or purposive activity to be the core of the person, his metaphysics is logically linked to human values. Affirming the freedom of individual persons to choose their own values, Bertocci distinguishes a person's will-agency from his will-power. A person's "will-agency" consists in his "capacity . . . to effect a change that is consistent with the approved end of the moment of choice;" and his "will-power is the amount of change that can be effectuated as seen from the point of view of the end contemplated."[109] He also distinguishes "person" from "personality."

> A *personality* is learned as a *person* interacts with other persons. More exactly, a person's personality is his more or less systematic mode of response to himself, to others, and to his total environment in the light of what he believes them to be, and what they actually are.[110]

From this theory of the person, therefore, follows a teleological moral theory. Values spring from personal needs and wants; personal development is directed toward the realization of values. The good life is the supreme moral value for the human person. The good life, moreover, exemplifies

> . . . the principle of most inclusive harmony in value experience. . . . In other words, the life best to live, at any stage of a person's existence, is the life that keeps a creative and mutually sustaining balance between the largest range of values open to him.[111]

The concept of the human person is a paradigm of the concept of God. As a person is "the kind of being who is a knowing-caring-unity in continuity,"[112] so is God. As a self-identity himself, however, God is not a unity of all other beings. As a unity-continuity, he is, however, "like the finite person, a Knower, a Mind or Spirit."[113] Since He is cosmic, He is omniscient. In addition, He is benevolent—in Bertocci's words, "a loving agent."[114] He is a cosmic creator who creates *ex nihilo*. And the finite human creators whom He creates are also creative, so that God is the "creator of co-creators."[115] Indeed Bertocci has described God to be a kind of "Conductor-Composer" with finite persons for players in His orchestra. In this symphonic pluralism, accordingly,

. . . the purpose of the Conductor-Composer in creating the
score was not simply to have the players follow the score
slavishly. His ultimate aim was to help the members to enter
creatively into the total value-meanings that he himself experienced. He is creating anew as he conducts *this* orchestra. And
he in turn undergoes a new moral-aesthetic experience as he
responds creatively to the performance of each of these players
and to the performance as a whole.[116]

CONCLUDING OBSERVATIONS

Idealism in America since 1900 has been a rich and vital type of
philosophy. It has embraced a wide variety of positions within the
framework of absolutism, and it has witnessed the formation of a
consistent body of doctrines within the personalist movement. While
idealism has favored values over empirical facts and theories, it has
nonetheless accommodated itself to the sciences and even, on occasion,
exploited the findings and methods of the sciences for its own constructive purposes. Although idealism has receded since its high tide
in American philosophy during the late nineteenth century, it is still
very much alive, especially in the area of values, in moral philosophy
and the philosophy of religion. The recent founding of the new journal,
Idealistic Studies, by its editor, Robert Beck, who also served as editor
of *The Personalist* in 1967 and 1968, may be a catalyst of greater
creativity among idealists in the future. Besides the living idealists
discussed in the present paper, others are hard at work: to mention
two, Errol Harris on the philosophy of nature, and Nicholas Rescher on
the reformulation of idealist theses in the philosophical idiom of the
present.

Historically idealism has revolved around the ancient metaphysical
problem of the One and the Many, and the story of American idealism
in the twentieth century has illuminated the gravity of the problem.
On the whole the decline and fall of the Absolute has occurred in the
past half-century. Personalism differs from absolutism in that the former
stresses the Many and the latter the One, yet the struggle between
monism and pluralism surfaces in both types of idealism. Absolutism
has spawned a variety of doctrines, with differing degrees of monism.
Similarly, personalism, which arose in protest against absolutism and as

a positive affirmation of the plurality of finite persons, has also been entangled in the issues of monism and pluralism, but in a new guise. The most critical problems of personalism hinge on the relation between the supreme person (God) and created finite persons—viz., whether He is infinite, and if so, how they can be independent and free; or whether He is finite, and if so, how they can be subordinate creatures. Yet in its most dynamic contemporary form idealism, having overcome absolutism and taking nourishment from the temporalism of process philosophy, has culminated in personalism.

NOTES

1.   Andrew J. Reck, *Speculative Philosophy* (Albuquerque: University of New Mexico Press, 1972).

2.   Maurice Mandelbaum, *History, Man, & Reason: A Study in Nineteenth-Century Thought* (Baltimore: Johns Hopkins University Press, 1971), p. 6.

3.   Charles Hartshorne and Paul Weiss, eds., *The Collected Papers of Charles Sanders Peirce* (Cambridge: Harvard University Press, 1965), VI, 24.

4.   See his letter to Charles Renouvier, dated March 29, 1888, in Ralph Barton Perry, *The Thought and Character of William James* (Boston: Little, Brown, and Co., 1935), I, 702-705.

5.   First published in George P. Adams and William Pepperell Montague, eds., *Contemporary American Philosophy* (New York: Macmillan, 1930), II, 13-27.

6.   Clifford Barrett, ed., *Contemporary Idealism in America* (New York: Macmillan, 1932), pp. 297-326. Hoernlé's essay closes the volume. The other authors and their contributions in the order of their appearance in the volume are: George Herbert Palmer, "In Dedication: Josiah Royce"; Clifford Barrett, "Introduction"; Charles M. Bakewell, "Continuity of the Idealist Tradition"; William Ernest Hocking, "The Ontological Argument in Royce and Others"; G. Watts Cunningham, "On the Meaning Situation"; Wilbur M. Urban, "The Philosophy of Spirit: Idealism and the Philosophy of Value"; Joseph Alexander Leighton, "The Principle of Individuality and Value"; Edgar Sheffield Brightman, "The Finite Self"; John Elof Boodin, "God and Cosmic Structure"; Radoslav A. Tsanoff, "The Theory of Moral Value"; and Charles W. Hendel, Jr., "The Meaning of Obligation."

Hoernlé was in good company when he greeted Whitehead's philosophy as a form of idealism. In chapter 16 of *A History of Philosophical Ideas in America* (New York: Ronald Press, 1949), W. H. Werkmeister also treated Whitehead as a "later idealist." Werkmeister's definition of idealism is broader than the one proposed in the present paper. Contending that "idealism in America has taken a variety of forms," Werkmeister applies the term "idealist" to all those thinkers who "have placed special emphasis upon the significance of values, and have presented views for which religious interests remained central." Yet Werkmeister counts Whitehead an idealist despite the fact that he "makes nature the central issue and thus represents a second basic orientation within the general framework of idealistic thought" (Ibid., p. 343).

7.   See Herbert W. Schneider, "Crises in Santayana's Life and Mind," *The Southern Journal of Philosophy* 10 (1972): 109-113.

8.   Hartley Burr Alexander, *Nature and Human Nature* (Chicago: Open Court, 1923), p. 3. Relevantly, Werkmeister treats Alexander as an exponent of "aesthetic idealism" (ibid., pp. 307-316). Yet Alexander's philosophy is dualistic to the point of being Manichaean. Undoubtedly, Alexander deserves a long overdue critical study. On the basis of my incomplete examination of his writings I doubt that such a study would demonstrate that Alexander was an idealist, except in some peculiar sense of the word.

9.   Josiah Royce, *The Religious Aspect of Philosophy* (Boston: Houghton, Mifflin, and Co., 1885), p. 423.

10.   Josiah Royce and others, *The Conception of God* (New York: Macmillan, 1897), p. 109.

11.   Ibid., pp. 98-99.

12.   James Edwin Creighton, *Studies in Speculative Philosophy*, ed. by Harold R. Smart (New York: Macmillan, 1925), p. 259.

13.   Ibid.

14.   Ibid., p. 271.

15.   Ibid., p. 272.

16.   Mary Whiton Calkins, "The Philosophic 'Credo' of an Absolute Personalist," in Adams and Montague, I, 200.

17.   Ibid., p. 201.

18.   Ibid., p. 203.

19.   Ibid., p. 209.

20.   Ibid., p. 202.

21.   John Elof Boodin, *A Realistic Universe,* rev. 2d ed. (New York: Macmillan, 1931), p. 73.

22.   John Elof Boodin, *Three Interpretations of the Universe* (New York: Macmillan, 1934), p. 499.

23.   John Elof Boodin, *The Social Mind* (New York: Macmillan, 1939), p. viii.

24.   Ibid., p. 141., For a full discussion of Boodin's philosophy, see Andrew J. Reck, *Recent American Philosophy* (New York: Pantheon Books, 1964), chap. 4, pp. 123-153.

25.   James Alexander Leighton, "My Development and Present Creed," in Adams and Montague, I, 427.

26.   Ibid., p. 441.

27.   William Ernest Hocking, *The Meaning of God in Human Experience: A Philosophic Study of Religion* (New Haven: Yale University Press, 1912), p. vi.

28.   Ibid., p. vii.

29.   Ibid., p. 229.

30.   Ibid., p. 206.

31.   William Ernest Hocking, *Human Nature and Its Remaking*, rev. ed. (New Haven: Yale University Press, 1929), p. 168.

32. William Ernest Hocking, *The Meaning of Immortality in Human Experience Including Thoughts on Death and Life* (New York: Harper and Bros., 1957), p. 59.

33. Ibid., p. 152.

34. William Ernest Hocking, *The Lasting Elements of Individualism* (New Haven: Yale University Press, 1937), p. 133. For further discussions of Hocking's philosophy, see Reck, *Recent American Philosophy,* chap. 2, pp. 42-83, and Leroy S. Rouner, ed., *Philosophy, Religion, and the Coming World Civilization; Essays in Honor of William Ernest Hocking* (The Hague: Martinus Nijhoff, 1966).

35. Josiah Royce, *Lectures on Modern Idealism*, ed. by J. Lowenberg (New Haven: Yale University Press, 1923), p. 237.

36. Wilbur Marshall Urban, *The Intelligible World* (New York: Macmillan, 1929), p. 64.

37. Wilbur Marshall Urban, "Philosophy of Spirit: Idealism and the Philosophy of Value," in Barrett, p. 106. For a full discussion of Urban's philosophy, see Reck, *Recent American Philosophy,* chap. 5, pp. 154-180.

38. Elijah Jordan, *Theory of Legislation: An Essay on the Dynamics of Public Mind,* 2d ed. (Chicago: University of Chicago Press, 1952), p. 170.

39. Ibid., p. 384.

40. Elijah Jordan, *Forms of Individuality: An Inquiry into the Grounds of Order in Human Relations* (Indianapolis: Charles W. Laut, 1927), p. 27.

41. Ibid., p. 3.

42. Ibid., p. 187.

43. For a full discussion of Jordan's philosophy, see Reck, *Recent American Philosophy,* chap. 9, pp. 276-310.

44. G. Watts Cunningham, "A Search for System," in Adams and Montague, I, 253.

45. Ibid., p. 261.

46. G. Watts Cunningham, "On the Meaning Situation," in Barrett, p. 78.

47. Ibid., pp. 98-99.

48. Perhaps it should be recalled that Parker edited the Schopenhauer *Selections* for Scribner's Modern Student's Library.

49. De Witt H. Parker, "Empirical Idealism," in Adams and Montague, II, 163-183.

50. For a full discussion of Parker's philosophy, see Reck, *Recent American Philosophy*, chap. 6, pp. 181-207.

51. James Ward Smith, "Stace, Walter Terrence," *The Encyclopedia of Philosophy,* ed. by Paul Edwards (New York: Macmillan, 1967), VIII, 2b.

52. Walter T. Stace, *The Theory of Knowledge and Existence* (Oxford: Clarendon Press, 1932), p. 443.

53. Walter T. Stace, *The Nature of the World, An Essay in Phenomenalist Metaphysics* (Princeton: Princeton University Press, 1940), p. 34.

54. Ibid., p. 36.

55. Ibid., p. 244.

56. Walter T. Stace, *Time and Eternity* (Princeton: Princeton University Press, 1952), p. 8.

57. Brand Blanshard, *The Nature of Thought,* (London: Allen and Unwin, 1939), II, 519.

58. Ibid., I, 518.

59. Ibid., p. 494.

60. Brand Blanshard, *Reason and Analysis* (London and La Salle, Ill.: Allen and Unwin and Open Court, 1962), p. 491.

61. For a full discussion of Blanshard's philosophy, see Andrew J. Reck, *The New American Philosophers* (Baton Rouge: Louisiana State University Press, 1968), chap. 3, pp. 81-119.

62. See Albert C. Knudson, *The Philosophy of Personalism* (Boston: Boston University Press, 1949), pp. 17ff.

63. Werkmeister, *A History of Philosophical Ideas in America,* p. 326.

64. For the platform of personalism, see ibid., pp. 326-328.

65. Ibid., p. 103.

66. Borden Parker Bowne, *Personalism* (Boston and New York: Houghton, Mifflin, and Co., 1908), p. 25.

67. Ibid., p. 37.

68. Ibid., p. 40.

69. Ibid., p. 69.

70. Ibid., p. 93.

71. Ibid., p. 197.

72. Ibid., p. 262.

73. Ibid., p. 266.

74. Ibid., pp. 266-267.

75. John Wright Buckham and George Malcolm Stratton, *George Holmes Howison: Philosopher and Teacher: A Selection from His Writings with a Biographical Sketch* (Berkeley: University of California Press, 1934), p. 125.

76. Ibid., p. 127.

77. Ibid.

78. Ibid., p. 133.

79. Ibid.

80. Ibid., p. 135.

81. Ibid., p. 136.

82. Ibid.

83. Ibid., p. 129.

84. Ralph Tyler Flewelling, *Creative Personality, A Study in Philosophical Reconciliation* (New York: Macmillan, 1926), p. 8.

85. Ralph Tyler Flewelling, *The Person or the Significance of Man* (Los Angeles: Ward Ritchie Press, 1952), p. 11.

86. Ibid., p. 332.

87. Ibid., p. 126.

88. Ibid., p. 321.

89. Ibid., p. 323.

90. Albert C. Knudson, *The Philosophy of Personalism* (Boston: Boston University Press, 1949), p. 87.

91. Ibid., p. 77.

92. Ibid., p. 80.

93. Edgar Sheffield Brightman, *An Introduction to Philosophy,* rev. ed. (New York: Henry Holt, 1951), p. 293.

94.   Edgar Sheffield Brightman, *Person and Reality: At Introduction to Metaphysics*, ed. by Peter A. Bertocci (New York: Ronald Press, 1958), p. 18.

95.   Edgar Sheffield Brightman, *Nature and Values* (New York: Abingdon Press, 1945), p. 56.

96.   Edgar Sheffield Brightman, *Person and Reality*, p. 226.

97.   Ibid., p. 250.

98.   Edgar Sheffield Brightman, *Persons and Values* (Boston: Boston University Press, 1952), p. 18.

99.   Edgar Sheffield Brightman, *The Problem of God* (New York: Abingdon Press, 1930), p. 113.

100.   Ibid.

101.   Edgar Sheffield Brightman, *The Finding of God* (New York: Abingdon Press, 1931), p. 186.

102.   Edgar Sheffield Brightman, *Is God a Person?* (New York: Association Press, 1932), p. 80. For a full discussion of Brightman's philosophy, see Andrew J. Reck, *Recent American Philosophy,* chap. 10, pp. 311-336.

103.   W. H. Werkmeister, *Man and His Values* (Lincoln, Nebraska: University of Nebraska Press, 1967), p. vii.

104.   Ibid., pp. 153-156. See also W. H. Werkmeister, *Theories of Ethics* (Lincoln, Nebraska: Johnson, 1961), pp. 285-365.

105.   Werkmeister, *Man and His Values*, p. 238.

106.   Peter A. Bertocci, "The Perspective of a Teleological Personalistic Idealist," in *Contemporary American Philosophy, Second Series,* ed. by John E. Smith (London and New York: George Allen & Unwin and Humanities Press, 1970), p. 248.

107.   Peter A. Bertocci, *The Person God Is* (London and New York: George Allen & Unwin and Humanities Press, 1970), p. 96.

108.   Ibid., p. 61.

109.   Peter A. Bertocci and Richard M. Millard, *Personality and the Good: Psychological and Ethical Perspectives* (New York: David McKay, 1963), p. 194.

110.   Bertocci, *The Person God Is*, p. 95.

111.   Bertocci and Millard, *Personality and the Good*, p. 331.

112.   Bertocci, *The Person God Is*, p. 20.

113.   Ibid., p. 22.

114.   Ibid., p. 26.

115.   Ibid., p. 34.

116.   Ibid., p. 222.

The Surveyor as Hero: Reflections on Ernest Hocking's Philosophy of Nature

Leroy S. Rouner

AS A YOUNG MAN Ernest Hocking was not primarily concerned with questions about nature. In the introduction to his doctoral dissertation at Harvard in 1904 he cheerfully made common cause with the idealists, noting that many who shared that persuasion were belatedly struggling to give the outer world of physical nature its metaphysical due. He was mindful that idealism had overstated its point in order to make it; that its triumphalist celebration of will and idea in the individual self could become irrelevant to the necessary human business of coping with natural fact. He welcomed this interaction between idealism and what he called natural realism. The twin influences of his two great teachers, the cerebral Royce and the earthy James, symbolized for him a fundamental and creative tension between idealistic and pragmatic values in American thought and experience. Furthermore, in his studies of Hegel, he had been impressed with the pragmatic element in the famous idealistic statement about the rational being the real. Hegel had said that the rational is *wirklich*, or that which really works in the world. Idealism and pragmatism seemed to him to belong together, and he welcomed the growing interest in questions about nature on the part of idealistic philosophers.

Nevertheless, this was not his primary problem. Idealism's absorption in the reality of individual selfhood had also obscured the relations between one self and another. His project was "to restore the stinging reality of contact with the human comrade."[1] Solipsism must be

overcome. His was to be a philosophy of community. As he mused on
the interrelationships among oneself, other selves, and natural objects,
he was determined to give each of these three items of experience a
measure of metaphysical independence. From the start he was committed to a dialectical method as the best guarantee of that independence.
His primary focus, however, was on the relation between the self and
the other self. For example, his criticism of Royce's dialectic of
interpretation was that it made our lines of connection with the other
person always indirect. Royce never solved the problem of solipsism to
Hocking's satisfaction. Hocking insisted that our communication with
our neighbors is as direct and immediate as it seems to be, and that we
need no Roycean "as if" to remind ourselves that all communication is
routed through our common human relationship to the Absolute.

As Hocking came to understand it, the objects of nature are the
coin of our communication with one another. The world of nature is
the world of mind because the objects of nature are what we think
about and therefore constitute the content of mind. He absorbed "the
outer world" into the individual self, but the "outer world" did not
lose its objectivity, because *my* perception of it is guaranteed by my
neighbor's common perception of it. Her world and my world are the
same world. Objective truth is empirically verifiable, but Hocking noted
that the empirical element is untrustworthy. It is public verifiability
which finally establishes fact, not any individual's empirical perception
of it; so he argued that natural fact is a public and therefore social
achievement. The world of natural objects is the means of solving the
problem of solipsism when its objects are seen as the content of the
common mind which I share with my neighbor. This is the significance
of the famous passage in *The Meaning of God* in which he describes
the experience of two separate minds meeting and sharing a common
experience.

> I have sometimes sat looking at a comrade, speculating on this
> mysterious isolation of self from self. Why are we so made that
> I gaze and see of thee only thy Wall, and never Thee? This Wall
> of thee is but a movable part of the Wall of my world; and I also
> am a Wall to thee: we look out at one another from behind masks.
> How would it seem if my mind could but once be *within* thine;
> and we could meet and without barrier be with each other? And
> then it has fallen upon me like a shock—as when one thinking
> himself alone has felt a presence—But I *am* in thy soul. These

things around me are in thy experience. They are thy own; when I touch them and move them I change *thee*. When I look on them I see what thou seest; when I listen, I hear what thou hearest. I am in the great Room of thy soul; and I experience thy very experience. For *where art thou*? Not there, behind those eyes, within that head, in darkness, fraternizing with chemical processes. Of these, in my own case, I know nothing and will know nothing; for my existence is spent not behind my Wall, but in front of it. I am there, where I have treasures. And there art thou, also. This world in which I live is the world of thy soul: and being within that, I am within thee. I can imagine no contact more real and thrilling than this; that we should meet and share identity, not through ineffable inner depths (alone), but here, through the foregrounds of common experience; and that thou shouldst be—not behind that mask—but *here*, pressing with all thy consciousness upon me, *containing* me, and these things of mine. This is reality: and having seen it thus, I can never again be frightened into monadism by reflections which have strayed from their guiding insight.[2]

Elsewhere he elaborates on this idea that the world is known as content of Other Mind by pointing out that even when we are alone in the process of perceiving an object such as a tree, we *know* that the tree is objectively real. How so? Not because our senses are infallible. It is because we sense a dimension of meaning in the world of natural fact. Nature, as symbol, is for him a realm of Other Mind. Even alone, he finds that we are companioned by a presence communicated through nature.

Hocking makes this discovery dialectically, in a series of reactions to a purposeless world of natural fact. He is not presupposing an Aristotelian principle of the world's natural intelligibility, and this is a distinction which needs to be stressed. Aristotle never had to go outside the relation between the subject and the object in order to explain the knowing process, since for him the object was naturally intelligible. His "object" belongs neither with the *res extensa* of Descartes nor the *Ding an sich* of Kant. Both these modern understandings of "object" assume that the knowing process takes place entirely within the mind. As a result, it is neither necessary nor possible to say what the "object" might be in and of itself. Descartes ventures no more than the assertion that an "object" is something extended in space. Kant, humbly noting that all our assertions are, after all, only our assertions, and therefore imply the prescript *Ich denke*, confesses that the nature of the thing in itself must always escape his capacities as a knower.

Aristotle, for his part, was not bothered by the modern "problem of knowledge" because knowing, as he understood it, was a natural process taking place in a naturally intelligible world. Aristotle observes that all natural objects have a "career" (Randall)[3] or "development" (Windelband)[4] made possible by their power to be that particular thing. This same power enables them to be known. Knowing does not take place entirely within the mind of the knower. It takes place at the point of meeting between the power of the knower to know and the capacity of the object to be known.[5] Aristotle's nature, like Whitehead's, is lively. A thing has its own natural power to be what it is.

Hocking is quite specific, however, in rejecting the Aristotelian and Whiteheadian idea that nature is somehow "alive." He agrees with Whitehead that the "bifurcation of nature," stemming from Descartes' separation of experienced reality into *res extensa* and *res cogitans*, must be overcome. Rather than regard Cartesianism as a disaster, however, he regards it as a necessary step. Dialectic must move beyond Descartes, but it must take seriously the cluster of philosophical problems which result from the Cartesian bifurcation, especially the body-mind problem and the problem of our knowledge of other minds. To be sure, he believes that Cartesianism requires some preliminary repair. As it stands, he finds the *Cogito ergo sum* incomplete. Descartes has fallen victim to the myth of the empty mind. We cannot simply think, Hocking notes; we must think something. This "something" is the necessary content of mind. Hence he revises the statement to make its implications specific: *Cogito aliquid, ergo sum et aliquid est.* I think something, therefore I exist, and something else also exists; for if mind is nothing apart from its content, an ontological affirmation of my own reality as mind is at the same time an ontological affirmation of the reality of mind's content, i.e., my experienced object world.[6]

The dialectical logic of Hocking's conclusion is offered as a description of our experience. Idealism, for him, is not a "school" of philosophy, it is the recognition that all philosophical enterprise, of whatever "school," is based on the twin assumptions that things have a meaning and that something at least of that meaning can be known.[7] But "meaning" is not initially a characteristic of logic or language. It is always fundamentally a characteristic of experience. Meaning is always in search of an idea in which to express itself. An idea is nothing more or less than an experience in shape for communication. Epistemology describes the experience of our learning about our world. And how does that experience run?

As Hocking sees it, our initial reflection on our experience of the world centers on the objective reality of nature. We find nature ready-made. Because it is the scene upon which we arrived, and is therefore prior to us, we must accept it obediently, as given. With one of his characteristic turns of phrase, Hocking observes that "Nature-drama goes on, careless of the seating of the house, or of the gossip there."[8] This natural realism is the thesis of his dialectic. The antithesis which this perception naturally calls forth in him is the reminder of subjective idealism that nature is always and only nature as it is known to us. But the further reminder that nature is necessary to mind, indeed, that it is creative of mind in us, leads into the synthetic judgment that nature is a realm of Other Mind, since the only thing which can create a mind is an other mind.[9]

There is nothing abstract about any of this. For all the fact that mind may shape its experience of particular natural objects and phenomena through "advance weaving on the part of ideas," the fact of the matter is that:

> What vividness and definiteness I now seem to possess comes, we must still think, chiefly through this flood of sense which irrupts upon my anticipative outgoings. Cut me off in earnest from my experience of nature, and I tend to become vague, indefinite, uncertain of myself. Let me lose a little in sight or hearing; and I find how much not only self but sense has been concerned in that influx. However vigorous the impetus of advance weaving on the part of my ideas—vigorous enough at time to falsify experience, displace feebler sensation—my own activity always accepts the irruptive material as its own authority and completion. Toward the Outer Reality I hold myself as toward that which sustains me from moment to moment in my present being.[10]

Hocking's dialectic then goes on to the Other Mind which is present in nature; discovers that it cannot be an empirical knower because empirical knowing is passive, and our experience is that nature is actively creative of mind in us; and turns to the ontological argument in support of its conclusion that the mind known in our experience of the natural world is that of an active Absolute Knower.

Hocking argues that nature is the realm of mind, but he insists that this argument must not qualify the objectivity of nature. Nature, as he sees it, including secondary qualities of objects, is first of all an objective causal network of events which is external to us, purposeless in its operations and meaningless in its significance. He protects the integrity of his dialectic by not resolving this initial "objectivity" of nature into anything else. But nature as objective fact poses a question for Hocking. He wonders not only why there should be anything in the first place—the classical ontological question—but, more specifically, why nature should present us with these facts rather than some other conceivable facts. Why, he asks, is nature purposeless rather than purposive? He answers that we would not be morally free to exercise our own purposes on nature if we were violating some hidden purposes of her own.

This is a crucial point for him, and he made it firmly and repeatedly, nowhere more baldly than when he wrote,

> The inanimateness of nature confers freedom to exploit and re-shape . . . A world of conscious enterprise and especially of social enterprise, would be impossible without such an impassive base; a world of meanings would necessarily include, and so give meaning to, such a world of the meaningless as abstract physical nature affords.[11]

This is why he insists that we begin with Descartes' division of reality into *res extensa* and *res cogitans*. This distinction has made possible an achievement in modern life and thought which Hocking is prepared to guard with all the wit and wisdom at his command. The spirit of "modernity," to which Cartesianism gave birth, elevated the individual self to a new position of primacy in the philosophy of civil rights, in the democratic theory of the state, and in the unique concern for individual human destiny as expressed in romanticism, depth psychology and existentialism.[12] This is Hocking's fundamental commitment. Selfhood is, for him, the ultimate category, because it is only selves who are creative, and creativity is his definition of reality. This commitment is his bond with the Boston personalism of Brightman, Bowne, Knudson, and Bertocci. But for Hocking the self is not an empty mind or a dreaming spirit; the self, for him, becomes itself only through activity. It needs something to think in order to know its own mind. It needs something to do in order to qualify as will. To an important extent the self shapes its own destiny, carves its own career. In order to do this it must have stuff to work on. Nature provides this stuff. Nature serves the self by providing those objects which become content of self (mind). Even more importantly, nature serves the self through its recalcitrant "over-againstness," by means of which mind (self) qualifies as will and enters on its destiny in the world.

Hocking was born and reared a midwesterner and a Methodist.[13] His philosophy reflects a traditional Christian view of nature as merely the stage on which the meaningful historical drama of salvation is. enacted. But at this point his regionalism may be more influential than his religion. The elegant neo-Hegelian dialectic, with its subtle touches of Husserlian phenomenology, strikes me as the European overlay of an essentially American pioneer philosophy. On metaphysical reflection, nature as symbol may provide infinite grist for the poet's mill. But in the primal encounter of the individual self with natural fact, the first order of business is to subdue nature. Hocking insists that only a purposeless nature can insure our freedom to shape our environment according to our own purposes. In a revealing metaphor, he argues that nature's purposelessness makes it possible for us "to dam rivers and fell trees" without fear of violating some hidden purpose of the natural world. The Harvard dialectician, I suggest, was a midwestern frontiersman at heart. In his philosophy of nature it is not the poet who presides. The surveyor is hero.[14]

I confess that my motivation for reexamining Hocking's philosophy of nature involves the uneasy suspicion that Americans have now dammed altogether too many of their rivers, and felled too many trees. But this personal prejudice leads into some of the unfinished business in Hocking's philosophical enterprise. Concerned as he was over the Cartesian "bifurcation of nature," he sought to move beyond this untenable dualism in modern thought to a new integration of selfhood, society, and physical nature. His philosophy of community sought a vision of the world as whole. This was his prophetic task as a philosopher: to provide a metaphysical foundation for the coming world civilization. Elsewhere, I have testified to my conviction that he was remarkably successful in doing this.[15] I want to explore his philosophy of nature, however, because it seems to me to be partly contradictory and partly inconsistent with the purpose of his philosophical program of forging a "passage beyond modernity." The crucial metaphysical issue here is one which I can only call the objective unreality of nature, for he has argued that nature is objective and at the same time unreal. Underlying this doctrine are two important assumptions: that we have an experience of nature as "purposeless" and that the knowing process takes place entirely within the mind of the knower.

Let me suggest what seems to me to be problematical. First, as to our experience of nature's purposelessness: because of Hocking's concern for creativity in the self, for him purpose always involves self-conscious decision. Now a tree, obviously, has not decided to be a tree; but then we did not initially decide to be selves either. Because the tree has no self-conscious purpose, as far as we can tell, does that mean that it can have no living or natural purpose? Or is this distinction metaphorical, or perhaps silly? I must persist. Are we justified in regarding the tree's being-in-the-world as purposeless on the basis of our experience? Hocking's use of "purpose" is built upon the radical Cartesian distinction between mind and matter. This usage is a limited one which common language does not seem to reflect. I doubt that one can describe an experience of natural phenomena adequately without recourse to purposive language, in the common sense of that word, and I believe that this language reflects a significant element in our experience. Later I will try to show that Hocking's description of nature's purposelessness as he experiences it is really a picture of contrary purposes, and not a lack of purpose.

Secondly, as to the locale of the knowing process: in outlining the "passage beyond modernity" Hocking has emphasized wholeness in our view of the world. He has done this without challenging the Cartesian and modern view that the knowing process takes place entirely within the mind, since his dialectic discovers nature as the content of mind. However, in order to guard our natural realism and the clarity and distinctness of our ideas, Hocking takes the mind-matter problem seriously. He has to decide which is really real. It is mind, of course, and therefore matter has to be explained. This means that nature is initially unintelligible to him. It is this unintelligibility which raises the question in his mind: Why should nature be this way? Does its meaninglessness mean anything? Does its purposelessness serve any purpose? He implies that those who do not raise this question lack metaphysical insight and courage.[16] His chiding of British empiricism at this point is a trifle ironic, because his question arises out of realistic presuppositions which he shares with that tradition, i.e., that nature, *qua* nature, is unintelligible. His radical realism in regard to nature's purposelessness gives rise to the dialectic of a purposive Whole.

Given his presuppositions, the question is a natural one. For a purposive being to discover oneself in an alien, purposeless world is to ask instinctively, "What am I doing in this strange place?"

But what if it doesn't seem like a strange place? For myself, I find that I do indeed want to know why there is something and not nothing; how it happens that I am here; and what I am to do. But I do not instinctively find myself asking why nature presents me with these facts rather than some others. I do not experience the facts in hand as radically uncongenial. For all nature's admitted over-againstness, I sense no total discrepancy between myself and nature to shock me into reflection on this issue. I sense faint elements of ontological continuity between my life and that of the tree. And so, of course, does Hocking. But for him, the continuity is derived from dialectical reflection of mind on the curious fact of "matter." To me continuity seems already present to a degree in the immediacy of my experience. Thus the knowing process seems to me to be centered in the natural relation between myself as knower and an inherently intelligible world of physical objects. Knowing takes place in this relation, as I understand it, and not within the confines of some "mind," because I sense no total discontinuity between "mind" and some "matter" which is totally alien to mind.

But Hocking also speaks of meaning as part of his immediate experience of nature, and of the purposelessness of nature as "abstract." I must confess perplexity at this point. My unresolved question about Hocking's theory of perception is whether the second movement of the dialectic, in which God is the creative agent in the perceiving process, doesn't cancel out the first movement of the dialectic, in which the object exists in its own right. At the conclusion of the dialectic Hocking seems to be saying that the object is established as real by virtue of being an idea in the mind of God. Earlier he was saying that matter has its own independent reality. What, then, is the final status of the object in Hocking's dialectic?[17] The answer to this crucial question seems to me to be unclear. I think the problem lies in Hocking's having accepted the Cartesian bifurcation in the first place. The division of reality into mind and matter robs nature of a dynamic which Hocking's dialectic strives mightily to restore. Clearly we need to reexamine what Hocking is saying and explore its implications in more detail.

He begins, as we have already noted, with the vividness and clarity of nature's objectivity, and therefore the fact that nature is over against us. Nature, he argues, is the source of whatever clarity, pungency, distinctness and objectivity that we (and Descartes) may hope to achieve in our thought. For all its inanimate purposelessness, nature provides the standards, or at least the examples, of what it is to be really real. In the course of his argument, Hocking accepts the objective status of secondary qualities. For him they are in the object, not simply in the mind. This confession makes him vulnerable to the naturalistic argument that nature, *qua* nature, is the cause of its own sense data. But if nature is to be its own cause, we are left with the Cartesian bifurcation between the mind of selfhood and the mechanics of nature, because a self-causing nature is independent of mind. Hocking argues that nature creates mind in one by providing the object-content of mind; and since only mind can create mind, the bifurcation cannot stand. We must admit, he says, that nature conceived realistically is incapable of being the cause of its own sense data. The cause must be sought in that Other Mind which we perceive through natural fact as symbol, but which transcends natural fact as immediately experienced.

Hocking is assuming the Cartesian and modern notion of cause when he speaks of nature as a realm of objective fact. Modernity accepted two of Aristotle's four causes, and rejected two. The material and efficient causes remain; the formal and final causes fall away. For Aristotle, on the other hand, the formal cause was the structural outline of development for any particular thing. His point was a simple one: the reason that acorns, under happy conditions, become oaks is that that is their nature; they cannot become maples because they are not that kind of thing. And the formal cause, I suggest, is no less a report of experience than the material and efficient causes. These kinds are reliable indications of the direction in which the career or development of the particular thing must move, and does move. If the formal cause is a report of our observation that kinds of things are subject to an unavoidable structure, final cause is recognition that each particular thing does indeed have the power to move toward fulfilling its potentiality as a particular kind. Here we are close to the heart of the matter, for "final cause" in Aristotle embodies much that I intend in the idea of a living or natural purpose. If experience is to be the touchstone of truth, I do not see how we can limit the observable "motions" of nature to a mechanics of cause and effect. This is an abstraction from experience. The thrust of the oak sapling toward its appointed end as an oak tree, in spite of numerous natural and man-made impediments, is surely enough to draw even a surveyor's grudging acknowledgment of the natural dynamism, or "desire," which literally "moves" the acorn to become an oak. The mystery of nature's career is quite wonderful but clearly observable. Because Hocking understands nature initially as a network of efficient causes, he has to move beyond our immediate experience of nature to an explanation of the final cause or purpose of the network as a whole. For him, the meaning of the natural network of cause, which is its final cause or purpose, is beyond nature. The Absolute, which as Self or Mind we know as God, is the source of that ultimate meaning on which nature, as symbol, depends. Nature, as the efficient realm of cause and effect, has no independent reality of its own. God is the transcendent meaning of natural motions.[18] Whether God is immediately involved in the immanent processes of nature is not clear.

My question is whether the richness of this transcendent meaning has not been bought too dearly. Hocking has limited our immediate experience of nature, as opposed to our reflective reaction to experience, to the narrow confines of cause and effect. As I read him, Hocking sensed this problem when he spoke of the need for a "widened empiricism" which would do justice to the wonder of our natural experience, as well as its mechanics.[19] But this element of mystery always seemed to him to require dialectical explanation. He was loath to regard it as a natural part of our experience for fear that it would qualify the freedom of the self to "exploit and reshape" the natural environment. As I shall suggest later, I think this fear is unwarranted.

But nature for him is not only a realm of sense data, it is also a realm of law. As he sees it, the causal network of natural law requires some source of initiation outside the network itself, lest the explanation of nature as a system of causes and effects becomes lost in the frustrations of infinite regress.[20] This source of the law which governs natural causality is purposive. He makes an important distinction here. Causality as we experience it immediately is efficient. We obey these laws in order to determine how best to "exploit and reshape" nature. He is concerned with nature as law in this sense when he quotes Bacon's famous dictum, "We cannot command nature except by obeying her."[21] Natural law is causal, not purposive. But ultimately causality for him does have a meaning which *is* purposive. The causal order of nature "may express a consistent will animating the whole cosmic order."[22] The purposelessness of nature is given to us for a purpose, that is, the fulfillment of our human purposes. Hocking argues a new teleology in which causality and purpose are not mutually exclusive.

Cause, after all, is not observed, it is only imputed, as David Hume made clear. Nevertheless, even the most committed British empiricists continue to speak of causes without apology, in spite of their inability to prove their existence. Hocking argues, by the same token, that every event may have both a cause and a purpose or meaning. Cause, however, is always individual, piecemeal, specific. Purpose, on the other hand, is a characteristic of the entire network of natural interactions. He argues for such a purpose on three grounds: that the natural network of cause results in an "assignable value"; that it preserves what it produces; and that it exhibits selectivity in the process.[23] I do not labor these arguments because I am more than ready to agree with them. But must they apply only to the causal network as a whole? Do we not have evidence, in experience, that the same logic also applies in the first instance to individual events within the causal network? Let me put the question directly. Does Hocking himself ever describe an experience of nature as purposeless?

In his own terms, grounding in experience is required. Now it may be that our awareness of nature as "over against" us is such an experience. In the development of his later thought, beginning with the essay "Establishing an Idealistic Metaphysics by a New Route" published at the end of 1941, running through the essays "Fact and Destiny" and "Fact, Field and Destiny," culminating in his final book, *The Meaning of Immortality in Human Experience*, there is a new sense of nature as a threat to our purposes. In his earlier writing the brute factuality of nature is a challenge, grist for the mill of our creativity, a necessary precondition for the hard work of thought. It is here that the pioneer spirit is most in evidence. In his later years he recognized that brute fact could in fact be brutal. The tragedies of history in the First World War and the Depression reminded him that nature, too, has a tragic dimension. He spoke of its "immensity, operating according to natural laws, opaque, silent, inscrutable, frequently cruel, and apparently uninterested in the lot of us poor human beings."[24] Ultimately there is still the conviction that "these appearances are not true," but the later Hocking is more aware of the threat of purposelessness as meaninglessness in nature than the author of *The Meaning of God in Human Experience* had been.

As a description, however, the picture of nature as "immense . . . inscrutable . . . cruel . . . (and) uninterested" is not a picture of purposelessness, but of a nature which is going its own way in spite of our purposes. May we say that it is pursuing its own purposes? I admit that common language can be misleading. If I cut my hand on the radiator fan of my car's engine, I may well speak of the cutting action of the fan as "cruel." This usage is purely metaphorical. I am projecting on to the engine a purposiveness which is not inherent in it. May not the same thing be said of the purposive language used to describe nature? My view is that we instinctively use purposive language to describe all experience, because we live in a world which is naturally dynamic in a way which means something. To put it differently, the flow of natural motions follows channels toward goals. In this sense nature is purposive. Machines, on the other hand, exhibit this natural dynamism only insofar as they incorporate natural materials and functions in which the dynamism is inherent. As an artificial product of human ingenuity, a machine is only a tool for fulfilling the purpose of the artificer. The spinning of my automobile fan is purposeless in itself, and not "cruel." This is an analogy to Hocking's view of nature, for in the relation between ourselves and our machines the purposeless does indeed exist for a purpose given to it by its creator. Because he understands nature as a causal order, and because he understands cause to be efficient and material in the Aristotelian sense, Hocking's view of nature fits readily into the conceptual scheme of Newtonian or "classical" mechanics. For him nature is a machine in the sense that it operates according to the laws of cause and effect, just as my car engine does, and quite unlike the operations of my mind.

Hocking has offered his realistic doctrine of nature as purposeless not only as a report of experience, but also as consonant with the prevailing view of modern physical science. I have already challenged his view that we have an experience of the purposelessness of nature. I also want to challenge his assumption that purposelessness in nature is required by physical science. His defense of nature as purposeless relies heavily on a principle of Newtonian mechanics which quantum theory has proven not to be an absolute law, and that is the principle of efficient causality itself. Efficient causality assumes that a body can only act upon, and therefore have an effect on, another body, when they are both in the same place. Efficient causality is always local. There can be no action-at-a-distance. You can't effect something unless you come into contact with it. Quantum mechanics, however, has first theorized and later proven experimentally that the motions of electrons can be altered without the presence of any locally causal forces. In reporting on one such experiment, Frederick Werner, Professor of Physics at Xavier University, Cincinnati, comments that "this kind of phenomenon is simply inconceivable in terms of classical mechanics, because here no local forces act on the electrons."[25] The significance of this discovery could be far-reaching and might even provide experimental openings toward theory building in a scientific philosophy of nature which could take full advantage of Aristotle's categories of formal and final cause. At the very least, however, it must qualify any assertion that we know nature to be purposeless. Causal efficiency as a universal law of natural order gave support to such a philosophical doctrine. Quantum theory must at least make agnostics of us all; nature may be purposeless or it may be purposive. If there is no scientific basis for arguing that nature is essentially a person, neither is there basis for arguing that it is essentially a machine.

Freed from the idea that contemporary physical theory requires a purposeless nature, it is possible to give a fairly simple answer to Hocking's point that we would not be morally free to dam rivers and fell trees if we knew that we were violating some hidden purpose of the tree itself. There are, for example, numerous illustrations in the folklore of the American Indian of respectful transactions between humankind and the natural world in which the life of the tree, or more to the point, the life of the deer and the buffalo, were in fact recognized as meaningful in themselves. Characteristically the hunter ritualized this interchange by acknowledging his need for meat, and asking the deer's permission to take its life for this purpose. Acknowledgment that the river or the tree has a purpose in being itself need not necessarily prevent dams or timber harvests, nor would it require a return to primitive spirituality. It would necessarily prevent only a heedless rape of nature; it would require only responsiveness to the reality of natural purpose, and responsibility for integrating it into a range of human purposes. The implications for a theory of knowledge are the reverse of the post-Cartesian view that knowledge takes place entirely within the mind, and that we do not need to know, nor are we able to know, very much about the natural object in itself. If we begin with the assumption that nature is purposive, then much difficulty in the "problem of perception" falls away, and the task is to describe the natural function of knowing in a naturally intelligible world. In this perspective the difference between the knower and the thing known will still be real, but it will not be radical. Because both minds and material objects are purposive beings, the absolute distinction between mind and matter will prove useful only in those situations where the principles of classical Newtonian mechanics continue to apply. As a metaphysical principle it would seem to be no longer valid.

Freed from the Newtonian view that the only natural causes are efficient causes, previously inconceivable possibilities of causal motion now demand serious exploration. Psycho-kinesis is one example. Ernest Hocking's dialectic is not inhospitable to these explorations. As it now stands, the radical realism of his philosophy of nature makes an inevitable dialectical demand for a radical mysticism in his philosophy of religion and an intellectualistic elaboration of the argument in the final synthesis. Modification of the dialectic's thesis of radical realism will not, I think, destroy the structure of the dialectic itself. Rather, it should make it possible to integrate immediate experience and dialectical reflection more closely than they are in Hocking's system at present. The details of readjustment in the dialectic will require separate treatment on another occasion. For the present it is perhaps enough to suggest that surveyors may not be the best possible heroes for a philosophy of nature.

NOTES

1. W. E. Hocking, "The Elementary Experience of Other Conscious Being in Its Relations to the Elementary Experience of Physical and Reflexive Objects," (Ph.D. dissertation, Harvard University, Cambridge, 1904), p. iv.

2. W. E. Hocking, *The Meaning of God in Human Experience* (New Haven: Yale University Press, 1912), pp. 265-266.

3. John H. Randall, Jr., *Aristotle* (New York: Columbia University Press, 1960), *passim*, esp. chap. 4, "Aristotle's Functional Concepts: Living and Desiring," pp. 59-80.

4. Wilhelm Windelband, *A History of Philosophy,* vol. I (New York: Harper and Bros., Torchbook, 1958), esp. chap. 3, "The Systematic Period," Section 13, "System of Development: Aristotle," pp. 139-154.

5. See Randall, *Aristotle,* chap. 5, "The Power of Selective Response: Sensing and Knowing," pp. 81-106.

6. W. E. Hocking, *The Coming World Civilization* (New York: Harper and Bros., 1956), p. 36.

7. W. E. Hocking, "What Does Philosophy Say?" *Philosophical Review,* 37 (March, 1928): 133-153.

8. Hocking, *The Meaning of God in Human Experience,* p. 283.

9. W. E. Hocking, "A World View," in *Preface to Philosophy: A Textbook* (with others) (New York: Macmillan, 1956), p. 462. "Mind is the only being that is known to create." For this reference, and others dealing with Hocking's view of nature as causal order, I am indebted to John Howie's stimulating paper

on "Self as the Key Metaphysical Element of Creativity in the Philosophy of W. E. Hocking" (unpublished) presented at the meeting of the *Society for Philosophy of Creativity*, New York, December 27, 1971.

10.   Hocking, *The Meaning of God in Human Experience*, p. 286.

11.   W. E. Hocking, *The Self: Its Body and Freedom* (New Haven: Yale University Press, 1928), p. 123.

12.   W. E. Hocking, *The Coming World Civilization*, Study II, "Passage Beyond Modernity," pp. 21-42.

13.   For a brief recounting of his early years and the influences which shaped his philosophy, see Leroy S. Rouner, "The Making of a Philosopher: Ernest Hocking's Early Years," in *Philosophy, Religion and the Coming World Civilization: Essays in Honor of William Ernest Hocking*, ed. by Leroy S. Rouner (The Hague: Martinus Nijhoff, 1966), pp. 5-22.

14.   On August 10, 1973, Professor and Mrs. Richard Hocking gathered a group of Ernest Hocking's friends and philosophical colleagues in the Hocking Library in Madison, New Hampshire, to commemorate the 100th anniversary of Ernest Hocking's birth. In the discussion on that occasion some of us expressed our questions concerning the realist side of Hocking's doctrine of nature, and Richard Hocking commented that it was indeed a picture of "the surveyor as hero." Without implicating him in the development of my views, I must gratefully acknowledge that the vividness of this image clarified several issues in Hocking's philosophy of nature, and lured me on into the work of this present essay.

15.   Leroy S. Rouner, *Within Human Experience: The Philosophy of William Ernest Hocking* (Cambridge: Harvard University Press, 1969), Conclusion, "Toward a World Perspective in Philosophy," pp. 311-322.

16.   W. E. Hocking, "Fact and Destiny II," *The Review of Metaphysics*, 4, No. 3 (March 1951): 230.

17.   Charles Hartshorne asks the same question in his "Idealism and our Experience of Nature," in Rouner, *Philosophy, Religion and the Coming World Civilization,* pp. 70-80. Hartshorne solves the mind-matter problem by reducing matter to mind. I hesitate to do this, partly because I have not thought through these issues as carefully as I need to, and partly because I'm convinced that the concepts of mind and matter have mutually informed one another, and if we are to give up either we must rethink *both* categories.

18.   Hocking, "Because the World Is Not, God Is," in *The Meaning of God in Human Experience,* p. 312.

19.   See Hocking, *The Coming World Civilization,* pp. 315-317.

20.   Hocking points out that the self, *qua* self, is outside nature, i.e., the mind is not locatable in either time or space as the brain is. Most tellingly, mind is self-transcendent. It can not only think and feel; it can also be the observer of its own thinking and feeling. See especially W. E. Hocking and R. Hocking, *Types of Philosophy* (3d ed.; New York: Scribner's, 1959), chap. 6: "Naturalism Examined," pp. 50-59.

21.   Hocking, *The Coming World Civilization,* p. 60.

22.   Hocking and Hocking, *Types of Philosophy*, p. 181.

23.   Ibid., p. 62.

24.   W. E. Hocking, "What is a Lost Soul?" *Chicago Theological Seminary Register,* 23 (March, 1933): 9-10.

25.   Frederick Werner, "Integrity," in Rouner, *Philosophy, Religion and the Coming World Civilization*, p. 105.

The Personal Dialectic
of the Impersonal

Richard Hocking

"What Is a Farm but a Mute Gospel?"

EARLY IN THE independent life of our country, Ralph Waldo Emerson declared a kind of philosophical independence, albeit anonymously, in a small book, *Nature*. This is his most nearly systematic work. Against the Newtonian view of nature as mechanical, he argued the view of nature as the embodiment of spirit and as the friendly home of human kind. "Spirit, that is, the Supreme Being, does not build up nature around us, but puts it forth through us, as the life of the tree puts forth new branches and leaves through the pores of the old."[1] The process of nature's becoming is organic and living and intimately involved in personal existence, human and divine.

Among the human "uses" of nature, Emerson identifies the moral one. "Nature is a discipline." Its material resistance to human effort, its inertia, its extension in space and time, its geometrical properties of shape and divisibility—all are stuff for the moral training of human wills. The apparently indifferent lawfulness of nature is seen with more penetration as a curriculum through which human persons find their concrete realization in physical terms. "The moral law lies at the centre of nature and radiates to the circumference." "What is a farm but a mute gospel?"[2]

This theme which is announced so early in the intellectual life of Emerson is one which he shared with the pioneering thinkers of the

Romantic period in English and Continental letters. As seen today in the context of our current recovery of Romantic insights, this awareness of the morality of nature on the part of our New England poetic philosopher nearly a century and a half ago takes on a new congeniality.

THE SHRINKAGE OF "NATURE"

Emerson's theorem that "nature is a discipline" needs to be appreciated in proper perspective. Let us undertake a supporting exercise in recollection and rehearsal.

Over the centuries, many are the philosophic works which have carried the title "Concerning Nature" or an equivalent one. These document a story of the shrinking denotation of the term "nature." Let us take an earlier and maximal sense of "nature" to be "all that generates." Under this ample formula, with its Classical inspiration, philosophers have found proper places for all things and all persons and God. A restriction in the sense of "nature" came with the more scholastic formula: "nature" comprises "all that receives existence," or simply all that is creaturely. "Nature" in this sense has places for all things and all finite persons, but not for God. Since the great scientific revolution of the seventeenth century, an extremer restriction of the sense of "nature" has been based on the concept of "all that is mechanical" (human artifacts excepted). This most shrunken "nature" is the domain of all things. There is no place in it for finite persons or for God. It is the "nature" of the Fechnerian night-view.

Such a simplified schema of successive narrowings does violence, of course, to a greatly subtle history. It also minimizes the cross issues of epistemology. But it does serve to transport us back to the situation of Emerson and his allies in their Romantic reflections *de rerum natura*.

THE ROMANTIC TURN

In such a historical perspective, the emphasis which Emerson gives to the moral aspect of nature takes its place as part of a recoil from the most shrunken view of nature. The classical Newtonian concentration on nature as "all that is mechanical" in the system of physical things was the appropriate, though unintended, preliminary to the reversal which I may be allowed to call "the Romantic turn." It was the

Newtonian perspective which brought about an unstable polarization: at one extreme, the moral order of persons, dismissed from nature; at the other extreme, the perfectly impersonal order of a thing-world. The Romantic turn consisted in the recognition that just such an impersonal and apparently amoral thing-world is the needed opposite which can offer a waiting field for the moral action of persons. The central moral vocation is the progressive embodiment of freedom in such a field. It was in these terms that the personal dialectic of the impersonal was made articulate.

We owe to Kant and Fichte together the philosophical work of preparation for this Romantic insight, namely that nature *qua* impersonal is morally necessary to freedom *qua* personal. The contribution of Kant is negative, that of Fichte, positive; but the one leads with systematic ease into the other.

THE NEGATIVE DIALECTIC

Few modern philosophers have so jealously sustained the Newtonian classical mechanics as did Kant. In Kant's cosmological doctrine, the principles of a mechanistic natural science are singled out as categorical and "constitutive" in their force. Teleological principles such as those of living organisms are regarded as merely "regulative" modes of inquiry which assist and energize the program of classical physics. Within nature the laws of inorganic things are well-grounded; the status of organisms, and *a fortiori* of persons, is highly insecure.

Kant's certitude about the metaphysical primacy of the community of all persons, "the kingdom of ends," is established in the fact of his philosophy of nature on the well-known strength of the moral *Faktum* of duty and the equally necessary postulations which reason requires in its practical employment. *That* the community of all persons is reality itself Kant claims that we know, practically; *how* it stands to the world of things (nature) he judges that we do not know.

Taking one more step, he finds in precisely this hiatus between the *that* and the *how* a teleological import for the life of persons. Consult the closing passage of the long Part I of his *Critique of Practical Reason.* Here we find a section (IX) entitled "Of the wise adaptation of man's cognitive faculties to his practical vocation." The position which Kant takes is that classical physics discloses nature as unfit to give comfort to an ethics of consequences. In this situation, we are left with the only alternative, an ethics of duty for duty's sake. As Kant proceeds to secure such an ethics, well out of reach of Newtonian categories, he observes that nature as disclosed by classical physics fortifies such disinterested moral action by its perfect denial of an account as to "how" the community of all persons stands to the world of all things. It is this negativity which he finds to be a "wise adaptation." "The inscrutible wisdom through which we exist is not less worthy of veneration in respect to what it denies us than in what it has granted."[3] Here we have the personal dialectic of the impersonal in negative form.

THE POSITIVE DIALECTIC

Fichte takes a positive step beyond this negative teleology of nature. Not content with Kant's doctrine of a freedom excluded from the flow of natural events, he sees that the unembodied freedom of persons is not the whole of their freedom but the formal part only, lacking material, that is to say, an abstraction. A personal freedom moving toward full realization requires the concreteness of nature in which to make itself concrete. The shrunken nature of classical mechanics provides what is requisite for just this concreteness. The materials of a resistant, intelligible, lawful, neutral, malleable thing-world are the materials for moral work.

We find an eloquent application of Fichte's insight in his political thought. In his outline of a kind of moral socialism he includes the dictum that each member of a political community possesses an unconditional right to a job. He is here applying the concreteness principle. The mere form of political freedom for all, without the matter of its economic embodiment in a job for each, is an abstraction. The realizing of freedom requires, for each person, a specific and disciplined hold upon some of the material resources provided by nature. Thus division of labor is linked with the moral imperative of concrete freedom.

Fichte's noted aphorism to the effect that this world is but the sensory material of our duty captures the intention of the concreteness principle. Once brought to light and made explicit, it has manifestly persisted as a principle of reflective practice down to our day. The various strands of dialectical philosophy have threaded it into their economic, political and theological doctrines. It has entered quite appropriately into New England transcendentalism. Thereby it has become effective in the diverse expressions of pragmatic thought in the New World and elsewhere.

MONADOLOGY COMPLEMENTED

Through the thought which we have been rethinking there runs as an undercurrent the opposition or polarity of person and thing. This opposition is uncompromising in the Kantian dialectic. Fichte, the more exuberantly Romantic of the two philosophers, is no purist in insisting on the stark, Newtonian aspect of the thing-world. But in his own measure he carries forward the Kantian recognition of nature's impersonal neutrality, its "blessed unconscious thinghood,"[4] as prerequisite to the freedom of persons.

The personal dialectic of the impersonal which emerges from the joint efforts of the two thinkers tends to a reshaping of the ontology of a community of persons. The more monadic conception which had prevailed earlier is blended with a complementary principle of limited but progressive consubstantiality.

The purely Kantian "kingdom of ends," taken strictly, may in retrospect be compared with the "city" of apperceptive monads for which Leibniz argued. The thought is of a society of timeless autonomies sharing law but not substance. In the light of Fichte's novel insight, however, we must conceive of this same Kantian "kingdom of ends" as so modified that the unique inwardness of each person is progressively worked out as a vocation in the public living room of nature. Community of persons does not grow from the zero of no bond save law. It grows from the minimum common bond which nature guarantees as the morally necessary material for concrete freedom.

SUPPOSING NATURE ALIVE

It was suggested as a premise that the very narrowness of the Newtonian focus on nature as "all that is mechanical" was an unintended provocation of "the Romantic turn." What should we say, then, as the age of Newton gives way to the age of Darwin? Does the personal dialectic of the impersonal lose its validity because a premise has been altered?

The biological sciences have assuredly and impressively come into their own in the course of the last century and a half. Their achieve-ments make up one of the greatest chapters in the history of science. The fuller understanding of cells, the doctrine of variation and of speciation through natural selection, the arguments for biogenesis, the discoveries concerning heredity and mutations all testify to a flooding tide of rediscovery of nature as a world of organic life. In consequence, an ampler awareness of living nature is a mark of our present intellectual climate.

Indeed, the Romantic impetus itself contributed to the recovery of a full sense of nature as a progress of growth and development and living action. Conversely, the coming-of-age of biology enriched Romantic thought. Whitehead's chapter, "The Romantic Reaction," in his Lowell Lectures, *Science and the Modern World*, suggests this mutuality of influence with supporting evidence drawn from English Romantic poets.

Another local parable of this reciprocal quickening is to be found in the little city of Weimar, Goethe's home. It was there in another center of Romantic thought that naturalists of Goethe's circle pursued studies of the fossil record so richly displayed in Thüringen, contributing by their work to the then young discipline of paleontology, and thereby to the rise of modern biology.

Philosophical prolongation of this renewed sense of life throughout nature takes forms well known to us in our day. One form is the doctrine that degrees of life are expressions of degrees of consciousness. We trace such panpsychist philosophies of nature from the "day view" of Fechner to the whole range of contemporary philosophies of organ-ism.[5] The genius of modern panpsychisms has proved to be their capacity to incorporate rather than reject the mechanistic point of view. Whitehead formulates this achievement in a delightful aphorism: "The only way of mitigating mechanism is by discovering that it is not mechanism" but "organic mechanism."[6]

A revolutionary change of our awareness of nature has been made possible by the intertwining of Romantic thought with modern biology. Nevertheless, the personal dialectic of the impersonal, which was initially predicated on a far narrower conception of nature, is neither invalidated nor superseded on account of this major enrichment. The reason is simple. Nature living is still essentially nature impersonal. The penetrations into the marvels of organic life have not discovered the personal principle, namely, the principle of a rational will seeking to embody its freedom.

There is a temptation to blend the principles of "life" and "personality." It is a temptation which has confusing consequences. If we suppose that the living principle in nature is *ipso facto* personal, even though in some low degree, then we might be persuaded that "the Romantic turn" was mistaken. Concrete freedom could not then be urged in terms of the dialectical opposition of persons and things. With thinghood gone, the imperative of concrete freedom would involve a moral offense. Somewhat as in the relation of master and slave, inferior personal beings would be exploited by their superiors as though they were things. But we must report that modern philosophical experience has not tended in this direction. On the contrary, the record shows dialectical philosophy and the philosophy of organism evolving side by side, preserving their distinctive qualities in interaction. The insight which is articulate in the personal dialectic of the impersonal has not been blurred by the rise of philosophies indebted to a mature biological science because nature's strict thinghood has been maintained.

Let us reconsider our schema of successive shrinkages in the denotations of "nature." The sequence was suggested by familiar stages of thought in Western philosophical experience. In the context of the schema, we should express the present life-centered awareness of nature in terms of a fourth idea: "all that is impersonally alive." This fourth aspect of nature would take its place as an interpolation between the narrowest sense of nature as "all that is mechanical" and the far ampler sense of nature as "all that receives existence."

Nature as "all that is impersonally alive" can satisfy the dialectical requirements of the Romantic turn. It is the principle of a theory of organic mechanism such as Whitehead offers. Nature alive but impersonal does not invalidate the dialectical dictum that this world is the sensory material of our duty.

GAIN IN COHERENCE

The philosophical experience which we have been reliving brings us significantly nearer to the goal of coherence. In Kant's time, the categorial gap or opposition between persons and things was the chief threat to philosophical coherence of thought. The narrowing of this gap from the side of persons began to take the form of a personal dialectic of the impersonal. Kant, and after him the greater number of his dialectical followers down to the present day, detected a personal purpose in this very opposition, as we have noted. Concrete freedom requires the thing-world.

Meanwhile, the coming-of-age of biology revived in philosophical experience the awareness of nature as living and organic. Nature's creative process presents itself in the new light of a varied ascent to higher forms having progressively closer analogies to the free existence of persons. Thus the categorial gap between things and persons is being narrowed from the side of the living thing-world.

The branch of biology which is especially concerned with the borderland between personal community and the social and communal aspects of the animal kingdom deals with animal ecology and animal sociology. This study is progressing dramatically in our century. The root terms which delimit the discipline: *oikos* (house) and *socius* (companion) express the awareness of analogies between human economics and society on the one hand and the higher reaches of animal sociality on the other. Those eloquent names for animal groupings which we inherit from unknown hunters and farmers of long ago are carried over into the more scientific study: "colonies," "hordes," "lodges," "schools," "swarms," "territories," "towns." Especially, the remarkable fact of "tradition" in some of the higher non-human societies, that is to say, activities learned and relearned rather than genetically inherited, is evidence of how close the ecology of certain animals approaches to the community of persons.

To be sure, the idea of community takes on startling meanings in biological usage. When the concept of a food chain and "trophic levels," and of prey and predator, are brought under the ecological meaning of community, one is acutely aware that this is not the community of persons but of things, albeit living things. We are encountering Darwin's risky metaphor of the economy of nature with its somehow benign warfare expressed in more advanced language.

Much is to be hoped for as ecological studies progress, and the precise terms of likeness and difference between natural communities and traditions and personal communities and traditions are established. It appears that the evidence will support the view of nature's creative evolution striving toward the type of community which is the unique achievement of free persons. Living nature tends toward concrete freedom.

NATURE AS EXISTENTIAL SITUATION

Recent dialectical philosophy is to be credited with an addition to philosophical experience which appears to complete the work begun by "the Romantic turn." The outcome of this achievement is the closing of the gap between persons and things from the side of persons in terms of the personal dialectic of the impersonal. I refer to the researches into "incarnate being" or "incarnate existence" as the pivotal fact of metaphysics.[7] The full impact of this freshly explored experience has not yet been felt and perhaps will not be so for a decade. It summons us to a new act of reflection, which is at best a difficult matter.

Beginning with the intention to understand personal being, we come to recognize that being a person is necessarily being "situated." This lesson we have learned from the whole movement of existential philosophy. A person's situation is that person's "world" brought to the unique historical focus of a concerned, decisive action or course of actions. As an unassuming example, the employment advertisements of olden times, under the caption "Situation Wanted" conveyed the pathos of a life contingent upon the search for a job. Some European languages offer the alternative idiom: "Existence Wanted," implying a will to better one's "Existenz." An unsituated person has lost his Existenz, speaking in concrete, historical terms.

It follows that being a person situated in the world is being in the presence of others. Here is a sense of *présence* which is active, as when we say: "The lady made her presence felt," or "So-and-so lacked presence." No science or deliberate art can generate this subtlety of *présence*. Marcel was right: such an attempt would be as absurd as a school for "charm." *Présence* reaches an ontologically profounder level than can be touched by any technique, and in fact is the ground which sustains every technique or objective science. Only persons make their presence felt, or fail to do so, never things, not even pets or prize livestock. *Présence* is evidence of a spontaneous epiphany of personal existence directed toward unique other presences.

To be in a "situation" in the "presence" of others requires, in our experience, the incarnate existence of persons. The immediate reflective awareness of "being my body" in a situation which includes the presence of others is an experience of "something which is inexhaustibly concrete at the heart of reality or of human destiny."[8] Note that this fact is at once personal and rooted in nature because "my body" is rooted in nature, and yet as "mine," not merely as "object." Scientific objectivity misses this fact and yet nature contains it. Marcel chooses to call it a "mystery," by which he intends a datum coupled with an intensely dialectical reflection. The same awareness which discovers this inexhaustible concreteness of "my body" cannot avoid acknowledging an identical concreteness of "all of nature as mine." This is to say that nature is the infinite existential situation for every incarnate person whose embodiment gives it a focus. The *Existenz* of nature fluctuates with the *Existenz* of persons. In this experience there is no longer any gap between the community of persons and existential nature as the field for incarnate existence. The work begun with "the Romantic turn" is carried to a conclusion.

The thesis that nature is the existential situation and the proper home of incarnate persons is a report of hard-won philosophical experience. Marcel calls this philosophical orientation Socratic because it calls into play a discipline of reflection (*réflexion seconde*) which is more penetrating and "recuperative" than that of objective science. The whole central experience manifestly brings with it the incentive to further exploration in the theological direction. For our immediate purpose, however, it clears the way for the coherent interpenetration of dialectical philosophy and the philosophy of "organic mechanism." And after all, nature as both creative process and dialectical discipline may properly evoke Emerson's village query: "What is a farm but a mute gospel?"

INTERSUBJECTIVITY AS *PRÉSENCE*

The insight into nature as infinite existential situation recommends itself on two counts. It incorporates the polarity of person and thing entirely within a personal dialectic of the impersonal. In addition, it does so consistently with the whole objective account of nature's creative process. By the test of philosophical coherence, the foregoing reflections appear to hold their own.

There is a corollary to our main line of argument which calls for further exploration of the nuclear ideas of "situation," "*présence*" and "embodiment." Once our philosophical experience centers on this complex datum in all its "inexhaustible concreteness," we gain a quite new perspective on the so-called "problem of other mind." In this more complete setting, we come to see that a misapprehension of this problem has prevailed. Despite much tortured discussion, we must conclude that the awareness of other mind is not a metaphysical problem at all but rather a primary fact. It may appear as a problem in the context of an impoverished experience such as characterizes certain monadic philosophies of human nature. But these are philosophies which have not yet permitted themselves to be complemented by the data of "the Romantic turn." I think of such careful analyses as those of Husserl and Prof. A. J. Ayer and Prof. John Wisdom. In ampler fact, the experience of "we" and of *"présence"* is original and hence beginningless. The nuances of solitude are subsequent. They are all experienced *sub specie absentiae*. The awareness of absence is the shadow cast by a prior presence. Personal history, and with it especially autobiography, support the sense that every "I" emerges from a "we" through a sequence of withdrawals. In each life history, the rhythms of presence and absence are infinitely varied; and always presence is the original fact.

Whoever reflects on the experience of incarnate existence and of nature as existential situation may conclude further that nature's impersonal quality is in some measure misjudged along with the "problem of other mind." Perceived more carefully, the impersonal or neutral aspect of nature is rather the evidence of a never wholly withdrawn presence. Such is of necessity a presence commensurate with the infinity of nature. We read in Emerson's *Nature*: "Spirit, that is, the Supreme Being, does not build up nature around us, but puts it forth through us, as the life of the tree puts forth new branches and leaves through the pores of the old." Nature's infinite process is forever the testimony of an infinite presence making itself felt to the community of finite persons.

Toward the Next Synopsis

It has been evident that our theme is especially associated with the philosophy of dialectical idealism. But to be faithful to the historical record, it is also shared with the philosophical offshoots of protest against idealism, namely, dialectical "materialism" and dialectical, or existential, theism. All three movements alike have contributed to "the personal dialectic of the impersonal," and have maintained variants of the doctrine of concrete freedom. This is their firmest common ground.

These three, and all dialectical philosophies in the modern period, share the character of being experiential philosophies, dialectically inductive and hence committed to mutual openness in the exploration of experience. As for the current rapprochement between dialectical philosophy and the philosophy of organism, the settled form which it promises to take will emerge in the time ahead. However, by way of a provisional conclusion to the present study, we may already single out three theses supported by the philosophical experience to which we have access in our time:

1. The impersonal aspect of nature is necessary for the concrete freedom of persons.

2. The organic aspect of nature evolves toward the community of persons as its norm.

3. The mystery of the presence of person to person is the original fact on which a coherent dialectic of persons and things is to be grounded.

These theses make complementary contributions to real teleology in metaphysics. A real teleology is at the heart of any philosophical synopsis, if we are to judge by the major synopses which have been achieved in the course of the Western centuries. Such teleological theses, then, are eligible for inclusion in whatever synoptic philosophy the future may hold in store. Without them such a synopsis would fall short of its goal.

NOTES

1.   R. W. Emerson, "Nature," *Miscellanies* (Boston: Osgood, 1876), p. 57.

2.   Ibid., p. 41.

3.   I. Kant, *Critique of Practical Reason,* trans. and ed. by L. W. Beck (Chicago: University of Chicago Press, 1949), p. 249.

4.   J. N. Findlay, *The Transcendence of the Cave* (London: Allen and Unwin, 1967), p. 137.

5.   C. Hartshorne, "A World of Organisms," *The Logic of Perfection* (La Salle, Ill.: Open Court, 1962), Chapter 7.

6.   A. N. Whitehead, *Science and the Modern World* (New York: Macmillan, 1925), pp. 107, 112.

7.   G. Marcel, "Incarnate Being as the Central Datum of Metaphysical Reflection," *Creative Fidelity* (New York: Farrar and Straus, 1964), pp. 11-37.

8.   Ibid., p. 66.

Science and Objectivity

Errol E. Harris

SCIENCE AS FACTUAL KNOWLEDGE

UNTIL COMPARATIVELY RECENTLY there were few who would have called into question the view that all reliable knowledge of facts about the world was scientific knowledge or, alternatively, that the knowledge disclosed by the empirical sciences is the soundest and most dependable knowledge available of the actual world. Even today, this contention is not likely to be disputed by many. Yet in recent years, from several different quarters and probably in mutual independence, critiques of the scientific enterprise have been mounted, the upshot of which, if we were to accept them, would be precisely to deny the above claim.

In the nineteenth century the claim of finality for scientific knowledge of the physical world was made rather too confidently. As Whitehead remarks:

> Clear-sighted men, of the sort who are so clearly wrong, now proclaimed that the secrets of the physical universe were finally disclosed. If only you ignored everything which refused to come into line, your powers of explanation were unlimited.[1]

The discoveries of Planck and Einstein, Bohr and Heisenberg, shook this confidence and made physicists of our own day more doubtful about finality but no less assured of the factual validity of scientific discovery, if only on the patent evidence of its practical results. But in some minds even the practical results, spectacular though they might be, raised problems and doubts which reflected upon the genuineness of scientific truth itself. And today, for a number of diverse reasons, doubt is spreading as we become more deeply enmeshed in problems generated by science and technology, with which our knowledge and capacity seem increasingly inadequate to cope.

It is not my intention to discuss this predicament directly, but only to consider the implications of some recent criticisms of the scientific discipline as such. Whether or not my reflections will have any bearing on the contemporary situation of our scientific civilization I shall reserve for further consideration at some other time and place.

TWO GROUNDS OF RELIABILITY

The claim of science to rank as the most dependable and objective form of real knowledge has been supported upon two main grounds: the rigor and unassailability of its mathematical reasoning and the empirical character of its data. These were the two pillars upon which the edifice of philosophical empiricism rested its defense of science as the exemplary form of knowledge. Scientific knowledge was seen as a growing accumulation of established facts, gleaned from experience by a method which derived general laws inductively from observation of particular instances. Once hypotheses had been inductively derived, deduction from them, in conjunction with fresh empirical material, should produce empirically testable consequences, experimental demonstration of which would either confirm or refute the hypothesis.

Despite widespread acceptance of this view and its almost complete domination of at least the English-speaking world in philosophy, it was never completely free from philosophical difficulties. Problems of inductive logic proved persistently intractable, while deductive and rationalistic aspects of scientific practice frequently seemed to belie the contentions of the philosophers that factual knowledge could not be attained by the purely analytic form of reasoning to which they reduced logic and mathematics. The account of deduction given by contemporary logic requires that it be purely tautological, so that no new factual information can be derived solely by its means. Yet, on the one hand, the actual procedures of practical scientists seem to include purely mathematico-deductive calculations which make new discoveries.

For instance, before positrons were even empirically observed, Dirac found by mathematical deduction alone that there are two solutions to the relativistic wave-equation of an electron one of which corresponds to the positron. In similar fashion Pauli discovered the existence of the neutrino by purely deductive reasoning. On the other hand, the alleged use of deduction in the hypothetico-deductive method of testing empirical theories, which empiricists themselves admit, should not be possible if deduction can never be synthetic in its results.

These were some of the internal difficulties of the received philosophy of science; but meanwhile, the whole position had come under attack from several diverse quarters, a convergence of critiques which, until the recent eruption of world problems resulting from science and technology, could be and was safely ignored.

THE NEW CRITIQUE

Apart from the criticism of the British idealists in the early years of this century, there were a few eminent physicists like Sir Arthur Eddington and E. A. Milne who, like voices crying in the wilderness, alleged that science imposed its own cognitive forms upon experience and (as Kant had maintained) discovered nothing in nature which it had not itself already put there. But their views were disregarded as the product of alien, largely idealistic philosophical influences. The argument of the idealists was that science as such and the special sciences in particular were forms of inquiry resting upon and circumscribed by abstractions from a richer and more concrete experience. The sciences succeeded within their own fields, it was alleged, only because they omitted from consideration vital elements of the comprehensive compactness of human experience. But this human experience, at least to the opponents of the idealist school, seemed at best and in every form merely subjective, so that even Whitehead, while recognizing the transformation of science in his own day, expresses the realistic predelictions of the age when he writes:

> The idealistic school, as hitherto developed, has been too much divorced from the scientific outlook. It has swallowed the scientific scheme in its entirety as being the only rendering of the facts of nature, and has then explained it as being an idea in the ultimate mentality.[2]

Since this was written, realism, empiricism, and objectivism have enjoyed a heyday of relatively unchallenged supremacy, and only in the last few years have certain convergent lines of criticism begun to attract attention.

Less subversive but still somewhat revolutionary was Sir Karl Popper's more recent modification of empiricism. He alleged that the hypotheses of science were conjectures, inventions of the human mind, the genesis of which was not susceptible of logical explanation, and which could never be confirmed by any inductive procedure. They are accepted only until they are refuted by the observation of singular falsifying instances, only one of which is needed to make the refutation conclusive.[3] It will be noted that this doctrine restricts our positive conception of the world to what we ourselves invent as hypotheses. They are not derived from that world, and its only effective influence upon them is to negate and disprove them when incompatible instances are empirically found. Popper asserts that no hypothesis is ever verified or even confirmed by positive evidence, for that entails inductive reasoning which, in his view, is logically unsound and (at best) psychologistic. But an even more unsettling feature of Popper's theory and one to which nobody, not even Popper himself, has given much attention until recently, is his assertions that no experimental evidence is ever free of interpretation and that there are no ultimately basic data in science. While he demands what he himself calls "basic statements" as falsifiers of general hypotheses, he maintains that what we accept as basic is ultimately a matter of convention.[4] The implications of this view on empiricism are quite devastating, but until attacks were made upon its stronghold from other quarters, nobody, including Popper himself, seemed to notice them.

A more drastic attack upon the objectivity of science has been launched by the phenomenologists and the existentialists, of whom I shall take the predominant figures of Husserl and Heidegger as representative. Husserl, diagnosing what he sees as the crisis of the European sciences, traces the malady back to the laudable but ultimately unsuccessful effort of Renaissance thinkers, Galileo and his successors, to realize the ideal of a completely translucent, precise, self-evidencing, and self-sustaining system of purely rational knowledge—the Greek ideal, of which they found the model in Euclidean geometry. To realize this ideal, the seventeenth-century thinkers reduced the knowable world to the field of pure extension in which idealized shapes could be mathematically related. The movement and spatio-temporal relations of bodies could thus be completely mathematized; and, to fulfill the aim of the new science, a quantitative counterpart had to be discovered of the purely qualitative properties of things as we experience them so that everything could be treated in terms of mathematics.

This aim was progressively achieved at the expense of omitting from the objectivized world everything pertaining to mind and consciousness. The new science, as it developed, had to objectivize everything in the form of observable phenomena which could be made susceptible to mathematical treatment. It did this through materialistic and mechanistic reduction. Consequently empirical psychology, the science of the mind, found itself faced with insoluble problems, and the metaphysical foundation of all science, its original derivation from a primary constituting consciousness, became undermined.

This, for Husserl, is the crisis of modern science. It is a crisis for humanity in that the physical sciences which are eminently successful in their own sphere are powerless to cope with the problems of mind and value, both social and moral, which are for man the most pressing and increasingly unmanageable. At the same time it is a crisis for the social sciences which have been constrained to adopt an objectivist attitude. Their subject is the mind and its cultural experience, but objectivism extrudes from its purview everything subjective. Yet not only is subjective experience intrinsic to mind, it is also originative of and prior to objectivity. The alleged sciences of the mind and its cultural activities in society are thus hamstrung from the very beginning, and can operate only on the periphery of their proper and professed subject-matter.

What is significant for my purpose, however, is Husserl's diagnosis. He does not belittle either the achievements of science or the efficiency of its methods—rather the contrary. But he sees its objectivism and the entire fruit of its enterprise as a secondary product. It is derivative from an original constituting activity effected by the transcendental subject of consciousness. The scientist presents to us and to himself, as spectators, the spectacle of nature as a delineated object; but the whole of his spectacle together with the objective viewpoint itself is derivative from the primordial experience of a "life-world" in which the subject is intimately involved, and by abstraction from which objective science has been constituted. Husserl writes,

As an accomplishment, it [mathematical science] is a triumph of the human spirit. But so far as the rationality of its methods and theories are concerned it is a thoroughly relative one. It presupposes at the outset the fundamental assumption which itself excludes true rationality. Since the perceived surrounding world, as merely subjective [experience] is forgotten in the scientific thematic, the working subject himself is also forgotten and the scientist is not made a theme [of investigation].[5]

The primary science should be transcendental phenomenology, the motif of which is (in Husserl's words) that

... of inquiring back into the ultimate sources of all forms of knowledge, of self-reflection by the knower into himself and his knowing life, in which all scientific structures which are valid for him have occurred as purposive activity, are preserved as acquisitions, and have become and continue to become freely available.[6]

The scientific world picture is thus seen as something subjectively constituted, and its very claim to objectivity is a subjective creation, even if the subjectivity is not psychological subjectivism but is transcendental idealism. The point is that scientific objectivity is not regarded as primary and fundamental knowledge of an independent world, but that the objectivism of its outlook and the independent status of the world itself is held to be a construction of the knowing subject.

Heidegger's critique develops this result still further and brings it curiously into agreement with other contemporary views of science which have no obvious connection with the work of the phenomenologists. For Heidegger, science is essentially research, rigidly specialized by a predelineation or *Entwurf* of its field.[7] This definition of the field determines at once its method and the nature of the objects it investigates. Only these objects count as real and independent, and only what the defined method recognizes can rank as evidence. Consequently science becomes the preserve of the institutionalized investigators, who form a closed professional group. The method prescribed projects the objective world as a "picture" which the investigator surveys from without. It thus isolates man as knower from the object known.

Heidegger's analysis reminds one immediately of Collingwood's doctrine that science rests on a constellation of absolute presuppositions which define its fundamental conceptions.[8] This corresponds to Heidegger's *Entwurf* (or predelineation of the field). Here again another contemporary philosopher of science agrees. Thomas Kuhn has declared that science operates within the limits of what he calls a "paradigm," an exemplar of method and procedure which at the same time defines the fundamental character and entities of the world for the scientist and sets his problems.[9] All three of these writers view the prescribed conceptual scheme as specific to the historical period. I shall presently return to the question of change. Both Heidegger and Kuhn assert that the scientific community is a specialized professional society to which its theories, methods, and standards are esoteric. What counts as "objective," or scientifically acceptable, is what the community of scientists recognize as valid.

For all three of these thinkers the source and origin of the presuppositions of science is irrational and unaccountable. For Heidegger the *Entwurf* is apparently arbitrary, a mere historical occurrence, and so is the constellation of absolute presuppositions for Collingwood. The latter admits historical continuity, but in no case and at no time can absolute presuppositions be rationally justified, because they are prior to all questions and all answers to questions and thus to all rational supporting argument. Kuhn espouses a similar view. The paradigm is established simply by its acceptance by the scientific community, usually from the exemplary work of some great man. The hypotheses that are contained in it are selected from among those which proliferated, it seems quite fortuitously, when the previous paradigm broke down. Popper also agrees on this point. The generation of new hypotheses, he maintains, is never logically explicable or justifiable, and all that scientists can do with them is to try to refute them empirically. The explanation of discovery can never be other than psychological. In short, it is a purely subjective phenomenon.

The progress of science, which in the classical view was one of cumulative addition of new facts to the body of objective knowledge, is a concept rejected by all these thinkers. Collingwood holds that constellations of absolute presuppositions develop "strains," of which he gives no clear explanation; but he says that when the strains become intolerable, new presuppositions are adopted. How and why such changes occur it is the task of the metaphysician to investigate. But the metaphysician is a purely historical thinker who uses logical analysis only to discover what has been presupposed by any scientific theory and how those presuppositions have changed from time to time. If presuppositions are absolute, they have no rational foundation; hence change can presumably not be rationally justified.

For Kuhn change of paradigm constitutes a revolution. It is occasioned when discovered anomalies become so numerous and obstructive that profitable research can no longer continue. The paradigm breaks down, new hypotheses abound, and finally one or a group of these is adopted as a new paradigm. But it is not a "better" one, or a more advanced or a truer world view; it is simply other. No comparison can be made between paradigms, because each prescribes its own criteria and its own rules of interpretation. They are mutually incommensurable, and the transfer from one to the next is of the nature of a gestalt-switch without rational justification.

The general effect of all these doctrines, as can easily be seen, is to relativize and subjectivize science. It is made relative to the historical period, relative to a special professional society, relative to subjectively conceived presuppositions, the origin and change of which are purely subjective, non-rational, psychological phenomena.

In yet one more respect recent philosophies of science call into question (by implication) the objectivity of science. This is the doctrine of the theory-laden character of observation. The British idealists at the turn of the century, drawing upon Kant and Hegel, had insisted on the equal status of conception with perception, but they were overwhelmed by the flood of empiricism in the 1940s and 1950s. Then Norwood Hanson, following out suggestions in Wittgenstein's *Philosophical Investigations*, drew attention to the formative and selective influence of theory upon how "facts" were observed.[10]

This fits exactly with the views we have just been recounting, especially that of Kuhn, for it is the paradigm that determines how facts will be seen, what will count as accurate observation, and how experimental results are to be interpreted. Kuhn maintains on the evidence of the history of science that anomalous occurrences tend not to be observed at all, to be misperceived, or simply to be passed over as irrelevant. More significantly, they are seen and interpreted in conformity to current theory, as when Uranus, before Herschel, was seen as a star and by Herschel at first as a comet. If theory is to be checked by observation, therefore, it is (apparently) by observation already loaded with theory, which we have already seen is a subjective construction.

The final dénouement comes with the view of Paul Feyerabend who exults in the subjectivity of science. For him theories are not merely mutually incommensurable; each is a product of the creative imagination without any rational basis at all. The greater the proliferation of alternatives and the more diverse and extravagant, the better. The adoption of any theory, he maintains, cannot be accounted for in any reasonable fashion.[11] What counts as "rational" depends on rules either accepted at the time by the scientific community or "invented in the course of development,"[12] and whatever rules may prevail at any one time, none are permanent or universal and all are historically transient. In science the human mind constructs a world view in its own way, prescribing its own standards and methods. The canons which are accepted in any period depend on taste just as they do in art and literature, the criteria of acceptance or rejection being primarily aesthetic in all three.[13]

Now the old classical notion of science as objective knowledge has dissolved away altogether. Fact and observation have become derivative from theory, theory is a subjective invention, standards of truth and accuracy dependent upon both of these are relative to the historical epoch. There is no such thing as progress in knowledge which is not recognizably advanced by scientific change, for none of these writers offers or acknowledges any criterion of advancement.

UNACCEPTABILITY OF SUBJECTIVISM

But no such position is tolerable, nor can it be consistently maintained. It is not acceptable because it leaves us without any form of objective knowledge. If science is not the knowledge of an independently real objective world, what is? Not even divine revelation would serve, because that is communicated privately to individuals and admits of no public test. If science is pure human invention, there is no knowledge, and for all we could know there might be no independent world. Even if there was, we could never claim to know what it was really like.

But no more can the position be maintained, for it involves a skepticism which destroys its own foundations. If everything is relative and subjective, no rational grounds are forthcoming for any theory, whether in or about science. The statement that all theories are relative and our choice among alternatives is a matter of taste must itself rest on some evidence. But if all evidence is theory-laden, it has no objective stability. If the statements have no rational grounds, they cannot be credited. If it is merely a matter of taste or temperament whether we accept or reject them, we may as well do the latter and pronounce them false. However, even that would be meaningless because the criteria of truth and falsehood have vanished. It will not serve to say that they may be true (or false) by present standards, but that these standards are not permanent, because if the standards are not universal and if what is taken as true now may prove false tomorrow, the alleged truth is bogus. And if tomorrow's standard is no more permanent than today's, then the rejection of today's truths has no more validity than their original acceptance. Unless we acknowledge, at least in principle, some objective conception of truth, no statement can legitimately be made and no position either held or defended. Some account of objectivity which will stand is therefore imperative or epistemology as well as science goes by the board.

OBJECTIVITY

A viable account of objectivity can be given, however, even on the basis of the very evidence to which most of these writers appeal. The case is not so parlous as it seems in the light of their theories, for there is a criterion of truth, whether or not it has always been openly acknowledged, which has been constant throughout the history of thought; and these very theories themselves point to it. We may begin by noticing their virtues.

The situation in the philosophy of science today is itself an example of a revolutionary transition such as Kuhn describes. It has all the features he notices, besides others which he misses and which are equally significant if not more so. The old empiricist view of science has broken down. The key notions of inductive and deductive reasoning could not be made intelligible or consistent either with themselves or with actual scientific practice. The new philosophies of science are the proliferating new hypotheses heralding a new conceptual system.

The new men are right in rejecting inductive generalization from particular observations as the method of generating hypotheses, for there can be no particular observations divorced from a systematically ordered experience in terms of which perceptions are interpreted.

Perception is never a purely passive registration of stimuli from without. Even the stimuli and their effects on our organs are interpretations by physiological (and other) sciences—as Husserl insists— within a wider and more primordial experience. Our basic experience is a primitive sentience undifferentiated into precise objects, which requires the activity of selective attention to discriminate data. These become recognizable as objects only as they are organized in schemata, which the activity of perceiving a systematically arranged world effects. Apart from that world, objects are not cognizable, and the perception of the systematized arrangement is always of a gestalt character, so that the whole determines the nature, function and significance of the constituent parts.[14]

This systematic world of objects is what we call the world of common sense. It is built up continuously in the course of experience, which (as it is a constant activity of systematizing) modifies and adjusts the schemata of arrangement so that they give coherent and consistent results. This experience of the world forms the pervasive and persistent background knowledge in terms of which all perceived objects are interpreted and recognized. Consequently all perception is always inter-pretation. It is always the totality of background knowledge that informs and determines how and what we perceive.

Popper is right, therefore, in his recognition that no observation is devoid of interpretation, and Hanson's insight that all observation is theory-laden is sound. All perception is inchoate judgment on the basis of schematized and conceptualized past experience. As Kant declared, perception without concepts is blind. So there always are schemata to delineate areas of investigation, and they do define the objects and evidence of the sciences. Synthesized into systems they constitute the presuppositions of research, the paradigms within which scientific investigation proceeds. So far our new philosophers of science are on the right lines.

But the fundamental underpinning of all this is the fact that thought and theory are the developed form of an organizing activity which is the essential character of all living processes. In this fact is to be found the underlying truth of Husserl's position. Theory is schematization, organization of experience, which begins in perception and is developed through common sense practice. The perplexities and contradictions arising out of our common sense notions give rise to scientific investi-gation, and science is no more than a further process of systematization. It is systematic thinking and its goal is complete unification, complete integration of diverse phenomena, without conflict or contradiction. But the systems it constructs are never perfect. Conflicts and inconsistencies constantly reveal themselves, especially when attempts are made to extend the applicability of the organizing principles to wider ranges of experience.

The interpretive theories which give significance to observation are complex and ramifying, and in specific cases some may come into collision with others in the same or in related fields. This occurs whenever "anomalies" are discovered; then the theorist's task is to find ways of modifying and adjusting the theories so as to remove the conflict. If the principles concerned are minor and peripheral, the removal of the anomaly is just a case of puzzle-solving, such as Kuhn attributes to the normal course of research within an accepted over-all paradigm. But if the fundamental concepts of the paradigm are involved in conflict, a total reorganization is required.

The reorganization is not effected in any haphazard manner, and new hypotheses are not unconnected with the old: they grow out of them by adjustment and modification until the requisite reconstruction of system is achieved. What usually occurs is that different thinkers discover different aspects of the required change without seeing how they can be systematically related until one man gathers them all together into a new integration.

The history of science gives repeated examples of this process. The classic case is the Copernican revolution. First contradictions appeared in the Aristotelian and Ptolemaic systems. Then isolated thinkers proposed piecemeal adjustments. Buridan introduced the notion of impetus (later to be transformed into momentum); Nicole Oresmé suggested that the diurnal rotation of the heavens could be explained as the rotation of the earth on its axis; Copernicus put forward the hypothesis that the sun might be the center of the system rather than the earth; Kepler worked out the orbits and the laws of planetary motion, and Galileo the laws of falling bodies. Finally, Newton integrated all these ideas into one coherent system which became dominant for the next two hundred years. In similar fashion the physiological revolution of William Harvey was heralded by piecemeal discoveries. Vesalius discovered the imperviousness of the septum of the heart, Colombo the lesser circulation of the blood through the lungs, Fabricius the valves in the veins; and Cesalpino suggested a circular flow without demonstrating it in detail. Harvey coordinated and substantiated all these fragmentary insights and developed with masterly demonstration the theory of the circulation of the blood.

In every case the criterion of a satisfactory theory is that it integrates without mutual conflict or inconsistency a multiplicity of experienced facts with the already systematized background knowledge which gives them meaning. Comprehensive consistency and coherence is the constant aim and, throughout history, the repeated achievement. That is the hallmark of objectivity. And this is the underlying and still unrecognized truth of the contemporary revolution in the history of science.

Popper has seen the anomalies of positivistic empiricism and recognized the prevalence of interpretation; Hanson has noticed the dependence of perception upon theory, and Kuhn that of scientific procedure upon conceptual schemes. Husserl realized (as have others before and since) that our intelligible experience (scientific and other) is the result of a constructive synthesis carried out subjectively on eidetic principles. He also insists rightly on the necessity for harmonious successive verification in accordance with these principles. Imré Lakatos has reached the stage at which he recognizes the necessity for mutual consistency among the related hypotheses by which the experimenter interprets first the initial conditions of his experiment and then the observed results. In short, what is emerging steadily from the seeming welter of diverse philosophical theories is the truth that comprehensive coherence is the final touchstone of objectivity.

Once this is recognized, the rational origin of new hypotheses no longer remains a mystery. They are prompted by contradictions in the old and result from investigation of the conflicts. They are attempts to modify and reconstitute the hypotheses hitherto entertained. Observe Kepler in his efforts to discover the orbit of Mars. First he adopts the existing view that it is a circle, but he modifies the Copernican version by measuring it from the center of the sun instead of from that of the earth's orbit. When his attempts to determine the circular orbit failed, he modified the hypothesis again to make the orbit ovoid (a circle with a lump on it). In doing this he used still older hypotheses assuming an epicycle on the circular deferent turning with reverse motion. When this hypothesis failed also he made the final modification and turned this ovoid into an ellipse. The object was to make the total theory coherent and self-sustaining.

Again, by recognizing comprehensive coherence as the mark of objectivity we regain the notion of scientific advance. For it is progressively towards wider and more integrated unification that science constantly moves. Newton unified the sciences of kinematics and celestial mechanics. Maxwell unified electromagnetic and optical theory.

Einstein integrated all of these into a single comprehensive and unified theory. At each stage the wider unification effects the elimination of conflicts and anomalies in the earlier partial theory. Newton removed the contradictions of Aristotelian science; Maxwell resolved those attendant upon mechanical theories of electricity, Einstein those which dogged the conception of the ether, itself an effort to make electro-dynamic phenomena conform to Newtonian principles. The progressive removal of contradictions and achievement of comprehensive unification free from conflict is the apposite description of scientific advance.

There is thus no need to succumb to relativism and subjectivism, no need to abandon ourselves to skepticism; for the historical facts and the actual course of scientific discovery give evidence of an actual progress towards a goal which scientists themselves, whatever their overt profession, recognize in practice as the objective truth about reality: that is, a comprehensive, all-inclusive, coherent, and unified system of harmonious experience of a common world.

NOTES

1.   A. N. Whitehead, *Science and the Modern World* (Cambridge: Cambridge University Press, 1930), p. 126.

2.   Ibid., p. 79.

3.   Cf. *The Logic of Scientific Discovery* (New York: Harper & Row, 1961).

4.   Ibid., pp. 94f, 107 n2, 104f, 111.

5.   E. Husserl, *The Crisis of European Humanity and Philosophy*, The Vienna Lecture of 1935, *Husserliana*, Gesammelte Werke (The Hague: Martinus Nijhoff, 1954), *Band VI*, p. 343.

6.   Husserl, *The Crisis of European Humanity and Philosophy*, p. 100f.

7.   Cf. M. Heidegger, "Die Zeit des Weltbilds" in *Holtzwege* (Frankfurt: V. Klostermann, 1952).

8.   Cf. R. G. Collingwood, *An Essay on Metaphysics* (Oxford: Clarendon Press, 1940).

9.   Cf. T. Kuhn, *The Structure of Scientific Revolutions* (Chicago: University of Chicago Press, 1962).

10.   Cf. N. R. Hanson, *Patterns of Discovery* (Cambridge: Cambridge University Press, 1958).

11.   P. Feyerabend, "Consolations for the Specialist" in *Criticism and the Growth of Knowledge*, ed. by I. Lakatos and A. Musgrave (Cambridge: Cambridge University Press, 1970).

12.   Ibid., p. 216.

13.   Ibid., p. 228.

14.   Cf. Errol E. Harris, *Hypothesis and Perception* (London: Allen and Unwin, 1970), chap. 8.

Whitehead and Leibniz: A Comparison

Charles Hartshorne

WHITEHEAD HAS IN COMMON with Leibniz and Charles Peirce, but with scarcely anyone else among modern philosophers, the fact of being all of the following: a mathematician of genius, a great logician, a contributor to theoretical physics, and a great original metaphysician. Like them, too, he took a positive attitude toward religious belief, was well read in the history of science and philosophy, and had still other interests not entirely covered by the foregoing list. In this essay I wish to inquire, with respect to Whitehead and Leibniz only, to what extent the common scope of their intellectual concerns and abilities, spanning an interval of nearly two and one-half centuries, led to or expressed their common convictions in metaphysics. The substantial areas of overlap between the two systems may, perhaps, be taken as suggestive of truths neutral to the advances of knowledge and insight during the interval between the two men. (I shall number the common doctrines by Roman numerals.)

Leibniz is in many respects in the main stream of Western thought, and that thought has almost always (at least until recently) tried to interpret becoming as a special (and inferior) form of being. However, Leibniz never denies the reality of becoming, although one of his most scholarly and sympathetic interpreters, Jalabert, holds that to be consistent he should have done so.[1] The world, for Leibniz, consists of beings rather than happenings or events; yet somehow these beings do involve or contain successive "states," so that becoming also has to be reckoned with. At this fundamental point Whitehead, whose basic category is "creativity" as endlessly protean, is rather far from Leibniz, and is much closer to the Asiatic tradition in its Buddhist form than to Western philosophy, at least before Hume and James. Yet there is still some agreement with Leibniz. For (I) neither thinker treats either being or becoming as "unreal" or "mere appearance." For Leibniz becoming is within being (and, says Jalabert, is reduced to mere succession); for Whitehead being is within becoming as its fixed aspect, including actualities already realized in the past and everlastingly "objectified" in all subsequent instances of becoming. (To be is to be "a potential for every [subsequent] becoming.")[2] But in either case both forms of reality are genuinely there.

Leibniz and Whitehead agree (II) that (contrary to Spinoza) many states of affairs are conceivable or possible which are not actual and, further, (III) that this is true by necessity. Not all possibilities can be actualized, for they are not all mutually compatible. There are, as Leibniz put it, "incompossibles." To this Whitehead would say, "I could not agree more." But there are other aspects of possibility upon which the two men disagree. For Whitehead there is no such thing as a possible world, or a possible individual. Possibilities, for the later thinker, are irreducibly nonindividual. What Leibniz calls a "complete concept," one which fully individualizes its object, must, Whitehead would hold, be no concept at all, but a percept; and its object must be more than a mere possibility. Even God knows no unreal individuals, but only real individuals and unindividuated possibilities. And if there are no possible individuals, still less are there possible worlds. Even if there were no other obstacle, this would suffice to prevent the Anglo-American thinker from accepting the idea that divine creation simply selects one of the infinitely many possible cosmic systems of possible individuals as the "best" system.

A severely compromised agreement between these two metaphysicians, or perhaps, more accurately, an almost complete disagreement but one in which Leibniz shows faint signs of knowing better than his system, is with respect to the temporal status of truth. Leibniz speaks now and then of "eternal truths," which he sometimes equates with necessary ones, as though there were another class of noneternal and contingent truths. But his system does not allow him to make the distinction in these terms, for all truth is timelessly known to God. On occasion Leibniz argues from this as a premise in support of his doctrine that truths about the future are true at any time, whether before or after the events in question. On this issue Whitehead is perfectly clear: some truths are indeed eternal, that is, truths about "eternal objects" as such, or about the primordial nature and existence of God, but not about concrete singulars or the particular contents of God as concrete or "consequent." Still, the two thinkers agree (IV) that at least some truths are eternal and necessary. (Whitehead is less explicit than Leibniz about the applicability of the latter term, but he speaks of metaphysical necessity.)[3]

Leibniz insisted upon what he called the principle of "*in esse*," the inherence of predicate in subject, as the ground of all truth. It might seem initially that Whitehead, with his scorn of the "subject-predicate logic," could not hold such a view. But there is a way of putting the principle which sidesteps the difference between the two men and finds them entirely of the same opinion (V).[4] The point is this: if there are definite truths, there must be definite entities of which the truths hold. There must be describable things which have the properties attributed to them by true descriptions. So far this may seem trivial and noncontroversial. But Leibniz, with his genius for sharp accuracy, realized—and Whitehead long afterwards, though using for the most part different words, essentially agreed with him—that the entirely definite entities of which the most definite truths hold cannot be things whose properties include both "essential" and also "accidental" qualities. For if a thing is to be perfectly definite, it is meaningless to ask whether it has a certain quality essentially or only as an "accident." No matter how trivial a quality is, were it lacking, the definite thing, as definite, must be another rather than the same entity. On the final level of definiteness or concreteness there can be no accidents but only essence. Either all the predicates are there or it is numerically another subject.

It can be shown that Whitehead has no quarrel with this. Quite the contrary, "definiteness is the soul of actuality," and the Whiteheadian "actual entity" exactly fulfills the Leibnizian requirement of having all the properties which it does have just in being itself. Given any other properties there would be a numerically different actual entity. Nowhere is there a suggestion of an essence-accident duality in "actual entities."

Neither for Leibniz (in one possible interpretation) nor (still less) for Whitehead does *in esse* mean that all truths become necessary. What is contingent, however, is not that a certain entirely definite entity, x, has certain properties rather than others, but that this definite entity, with its properties, exists. There could not have been the same entity with other properties than those it actually has, but there could have been another entity with other properties instead of this entity with these properties. Contingency lies in what entities exist, not in what properties the entities have.

Both Leibniz and Whitehead confronted the Aristotelian common-sense tradition according to which the world consists of enduring individuals, some of whose properties are "essential" to the entities and some inessential. Both men object that this tradition fails to specify the definite constituents of reality. But they seek the remedy in opposite directions. Leibniz agrees with Aristotle (or at least with what may easily be taken as Aristotle's view) that individuals lasting through changing states are the fully definite things described in true descriptions; but he infers that the so-called accidents are really essential to the individuals. He thus departs both from the learned tradition and from that aspect of common sense according to which a certain man, while remaining numerically the same entity, can take on, or fail to take on, various qualifications. Thus, we ordinarily suppose that a man in freely choosing a certain course of action remains himself, but that had he chosen otherwise, he could in that case too have remained himself. No, said Leibniz, this would have been a numerically different individual. The actions John Smith takes are the only ones he could have taken. Moreover, all changes in John Smith, whether chosen by him or not, are essential to his being himself. Thus Leibniz could have said that in creating Adam God had determined once for all the entire future career of Adam (and indeed of all humanity; but this involved further considerations.)

Whitehead takes the one remaining way to secure *in esse*: he rejects the assumption that the changing yet "identical" individual is the most definite type of entity.[5] Instead it is the momentary "states" of individuals which are definite, while the individual as always one and the same is a somewhat indefinite abstraction. This is a fairly radical departure from Aristotle and still more from Leibniz. Personally I see no fourth option comparable in merit to any of these three.

Aristotle gives us a view congenial to common sense partly because it implies contingency and freedom and partly because of its relative simplicity. Instead of millions of states making up a human career, for example, there is simply the one individual plus the general idea of successive changing states and the somewhat vague distinctions between form and matter and between essential and accidental properties. But this view fails to make fully clear that the entirely definite truths refer to states and already actualized careers, not to things or persons. It leaves the application of *in esse*, and with it truth, somewhat ambiguous. Leibniz unambiguously affirms the definiteness principle; but because he combines this with the supposed finality of the changing subject of change, he must (in spite of some special pleading now and then) reject the common sense insight into the freedom of the individual to do either this or that instead, and also the insight into the distinction between what an individual has been up till now and what he may or may not be in the future. Thus we have the paradoxes that when an individual begins to be, all his future adventures are already real, and that actions are "infallibly inclined but not necessitated." Whitehead stands by common sense as to freedom and the reality of the past-future distinction, but rejects the assumption, which is technical rather than commonsensical, that individuals rather than events or states are the most definite or concrete realities. There is scarcely a more important technical decision a philosopher can make than this. Buddhists made it two thousand years earlier, but in the West Whitehead, with some help from Hume and James, was its chief originator. Leibniz, I imagine, could have been made to see the point.

Like Leibniz, Whitehead is a pluralist (VI) holding that there are many definite entities, not merely one. As Leibniz disagreed with Spinoza on this issue, Whitehead disagrees not only with that daring and eccentric thinker but also and more particularly with Bradley.[6]

Whitehead heartily shares Leibniz's conviction (VII) that in a certain sense all definite unit-realities (in Leibniz's term "monads" or "singulars") are of one basic kind. In this sense both men are monists. Moreover, they agree as to the basic kind of actuality. The earlier thinker expresses this by attributing "perception" to every singular; Whitehead prefers the term "feeling" or "prehension." The entirely definite "subjects," whose predicates render true whatever statements about existence are true, are subjects in the psychical as well as the logical or ontological sense.[7] They are never mere objects or mere bits of matter.

(VIII) Both men explain in essentially the same way those facts of experience which have led to materialistic or dualistic theories. They say (a) that our perceptions are largely lacking in distinctness with respect to the singulars which are there to be perceived and (b) that extended physical things, as perceived by us, are never mere singulars but are always large masses of singular actualities of humble kinds too numerous in any small region of space to be perceptible one by one. Whitehead's theory of "transmutation" is exactly his version of this

doctrine of pervasive perceptual indistinctness. This does not mean that
he would have agreed with one connotation of the Leibnizian view:
that the adequate approach to reality is intellect rather than perception.
Not even God can know a concrete reality in the world by mere
thought. Rather he too must have perceptions, but distinct, unconfused
ones. That ours are indistinct is merely a function of our not being
divine. Thus a different idea of God from the Leibnizian concept is, as
we shall see, involved here.

It is clear that both metaphysicians are antimaterialists and anti-
dualists. Both reject utterly the notion that the psychical, or experience, is "inextended," if this means that it is unable to constitute the
world given to us as extended, so that something else, say matter, must
also be assumed. Leibniz would have agreed with Whitehead's dictum:
apart from experiencing subjects there is "nothing, nothing, bare
nothingness."

In their conceptions of animals the two men (apart from certain
fantasies of Leibniz, and allowing for the vast increase of biological
knowledge since 1715) are in striking agreement (IX). For both, the
mind-body relation is a one-many, not a one-one relation. The body is a
system of actualities under the guidance of what Leibniz calls a "dominant entelechy" or dominant monad or what Whitehead calls a
"society of presiding occasions." For both, what distinguishes an animal
from an inanimate object is that the latter (even in a momentary state)
is a composite, aggregate, or group, of many singulars, the group itself
being a singular only in a weak sense sharply relative to the standpoint
from which it is surveyed, and lacking any singular with predominant
powers over the entire system. As to plants, Leibniz seems to hesitate
whether to assimilate them to the animals or to the unorganized
aggregates. Not without some misgiving, he inclines toward the former.
Whitehead takes a stand here, thanks partly to the expansion of botani-
cal knowledge: "a tree is a democracy." In other words, there are no
presiding tree occasions. For both men the question is empirical rather
than metaphysical.

Although Whitehead rejects the absolute and concrete identity of the
individual enduring through changing states, he grants him a somewhat
abstract identity, which is made possible by a certain indefiniteness in
the idea of the "self." Moreover, (X) he agrees with Leibniz that the
present state of the individual implicates all of its past states. He rejects,
however, the notion that the present state implicates future states.[8] "I-
now" implicates my childhood, with all its peculiarities, but not pre-

cisely my further career and its detailed qualities. Here the two philosophers quite definitely disagree.

Leibniz is famous, among other things, for having denied interaction ("windows") between unit-realities, his "monads," and for having asserted that any correspondence between them is merely the expression of a preestablished harmony explicable only by supposing that God, in deciding which among possible monads should be created, wanted to produce the most harmonious yet most diversified world, that is, the best possible. As this stands it is far from Whiteheadian. Nevertheless there is partial yet exact agreement (XI). Whitehead holds that the present state of any one individual is uninfluenced by the present state of any other individual, although past states of other individuals, if either near enough spatially or far enough temporally, will have influenced the present state of the individual in question.[9] Thus, as in relativity physics, all contemporary events (and some event sequences) are mutually independent. Moreover (XII), any correspondence (for Whitehead an imperfect one) between such events is in a sense "preestablished," being the result of the truth that the causal past of what happens here and now partly overlaps the causal past of what happens somewhere else in the contemporary world. Also, God, as the "ground of order" in the world, is required to give the world process sufficient causal regularity to make a certain degree of correspondence among contemporary events an intelligible possibility, in spite of their independence of one another and in spite of universal creaturely freedom.

One must now consider the fact that both men accept an idea of God, though not the same idea. Both hold (XIII) that definite realities divide *a priori* into two kinds, ordinary and divine. Leibniz would have said "imperfect" and "perfect." Whitehead occasionally uses the last word in reference to God, but it is not a technical term in his system. Both men agree that extraordinary or divine reality is (at least in some aspect) eternal, i.e., ungenerated and indestructible, as well as exalted in principle above all others. But Whitehead insists that any concept of the divine uniqueness and unrivaled excellence must take into account the following: (a) becoming—the definite units of which are events, states, "occasions"—is the concrete and inclusive form of reality, so that God, unless he is to be a mere abstraction, cannot be in every sense immutable; (b) value possibilities (even in their positive or good aspects) partly conflict, and hence the Leibnizian definition of perfection, essentially the classical one found even in Plato (the union of all possible positive

and good qualities), is intrinsically absurd or impossible. Any value
possibility that could be actualized for or by anyone could and would
be an actual possession of God (for he could and would have adequate
experience, perception of it); but that all such possibilities should be
exhaustively actualized once for all in the divine perfection (or any-
where else) is metaphysically impossible. (Kant suspected this might be
so, but failed to draw the appropriate conclusion, which is not, "We do
not know there could be such perfection," but rather, "We do know
there could not be," and hence God is to be conceived, if at all, in less
traditional terms).[10]

Points (a) and (b) in the previous paragraph taken together imply
that the only admissible idea of deity is as an exalted form of becoming,
not as mere being, and that the perfection of God cannot be an achievement in a final actuality of all possible good, but must be progressive,
an endless pursuit of further good. Since any actuality must fall short of
"all possible good," and since there is no clear meaning for the notion
of "best possible" good other than all possible good, it would be absurd
for God to rest content, as it were, with a definite creation. No matter
what exists, the appropriate divine view must be, "There could be more
value; therefore, let there be more."

On the one hand, Whitehead holds, God's capacity for value is
"absolutely infinite"; on the other hand, by the very meaning of
"actual," any actual value is in some respect finite, definite, this instead
of that. Accordingly, the only appropriate relation of the divine capacity to actuality is through an unending process of actualization.
(Fechner and others had said it before, but less clearly and not in a com-
parably powerful metaphysical system.)

In spite of all this, there are real aspects of agreement between
Whitehead and Leibniz as to God. Both hold that God exists and is
incomparably exalted above all other individuals, being alone cosmic,
primordial, and everlasting in influence, incorruptible, ideally wise and
beneficent, and the "ground of order."

It follows from what has already been said that Whitehead must
reject the Leibnizian idea of divine creation as selection of the best one
out of many "possible worlds" each fully definite apart from its
actualization. The Whiteheadian objection is not that too much power
is thus attributed to God, but that both possibility and power are here
misconceived. A Whiteheadian actual entity, no matter how humble, is
in some degree self-determined or self-created (*causa sui*), and any
definition of omnipotence or of possibility which contradicts this is

merely absurd or self-contradictory.[11] Creation as God's mere selection, or sheer determination, of other actualities would just not have other actualities as result. Such formulae are for Whitehead merely verbal. In consequence, whereas Leibniz is caught in the toils of the problem of evil in its worst form, Whitehead faces no such problem. In details each creature finally determines itself, utilizing data furnished by its predecessors. The creature is profoundly influenced, to be sure, by God, but the final definiteness in every case is outside any divine choice. God sets limits to the possible evil in the world but more cannot, according to the categories of this philosophy, be done in or for any possible world or by any possible power. Risk is inherent in the principle of principles, creativity, of which God himself is the eminent form.[12]

A famous Leibnizian doctrine (XIV) is the "identity of indiscernibles," or the qualitative uniqueness of every singular actuality. Whitehead is as convinced of this as his predecessor, though there are some differences in the way the idea is worked out in relation to other doctrines. Both men connect qualitative uniqueness with the perspectival nature of subjects each of which "expresses" or perceives the rest of reality from its own standpoint. But for Whitehead "the rest of reality" has a more restricted meaning, being limited to realities temporally-causally prior to the actuality in question. Also, for Whitehead the uniqueness of enduring individuals is but a somewhat abstract derivative from the uniqueness of each momentary state or unit-event. Such a unit does more than "express" other units by correspondence via God and the preestablished harmony; it is an effect of them (so far as temporally prior), intuits or prehends them, and strictly requires them for its own reality.

The difference between the two men here is connected with Leibniz's denial and Whitehead's firm assertion of irreducibly relative predicates (prehensions).[13] Leibniz seems implicitly committed to such predicates, though in a manner of which he is scarcely aware. He speaks of "states" and admits that each state is complex.[14] Must this not mean that a state is really a singular subject with a number of predicates? If so, these predicates are essentially relative ones, for they must somehow include the law which relates them to their predecessors (and successors) in the unity of the one monadic subject. Whitehead, arguing that the most definite singulars are states, takes their predicates as relative with respect to preceding states but as non-relative with respect to succeeding ones. Thus Whitehead, like Leibniz (XV), admits both relative and absolute properties, but his application of *in esse* to unit events or states, rather than substances or individuals, enables him to avoid treating the unity of states in one individual career as absolutely different from the unity which makes one cosmos of many careers.[15] Just as my present state derives its qualitative uniqueness in large part from the uniqueness of my past career compared to anyone else's, so it also owes much of its uniqueness to the fact that my causal past, my "actual world," only partly overlaps with anyone else's.[16] (Whitehead here thinks in terms of relativity physics. But the idea makes metaphysical sense.) Since causal influences take time according to distance, no two individuals occupying a different spatial volume can inherit from entirely the same past events. And Whitehead can, as Leibniz cannot, free himself from the most limiting—I am tempted to say vicious—aspect of the "subject-predicate logic," its denial of ultimately relative predicates, and yet retain in full force a principle of *in esse*, or of ontological definiteness.

(The remarkable fact is that Bertrand Russell, though agreeing with Whitehead on event-pluralism rather than substance-pluralism, agrees with Leibniz in denying relative predicates. For his "relations" are as external as Hume's, and so are not genuinely predicates, parts of the definiteness of singulars, at all. Thus Russell has the worst features of both Hume and Leibniz and of logic prior to the modern study of relations. Paradoxical as this is, I submit it as fact.)

A further similarity (XVI) between the two world views is that both philosophers, though in rather different ways, take actuality to be numerically infinite. Leibniz expressly says that there are infinitely many monads, indeed even in a part of the world as small as you can conceive spatially. Whitehead has no such idea. But since his actualities are momentary unit-events, either the creative process has had an absolute beginning, and this is contrary to the very definition of an actual entity (which is constituted by its "prehending" of temporally antecedent events), or the process is beginningless and the number of actualities already created is infinite. There is, however, no suggestion that the number of contemporary actualities is ever more than finite. In this respect I take Whitehead to be an ontological finitist, unlike Leibniz. But neither man is a finitist if past time as well as space are taken into account.

Leibniz offers as the criterion of best possible world that it is at once the most unified and yet the most diversified of the possible world systems. If beauty is unity in variety then Leibniz's criterion is, broadly speaking, aesthetic. Whitehead's criterion is, insofar, the same (XVII), though he denies that there is or could be a maximal value under this criterion. For Whitehead no possible unified variety is the greatest possible.

Leibniz deduces that this is the best possible world from his conception of God and the principle of Sufficient Reason, which he thinks God must, as it were, consult in choosing what sort of world to create. Leibniz gives no reason for supposing that one among possible worlds must be best other than this: were it not so, God would not know what world to create. Yet Leibniz himself has pointed out that there can be no greatest number; how does he know there can be a greatest harmonized variety? He assumes also that God simply selects the world in a single eternal act, leaving the creatures selected with no further indeterminacies to resolve. A philosophy of becoming alters all this radically, as we shall see more fully presently.

Whitehead would grant (XVIII) that any contingent entity has "necessary" antecedent conditions without which it would be impossible. What he denies is that there are any "sufficient" conditions (or "reasons") in the strong sense of sufficient, meaning that, given the conditions, what happens in all its concreteness or definiteness is uniquely implied, or as it were guaranteed. Causality of course narrows down what can happen here and now to a limited range of real possibilities, but does not, Whitehead holds, narrow it down to precisely what happens. This is why becoming is termed "creative." Events strictly require their predecessors, but only approximately, or statistically, their successors. Thus the man must have been a child and the child that he was, but the child, even granted all the circumstances, could have become a somewhat different man or could have died in childhood.

To summarize what has been said so far, the common doctrines of the two metaphysicians (to my mind the greatest the modern world has seen) include:

I.   Reality includes both being and becoming;

II.   Not all possibilities are, or (III) could be actualized—doctrine of incompossibles;

IV.   There are eternal and necessary truths;

V.   There are entirely definite singular things, units of reality to which the distinction of essence and accidents does not apply, but which yet are contingent (doctrine of *in esse*);

VI.   The definite things are many, not one only (pluralism);

VII.   The singulars are all of one type in that all are subjects rather than mere objects or mere bits of matter;

VIII.   In subjects (other than God), perception is largely indistinct so far as details of the perceived are concerned, and extended phenomenal objects are masses of singulars too radically subhuman, and for us insignificant, to be accessible to our direct and distinct observation;

IX.   An animal (at least above a very low level) is a compound of singulars with a dominant member (or—Whitehead—a "presiding" and linear society of singulars);

X.   Any momentary state implicates all earlier states (Leibniz, only if they are states of the same individual);

XI, XII.   There is at least some (Leibniz, a perfect) correspondence or harmony (but not interaction) between contemporary states, this correspondence being (XII) preestablished, i.e., grounded in some antecedent factor (Leibniz, God) or factors (Whitehead, God and the overlapping portions of the past worlds of the contemporary states);

XIII.   There is an eternal (for Whitehead not in all respects immutable or uncreated) individual, exalted in principle above all others, and the ground of order among them;

XIV.   Every singular actuality is qualitatively and perspectively unique (more radically so in Whitehead);

XV.   There are both absolute and relative properties (Leibniz: only if states, or monads in relation to God, are taken as logical subjects);

XVI.   Definite actualities are infinitely many (Leibniz, in each part of space; Whitehead, in past time);

XVII.   Value, at least in the world, is measured by the extent to which variety is embraced in unity, and insofar is aesthetic;

XVIII.   "Sufficient Reason" (Whitehead, if relaxed to allow some degree of creativity in all cases) is universally valid, and for each concrete actuality or contingent thing there are at least necessary conditions without which it would not have existed.

Of these eighteen doctrines, only I, IV, VI, and XIII were, in the Leibnizian form, merely traditional. The others seem to be in some measure original with Leibniz.

Particularly in V, VII, VIII, IX, XI, XII, and XIV Leibniz showed himself a great originator. Without these seven points Whitehead's philosophy would have been radically different, nor can we be sure that he could have come upon them all independently. The remaining seven points he probably could have originated without help from Leibniz. But in all of them I suspect that the example of Leibniz was helpful and saved the later man's energy for other matters.

The Xth, XIth, and XVth common doctrines together imply that each man affirms both external and internal relations. Relations of earlier states to later, whether or not belonging to the same individual sequence or society, are for Whitehead external to the earlier; relations of contemporary states are external for both thinkers; relations of later to earlier in the same sequence (for Whitehead, in any sequence) are for both internal to the later. It is true that there is, as will be noted later, an ambiguity in Leibniz's assertion of external relations between monads if God and the principles of plenitude and of each monad's "expressing the entire universe" are taken into account. Still, Leibniz means to avoid an unqualified assertion of internal relations (as in Spinoza) and he certainly means to deny an unqualified assertion of external relations, as (later) in Hume or Russell. And both Leibniz and Whitehead regard the relations of nondivine to divine existence as internal to the former. But in Leibniz this is, as Whitehead says, a glaring, even though inexplicit contradiction.

The ambiguity mentioned above is typical of metaphysicians insofar as they are the victims of some mistaken axiom, but are also aware of truths inconsistent with that axiom. To escape ambiguity and inconsistency while making definite affirmations is the goal or ideal in metaphysics, but history shows that the goal is not easy to reach. The truth that both Leibniz and Whitehead were aware of is that neither external nor internal relations is the whole story. Whitehead sometimes writes as though all relations were internal, and some critics have taken these passages literally. But this simply wrecks his system and makes nonsense of innumerable passages. The two men were alike in trying to construe both dependence (in a sense which escaped Hume and Russell) and independence (in a sense which escaped Spinoza and Bradley) as genuine aspects of reality.

There is one enormous difference between the two thinkers which is rather to be expected in view of some recent changes in science. For Leibniz diversity in space, I here and you there, has a totally different meaning from diversity in time, say I-now and I-yesterday. That my present experience is influenced by my past experiences is because I am the same entity now and in the past. Thus identity is here put in the place of causality. But that someone else's past appears to influence me now must then be in spite of the sheer nonidentity between myself and him. Yet for science the same causal principle is at work in both cases. Past events influence later events regardless of what individuals the events belong to, locus in space-time being what matters. From this standpoint Leibniz's system seems fantastically artificial. Also, if self-identity were the key to the influence of past upon present states of an individual, there is no reason why memory should point backward in time rather than in either direction indifferently. Mere identity has no direction. And then the obvious influence of past states of other individuals (including, for Leibniz, the cells of one's own body) upon one's present state is made into an utter mystery by the sheer non-identity between individuals. Here Whitehead has an enormous advantage. But this advantage is made possible only by a combination of several differences from Leibniz.

First, by taking states, not individuals, as the definite or concrete units, Whitehead is enabled to take memory of "one's own" past and perception of happenings in other individuals as basically analogous. In doing this he must discard the assumptions that in memory or perception what is immediately given is only present mental states or that the object known in perception is strictly simultaneous with the perceiving. Leibniz held both of these views; Whitehead rejects both. In perception as well as memory, he holds, some part of the past is directly given. The earlier events are still real in the later ones which remember or perceive them. Process, as Bergson was perhaps the first to say clearly (though essentially Peirce had said it),[17] is cumulative and embraces its antecedents. With this understanding, the causal principle covers all dependence of later upon earlier events, and the "identity" of an individual is merely a special form of the general principle of causal "inheritance" of experience from previous experience, whether the previous experience is "one's own" or not one's own. This is an economy of first principles. The causal structure of the world is taken as *the* structure.

Inheritance, taken from the side of effects rather than causes, is "prehension," the common element of memory and perception, the intuitive grasping by a later experience of its temporal antecedents or causal conditions. As I have written elsewhere, "an experience is an effect which intuits its own causes." If these causes have that special relation to the experience which makes them members of the same individual career, then we call the experience memory; if not, we call it perception. While Leibniz made perception and memory totally different in principle, Whitehead derives both from a single general principle, present intuition of earlier events.

It is absurd to criticize this view on the ground that earlier events "no longer exist" and so cannot now be intuited. For by the same logic earlier events cannot now produce effects, since the nonexistent cannot act! Moreover, if the past cannot be intuited, nothing worth knowing can be intuited. Our knowledge is throughout an interpretation of past happenings as causally implicative of approximately what is now going on around us and about to go on in the future. On this point Whitehead, Peirce,[18] and Bergson (the last two much less clearly) almost alone among philosophers seem to me to have grasped the essential truth. Experiences do not have themselves or their contemporaries but their predecessors as data, and it is a secondary question which predecessors belong to the same individual sequence, the same "stream of consciousness," rather than to other sequences.

Among "other sequences" bodily states are included. For it is one thing to say one intuits one's own (antecedent) mental states, and another to say one intuits one's own (antecedent) bodily states. The body is a part of the subhuman physical realm in the definite sense in which a human cell is a subhuman individual. It is not a man and it entirely lacks human "rationality." To intuit it is not to intuit one's own thoughts or feelings.

It may seem strange that I have not mentioned as common to Leibniz and Whitehead the rejection of absolute space, the realization that space is but a relational order among things, not a thing on its own. Certainly there is some common ground here. But there are important qualifications. By treating space as an order between and time as an order within identities, or space as relating individuals and time as relating states of individuals, Leibniz from one point of view missed the union of space-time more radically than anybody else. For this reason alone, and I suspect there are others, Leibniz is not necessarily closer to Einstein or Whitehead on this issue than was Newton, and perhaps not even as close. Both space and time are constituted fundamentally by relations of events rather than things. Leibniz almost put his finger on the difference between spatial and temporal relations when he spoke of space as an order of coexistence and time as the order of succession. What matters is that coexistence is symmetrical and succession is not.

There may seem to be an inconsistency on the part of both metaphysicians in combining the principle of *in esse* with the admission of external as well as internal relations. However, the trouble here is merely semantic and the inconsistency is not genuine. The relational properties which a definite entity really has it has essentially, not accidentally. However, external relations are only nominally "properties" of the thing said to be externally related. Thus, if I think about

Plato, this thinking is a real quality in me, relative to Plato. But it puts no quality, new or old, into Plato. No one needs, in order to know Plato's character or life, to know that I think about him, or that I exist. But to adequately understand me he must know that I think about Plato, that he existed, and what Plato, or at least his work, was (and in a sense still is) like. Of course, when I think about Plato he is "in" relation to me. But it does not follow that this produces any qualitative change whatever in Plato, as a man living and working many centuries ago. Relations of something to a whole which includes it do not need to be intrinsic, part of the definiteness of the thing. The contrary supposition, that all wholes qualify their parts, or are "organic," is an error which both Leibniz and Whitehead avoid. The part or constituent contributes to the definiteness of the whole, but only with organic wholes does the whole contribute to the definiteness of the part. To take all wholes as organic is to assert a mystical monism according to which plurality is entirely illusory. But then there are no parts and, in the proper sense, no wholes either. Bradley conceded this, as did Sankara.

In one respect, Leibniz did not entirely avoid falling into the organicistic or monistic trap. For, he holds, the existence of a monad requires God's creative act, and this act takes into account all other monads as essential to the best possible cosmos. In this somewhat complicated way the parts do implicate one another and the whole, and so all relations are internal after all. Leibniz wanted it both ways here. For he did seek a genuine pluralism. Whitehead is more clearly pluralistic. God's creative act or acts required for my existence did not, according to Whitehead, take into account my contemporaries and successors, but only my causal antecedents.

Leibniz got into the steep slope leading to monism because he assumed: (1) the absoluteness of individual identity as the final referent of definite truths, (2) the equal definiteness of actual and possible unit-realities (whereas for Whitehead "definiteness is the soul of actuality"), (3) a uniquely best possible combination of units, and (4) the most extreme version of the monopolistic conception of divine power, with (5) the strongest possible version of the principle of Sufficient Reason. Whitehead rejects every one of these, substituting states rather than individuals as alone fully definite, regarding possibility as less definite than actuality (though his "eternal objects" doctrine is perilously close to compromising this point), taking possibilities to involve an infinitely open value hierarchy with no upper limit, taking even divine power to influence, not determine, events, and substituting a weaker version of Sufficient Reason.

It is interesting to compare the two systems from an ethical point of view. Leibniz is one more Western individualist who finds the ground of right action in the allegedly complete harmony between the individual's happiness in the long run and the goodness of his actions. This harmony is to be effected by omnipotence guided by divine wisdom. Whitehead is free from this idea of eventual rewards and punishments, freer than most Buddhists or Hindus. For him each momentary actual entity enjoys itself, and an essential element in this present happiness, at its best, is in the sense of contributing, as well as it can, to the futures of those whom it is in a position to influence.[19] "One's own" future personal career is merely an important possible or probable recipient, among others, of the contribution one is now making. Ultimately what matters is the contribution made to the divine life.[20] Thus Whitehead's in one sense radically pluralistic metaphysics (self-identity being taken as a relative and only relatively important factor), enables Whitehead to escape the ethical curse of ordinary pluralism, which is the enthronement of self-interest as the absolute motive—in spite of the ancient commandment, "Love thy neighbor as thyself." The Buddhists would understand Whitehead's point. Could Leibniz have done so?

A somewhat vague overlap between the eighteenth and the twentieth-century systems is that in both, continuity plays an important role. For Leibniz this meant that "nature makes no leaps," but since the introduction of quantum mechanics a physicist can hardly be expected to say this. It was in any case always a dubious thing to say, since—for example—each new offspring of an organic species differs finitely from its parents and in this respect nature always makes leaps. Yet Whitehead does talk about the "extensive continuum" as a basic scheme of "real potentiality" in nature as in our cosmic epoch.[21] He is clear, however, that it is potentiality not actuality that is thus continuous. Even for Leibniz, it seems, actuality was not altogether continuous in space, in that a spatial half of a man is not a smaller man, or even a smaller animal, as half a region in geometry is a smaller region. Only on the level of abstract possibility is continuity a reality. Whitehead, unlike Leibniz, applies this to time as well as space.[22] The experience of a man within a millionth of a second is not human experience at all, and entirely within a sufficiently small fraction of a second there would be no actuality of any kind. As Whitehead says, reality is rhythmical or vibratory, and there is a minimal time within which a vibration of even the most rapid kind can occur. Yet Whitehead could agree with Leibniz that to understand the world one must be able to thread the "labyrinth of the continuum," to know how to relate the continuous and the discontinuous.

The changes Whitehead makes in the Leibnizian system seem largely in the direction of good sense and greater intelligibility. No longer must one try to find a difference between that which follows infallibly from an ultimate and eternal reason and that which is necessary; no longer must one defend every evil as essential to the perfect whole; no longer must one explain that, although everything is *as if* causal influence moved between individuals rather than merely from one's own past to one's own present, this is nevertheless not so at all; no longer must one deny creative freedom (or reduce it to mere voluntariness), or deny the partial indeterminacy of the future as such, or try to conceive divine purpose, knowledge, or love as properties of an immutable actuality complete once for all, and by definition uninfluenced by what happens in the world. Also no longer must one hold that one directly perceives only one's own mental states. The relative independence and relative interdependence of individual careers can be alike recognized. Both science and common sense, in these respects, have come into their own.

It seems that there should be some aspect in which it is Leibniz, rather than Whitehead, who was right. True, Whitehead had the advantage of coming later, after enormous intellectual advances; still, being human, he might have made some mistake which the earlier thinker avoided. Also changes of fashion, even in intellectual matters, are sometimes partly retrogressive.

I see only two significant possibilities here. Leibniz was extremely clear, and in my opinion profoundly right, about the importance of the a priori, or of what he and Descartes, not too happily, termed "innate ideas." What they meant (poorly understood by Locke) was nonsensory ideas, ideas which, though they cannot be entertained by a mind simply without concrete perceptions, would be entirely possible for beings whose senses were as different as you please from ours, in a world with different natural laws, and in which all particular events were in some way different from those we observe—provided only that these beings could think freely and reflectively, that is, could think about thinking, as well as about their concrete experiences.

In a way Whitehead, with his doctrines of eternal objects and the primordial aspect of deity which every actuality prehends, is with

Leibniz in all this. Yet he somehow manages, now and then, to give an impression of being a complete empiricist, to such an extent that Victor Lowe thinks one ought to try to purify the system from any non-empirical elements.[23] And Whitehead did call metaphysics a "descriptive science" (in an unpublished lecture only, I think). Here is where Popper's falsifiability criterion of the empirical is relevant. Metaphysics seeks the "necessary" aspects of experience, those which no conceivable experience could fail somehow to exemplify or corroborate. This is certainly what Whitehead has in mind, but I find Leibniz clearer on the limitations of the empirical, though of course Whitehead is far clearer on the limitations of the a priori, and especially on the fallibility of our human grasp of the a priori.[24]

The other aspect of Leibnizian superiority is his wonderful sense of the difficulty of making direct use in natural science of the metaphysical truth that ultimate explanations must be psychical or spiritual. Leibniz insisted upon thoroughgoing mechanism in physics and physiology, even though for him the only real forces were appetitions, such things as desires, emotions, or purposes. But he saw that science has to think largely in other terms, referring to phenomena rather than things in themselves, and apparent rather than real forces. Today the issue is somewhat changed. Quantum mechanics is hardly mechanical in Leibniz's sense, and neither is neo-Darwinian biology. Still, both are strictly behavioristic; they do not try to describe the "perceptions" or "appetitions" of singulars. Also it is still true that, as Leibniz advocated, idealistic or psychicalistic ontology is not appealed to in discussing specific problems in natural science, although some few physicists and biologists have made efforts in this direction.[25]

The disappointing thing about Whitehead is that he scarcely seems to see the methodological problems here. The behavioristic drive in all natural science is scarcely mentioned by him. He speaks of the "nascent science of psychological physiology," by which he means the attempt to get at the psychology of human cells and the like, rather than of human beings as wholes. But we are given no hint as to how this inquiry should proceed. Leibniz apparently thought that no such program could be usefully undertaken, even though the real truth is that every part of nature does illustrate psychical principles. In his metaphysics Leibniz, like Whitehead, generalizes ideas derived from introspection; in his program for science he relies upon quite other principles, apart from the extremely abstract principle of plenitude (that nature is ideally varied and yet orderly).

I suspect that the truth about the ultimate possibilities of science is more subtle than either man clearly saw. But so far as the challenge of behaviorism is concerned, Leibniz seems more in the spirit of the twentieth century than Whitehead, who was still less of an experimental scientist than his predecessor. In this respect Peirce is the best of the three. He outlines the behavioristic method for psychology, yet his ontology is idealistic. He knows the need in science for intersubjective observability, but he believes in mere dead matter no more than either of the other two. On the first point his fairly extensive work in experimental science no doubt influenced him considerably.

It is, I submit, a striking fact that the three most creative physicist-metaphysicians of the modern period should agree so completely on the proposition that, in Peirce's lively phrase, mind, as "the sole self-intelligible thing," should be regarded as "the fountain of existence." Many others of lesser note have held this opinion. I have no doubt that it will in time be much more widespread than it is now. It has been the doctrine of most Asiatic metaphysicians. It is the only hope we have of understanding the world in depth.[26]

NOTES

1.   J. Jalabert, *La théorie leibnizienne de la substance* (Paris: Presses universitaires de France, 1947).

2.   A. N. Whitehead, *Process and Reality* (New York: Social Science Bookstore, 1941), p. 33.

3.   Ibid., pp. 5, 300, 517.

4.   For Leibniz on *in esse* see his *Discourse on Metaphysics,* VIII. Whitehead's view on this point is implied by his statements that actual occasions are "devoid of all indetermination" (Whitehead, p. 44), that in them "potentiality has passed into realization," and that "actual entities . . . do not change" (Whitehead, p. 52). Note also p. 471.

5.   Whitehead, pp. ix, 28, 32, 44, 116.

6.   Ibid., pp. vii, 10, 69.

7.   Ibid., pp. viii (item vii), 35, 43, 253.

8.   Ibid., p. 328. See also *Adventures of Ideas* (New York: Macmillan, 1933), 247f. For Whitehead's views on Leibniz see pp. 167ff., 300 of this book; also Whitehead, *Process and Reality,* pp. 29, 40, 47, 76, 124, 289, 384.

9.   Whitehead, *Adventures of Ideas,* p. 251.

10.   See Kant's essay, *Versuch den Begriff der negativen Grössen in die Welt-Weisheit einzuführen.*

11.   Whitehead, *Process and Reality,* p. 135.

12.   This is why "the dream of youth," because of the very "nature of things," is followed by "the harvest of tragedy," or why the Adventure of the

Universe "reaps tragic beauty." Whitehead, *Adventures of Ideas,* p. 381. See also Whitehead, *Process and Reality,* p. 339.

13. Ibid., pp. 32, 80 (ii), 88f., 350. Whitehead, *Adventures of Ideas*, p. 197. Leibniz's denial of relative properties is contained in his saying that there are "no extrinsic denominations," that is, the internal constitution of a substance is fully describable without mentioning other substances. Yet relation to God, at least, must be an exception.

14. "L'état passager qui enveloppe et représente une multitude dans unité ou dans la substance simple" (*Monadologie,* p. 14). Because Leibniz believed in the continuity of becoming, he could not have a definite idea of a genuinely single "state" of experiencing. It could not be instantaneous; for an instant is, he holds, a mere "limit" or "extreme." Nor could it have a definite finite time length, for this would break the continuity. In this respect too I think Jalabert's point has force: Leibniz has no viable theory of becoming or of time. But neither have most philosophers. Continuous becoming means that there can be no definite succession, for there are no definite entities to sustain this relation. There is only all becoming, taken as a single entity. But this spatializes time, eternalizes it. For the other side of this argument see H. N. Lee, *Percepts, Concepts and Theoretic Knowledge* (Memphis: Memphis State University Press, 1973).

15. Whitehead, *Adventures of Ideas,* pp. 243f.

16. Whitehead, *Process and Reality,* pp. 33f. (Category V).

17. In his dictum "the past is the sum of accomplished facts." See C. Hartshorne and Paul Weiss, eds., *The Collected Papers of Charles S. Peirce* (Cambridge: Harvard University Press 1931-1935), 5.458ff. See also 7.547.

18. Ibid., 1.38; 1.358.

19. Whitehead, *Process and Reality*, p. 531.

20. Ibid., p. 533.

21. Ibid., pp. 95ff.

22. Ibid., p. 105.

23. Victor Lowe, *Understanding Whitehead* (Baltimore: Johns Hopkins, 1962), pp. 311, 325ff.

24. Whitehead, *Process and Reality*, pp. 19, 138f., 294.

25. J. M. Burgers, *Experience and Conceptual Activity: A Philosophy Based on the Writings of A. N. Whitehead* (Cambridge: M.I.T. Press, 1964); D. Bohm, *Toward a Theoretical Biology,* ed. by C. H. Waddington (Edinburgh: Edinburgh University Press, 1969, Vol. 2), pp. 42f., 48; C. H. Waddington, *The Nature of Life* (London: Allen and Unwin, 1961); W. E. Agar, *A Contribution to the Theory of the Living Organism* (Melbourne: Melbourne University Press, 1943).

26. Whitehead, *Process and Reality*, p. 471; Whitehead, *Adventures of Ideas,* p. 281. See also my essays: "The Case for Idealism," *The Philosophical Forum,* 1968, I, No. 1 (New Series); and "The Synthesis of Idealism and Realism," in my *Reality as Social Process* (New York: Hafner, 1971). The latter essay was first published in *Theoria* (Sweden) 4 (March 12, 1949): 90-107.

Faith and Knowledge:
Is the Ineffable Intelligible?

John H. Lavely

WHEN I FIRST READ Professor Bertocci's *Introduction to the Philosophy of Religion* in 1951, the chapter which most intrigued me was the one entitled "Do We Know God Directly in Religious Experience?"[1] In this chapter, Dr. Bertocci develops a strong negative answer to that question. That is, he denies that religious experience is cognitive. I could not help but agree with him if the cognitive value of religious experience is taken to mean that "there is an immediate experience of God which provides indubitable knowledge of the existence and nature of Deity"[2] and that such knowledge is arrived at "by religious experience alone, unrelated to other parts of experience."[3] In short, I shared with Dr. Bertocci—and still do—the view that religious cognitivism or, as I prefer to call it, religious objectivism (the position that religious experience as such is self-authenticating, self-validating, self-verifying) is untenable.

But I came to be puzzled, if not troubled, by an important part of Dr. Bertocci's argument against religious cognitivism. He seemed to believe that in order to deny "the *independent* validity of religious experience as a source of knowledge,"[4] he had to show that there is no "common core" in religious experience. He argues that "there is no broad agreement as to what the experience contains as *nonsensory qualitative data*"[5] and that the diversity of interpretations (he cites William James, Rudolf Otto, and Henri Bergson) shows there is "not . . .

enough stability in the nonsensory religious data experienced" to "control" such interpretations.[6]

This line of reasoning seemed to me to be in danger of conceding too much, especially since Dr. Bertocci confesses that the content of religious experience lacks that obdurate character of sense experience on the basis of which the objectivity of our knowledge of the physical world stands. It seems, therefore, somewhat anomalous for Dr. Bertocci to conclude his argument in support of the hypothesis of a personal God by holding that religious experience is confirmatory when it is not quite clear how the notion of God in its distinctively religious meaning could even be derived from such elusive variable data as he suggests constitute religious experience. It is true that Dr. Bertocci does say, "we are not seeking to *deny* the fact of religious experience;" but in the next sentence he speaks of the "*cognitive* or *evidential* value for belief in some sort of God"[7] in a way which clearly suggests that "cognitive" and "evidential" are interchangeable terms.

I wondered: cannot religious experience be evidential even if it is not an independent and indubitable source of religious knowledge? Is there no discernible character, no primitive experiential base for religious concepts and/or symbols?

Actually, although Dr. Bertocci seems to subvert the evidential significance of religious experience, in other respects he seems to assume its evidential import. He speaks of religious experience "as a source of moral power and inspiration, and as an experience worth having for its own sake."[8] Furthermore, his minimum definition of God (as Sponsor or Source of values)[9] presupposes the steadiness and the referential character of the value dimension of experience. Religious experience seems, then, to have a pervasive and persistent character, even if it is not a "special way of knowing" or has no "common core."

I have reviewed Dr. Bertocci's treatment of religious cognitivism here not as a prelude to a full-scale critique of his position but rather to credit him for stimulating my own efforts to grapple with the central problems of religious epistemology. It is precisely because of the ambiguities in his view that I have found it so provocative, and I am grateful to Dr. Bertocci for getting me started on an inquiry to which I have devoted considerable time during the years since I first read his book. Whether I have managed to resolve any of the problems or overcome any of the ambiguities alluded to above is not for me to say; what I want to report here is the main lines of my attempt to do so.

The thesis I want to maintain and test is this: religious experience is evidential but not as such cognitive. There is such a thing as religious matter of fact. I do not mean a pure religious given or an abstract religious essence, but rather an intrinsic religious dimension the interpretation of which would be religious knowledge.

In taking this position, I share with Dr. Bertocci a dissatisfaction with what he calls "psychological dogmatism"[10] or what I call religious subjectivism: for this view religious experience is not even evidential; and, as indicated above, I agree with him that religious cognitivism is inadequate. But I am not convinced, for reasons I have already indicated, that Dr. Bertocci has a viable alternative.

It is also clear to me that such a middle way, an alternative to religious subjectivism and religious objectivism, should not be confused with the stance expressed in William James's three conclusions about mysticism. Cryptically stated in the contents of *The Varieties of Religious Experience*, they are: "(1) Mystical states carry authority for him who has them–(2) But for no one else–(3) Nevertheless, they break down the exclusive authority of rationalistic states."[11] This amounts to saying that religious objectivism is true for those who have had mystical experience and religious subjectivism is true for those who haven't. But this simply describes the prevalence of what I call the insider/outsider dilemma: mutually incompatible views are entertained by different people. A temporary truce between faith and knowledge does not resolve the hiatus. It is true that the persistence (we might even say the stubbornness) with which the authority of religious experience is upheld by some does "break down the exclusive authority of rationalistic states" for some others. The result is simply a juxtaposition of religious subjectivism and religious objectivism, one which in effect concedes the inadequacy of both but has no way of resolving the conflict. Such a position is little more than a marriage of convenience which disguises a deep-seated incompatibility.[12]

Now there is no hope of dealing with this problem unless we can determine what there is about religious experience which would give it evidential import, unless we can locate clearly and characterize intelligibly those features of religious experience which would enable us to speak of it, in some justifiable sense, as evidential or factual. If we turn to the testimony, the reports, the claims, of those who purport to be describing religious experience in what Buber calls "the unreduced immediacy of the moment,"[13] we keep hearing that religious experience is ineffable, that it is unique, that it is immediate. On the surface, this kind of language would seem to throw a road-block in the path of rational comprehension. References to the ineffability or immediacy of religious experience seem to be explicitly proclaiming that faith is incommensurate with knowledge, that mystical experience is inaccessible to conceptual analysis.

I want to challenge this initial reading: there is a hermeneutic problem here that calls for more subtle decoding. Is the ineffable really unintelligible? Is the unique really beyond understanding? Is the immediate incapable of mediation? Perhaps the use of terms like "ineffable," "unique," and "immediate" (or their equivalents) is an oblique way of telling us something positive and meaningful about an intrinsic religious dimension. A careful examination of these concepts (or their cognates) in some cases to which they are applied may help us decide.

Let us begin with the notion of ineffability. It is quite possible that the ascription of ineffability to religious experience is an overlapping or even alternative way of saying the same thing as the attribution of uniqueness or immediacy intends. We can sort this out when we come to the latter two concepts. Here I want to concentrate on deciphering the special suggestions of ineffability.

It is almost a standard response on the part of someone who is asked to define religion to reply that religion cannot be defined because religion is in essence ineffable: it "transcends what can be expressed in words" and "there is no doctrine which can be taught,"[14] to use Buddhist idiom. That such statements already tell us quite a bit is often overlooked: they presuppose a distinction between the inner experience and the outward form, identifying "essential" religion with the former. That is, the term religion is taken to mean fundamentally a private, first-person experience rather than any symbolic forms (such as a written creed, a set of moral precepts, or overt ritual practices).

This emphasis on ineffability is often given systematic formulation as a view of religion. For example, Professor Jacobus Waardenburg[15] holds that a religious meaning is one not able to be expressed adequately either in words or actions; it is what he called a surplus value. A dramatic version of this theme is found in the story of a Chinese Zen master who was once asked: "What is the First Principle?" He answered: "If I were to tell you, it would become the second principle."[16]

Whatever else may be suggested by the emphasis on ineffability, it at least identifies the primitive point of departure religiously with an intrinsic dimension of experience. This intrinsic religious dimension cannot be derived from something else, nor can it be translated without remainder into anything else. To say it is inexpressible is to say it is generic and cannot be reduced to or equated with any form, symbol, or other expression. Since the intrinsic religious dimension is thus in the class of experiences, of actual inner occurrences, of first-person human happenings, it cannot be observed from the outside.

Consequently, what we learn about religious experience depends on reports about it or expressions of it. In this is a paradox: the religious experience, we are constantly being told, is inexpressible, but at the same time the religious experient seems almost obsessed to utter the unutterable. As Hocking says, "the mystic is under some radical necessity of propagating his truth,"[17] the truth being the contents of his intrinsic experience. Words pour forth endlessly to tell us about something beyond words. The whole range of man's symbolic expression is drawn on to convey what is beyond symbols. We have here a virtual criterion of the intrinsically religious: not only is the experience felt as qualitatively ineffable, but it is felt as needing to be expressed or articulated. That is, I *must* report my experience (its "meaning" or "message") but I am never satisfied with the report. A prayer of Shankara illustrates this motif:

> O Lord, pardon my three sins.
> I have in contemplation clothed in form Thee
>   who art formless:
> I have in praise described Thee who art
>   ineffable:
> And in visiting temples I have ignored Thine
>   omnipresence.[18]

In this paradox, then, we have the phenomenological root both of the danger of idolatry and of the counter to this danger. In other words, the emphasis on ineffability may dramatize the tension in religion between the tendency to isolate the "pure religious event" and the tendency to equate the mystery with some determinate forms or symbols. The perennial suspicion of confusing the nature of deity with an image (and what symbol is not an image?) leads to many variations on the theme of ineffability, some of them extreme and exaggerated.

The correction of the danger of idolatry is itself a danger: that is, to say that the unutterable mystery cannot be captured is either already an evaluation and an interpretation or it so segregates the experience that what I call mysteriosclerosis sets in—the mystery hardens when cut off from any expression. As John Donne puts it in "Ecclogue": "To know and feele all this and not to have/Words to express it, makes a man a grave/Of his owne thoughts." The life-blood of faith (the intrinsic religious dimension) needs vessels (religious symbols or forms) to carry it. The word can indeed be reified, the symbol can certainly become idolatrous, but word and symbol can also be recognized as vessels for living water, which spills over any container.

Now if we do not take the claim of ineffability literally, there is nothing unintelligible about it. The claim does not depend on special pleading or privileged access, but it does reflect an intense insistence on the priority of the inner religious quality over any outer forms; the latter are always (or should be) derivative and ancillary. ("The Sabbath was made for man, not man for the Sabbath.")

If this is correct, we are dealing in religion with the general epistemological problem of the relation between experience and language (or more generally symbolic forms and human cultural products). As Whitehead says, "Expression is the one fundamental sacrament. It is the outward and visible sign of an inward and spiritual grace."[19] Whether in religion or in knowledge generally, the relation of experience and expression has been perennially elusive. It would be wrong to foreclose or prejudice an issue of such theoretical importance for philosophy. And it may be that statements about the ineffability of religious experience presuppose some commitments regarding the relation of inner experience and outer expression. The point I want to make, however, is that there is nothing about the language of ineffability in religion which makes it essentially ineluctable in contrast to other dimensions of human knowledge. The religious dimension is hence no less amenable to understanding than any of the other structures of human knowing. Unless we are to accept a suicidal polarization of formless faith (pure ineffable religious experience) and faithless form (without any inner meaning), it is quite intelligible to maintain that inner faith and its outward expressions are coordinate.

On this basis, the generic character of the intrinsic religious dimension is preserved but not its isolation or independence. Religious experience interpenetrates other experience by means of religious symbols or forms. Religious experience and religious forms are interdependent: neither can be reduced to the other, yet neither amounts to much without the other. It is a paradox of the religious life that the intrinsic religious dimension is of inexpressible value but that it also initiates further expression. Religious forms are necessary to the full richness of the religious life. Though religious forms may not be the substance of religion, they can serve as vehicles for permeating all of life with religious quality. Religious forms can be reflections of religious experience and instrumental to further religious experience both for oneself and for others. Religious forms are thus both expressive and evocative, though they are not automatically efficacious in either respect.

There is, of course, the perennial danger of supposing that religious forms constitute religion per se. Religion is thus reduced to its symbolic manifestations and becomes religiosity. I have already commented on the opposite danger, that of isolating the intrinsic religious dimension and granting it absolute autonomy. Because of the indiscriminate and ambiguous use of the term religion to cover both private religious experience and public religious forms, it is essential for an analysis of religion to distinguish between the intrinsically religious and its symbols. The value of distinguishing the two is to avoid separating or dissociating them.

Now where does this leave us vis-à-vis the claim of ineffability? It clearly leaves us with a powerful emphasis on something primary, underivative, on something which could not be replaced by or equated with anything formal or humanly constructed, hence on a religious primitive or fact. We must also conclude that to call such an experience ineffable is to evaluate it and to interpret it. We must reiterate that the experience is unutterable in the sense in which an inexpressible love requires me to proclaim it. ("There are no words to tell you how much I love you.") This value character of the appeal to ineffability can, I believe, be brought out more fully in connection with the ascription of uniqueness to religious experience. To this we will turn in the following section.

Another dominant theme in references to or reports about the intrinsic religious dimension is the emphasis on the uniqueness of the experience. It is hard to exaggerate the intensity with which this claim is made. All the devices of language, though they are used, are not enough to do justice to the absolutely distinctive dimension, the utterly unique quality, of religious experience. It may be that the appeal to ineffability is a way of expressing this sense of uniqueness. That is, religious experience is ineffable because it is unique. If so, our exploration of the claim of uniqueness will help to elucidate the meaning of ineffability.

What does it mean to say that religious experience is unique? It is clearly an assertion of the importance or worth of the experience. There is something so special about the experience that only the language of superlatives, of the ultimate, of the total, can express it. Nothing can compare with it. As Professor Waardenburg puts it, an absolute meaning is religious and no relative meaning is religious. Tillich says: "Our ultimate concern is that which determines our being or not-being."[20] That is, our total existence is at stake, and it is here that the intrinsic dimension of faith is located. The claim of uniqueness thus discloses the supremely normative character of the intrinsic religious dimension.

But we need to probe this normative character further. We soon find that the content of the experience is identified in terms of highest worth, preeminent fulfillment, or maximum meaning (relative, of course, to the individual or group and the time and tradition). We also find, however, that religious experience does not merely turn inward reflexively or introspectively, it takes its fullness or joy or salvation (or whatever value term is used) as a function of a transaction or relationship with some other "reality" or "object." The intrinsically religious is thus identified with a sense of meaning or worth in transaction, with a relationship in which preeminent fulfillment takes place.

This abstract way of characterizing the content of religious experience needs to be clarified and documented both in terms of the human side of the transaction or relationship and in terms of its alleged referent. Since we have specified religious experience as a kind of relationship, perhaps it will help to put this question: What is it about anything which would make relationship to it a distinctively religious relationship? What are the properties of anything in virtue of which it would be "an adequate object of religious attitudes,"[21] to use Professor John Findlay's phrase? If we use the term "God" for such an object, how do we identify any object or reality as God?

If God is thought of as worthy of worship, the meaning of "worship" may provide a clue. Etymologically the term "worship" is derived from the Old English "worthship." The suffix "-ship" comes from a root meaning to shape or create. On this basis, we can say that God is God (that is, is worshipped) in that he/she/it[22] *shapes or creates worth.* The religious authority of God consists in God's being "the author of all good." To say, "O Thou who art the giver of every good and perfect gift," is thus equivalent to saying, "O God." The generic and indispensable religious meaning of "God" is thus "Source of Value."[23] (One can just as well say Sponsor or Sustainer or Ground of Value; there are many other formulations.) This is the property in virtue of which any object is sacred or divine.

Evidence of this valuational content of religious experience is so pervasive we hardly need cite illustrations. Anyone can test this claim by looking almost at random into any book of prayers or hymns or any religious scriptures.[24] Let me mention one case in point. If death is the negation of human existence and the fulfillments found in it, the following lines from a Peruvian hymn to the high god, Viracocha, exemplify this theme:

> O hearken to me,
> listen to me,
> let it not befall
> that I grow weary
> and die.[25]

Compare this primitive appeal with the high assurance of these words from the Gospel of John: "Truly, truly, I say to you, if any one keeps my word, he will never see death."[26]

The concept of God with which we are here dealing is thus not an academic inference but is experientially derived. It is a transcription, as it were, from religious experience. The religious experient reports that consummate fulfillment actually occurs and he or she takes it as a product of relationship with something real. As Brightman says, "the religious value is experienced as a relation of the human individual to the Divine."[27] And the unique quality of religious experience is the meaning (or fulfillment or value) found in relationship to that without which, or whom, no meaning would be. Both Buber and Whitehead state this insight in instructive ways. Buber says:

> Religion ... insofar as it speaks of knowledge at all, does not understand it as a noetic relation of a thinking subject to a neutral object of thought, but rather as mutual contact, as the genuinely reciprocal meeting in the fullness of life between one active existence and another. Similarly, it understands faith as the entrance into this reciprocity, as binding oneself in relationship

with an undemonstrable and unprovable, yet even so, in relationship, knowable Being, from whom all meaning comes.[28]

For Whitehead,

> the peculiar character of religious truth is that it explicitly deals with values. It brings into our consciousness that permanent side of the universe which we can care for. It thereby provides a meaning, in terms of value, for our own existence, a meaning which flows from the nature of things.[29]

It is thus by virtue of its value-producing properties that any reality gets its religious character, that any object or process or being is treated as sacred or known as God. The index to the religious character of any reality is actually experienced values. In religion, values (actual fulfillments) are taken as revelatory experience.

To say that God exists in the distinctive religious sense is to say that some existing reality is the source of the actually experienced fulfillment or that there is an objective source of value or, as above, that reality has value-producing characteristics. It is obvious that conceptions of God are seldom this pure or bare,[30] but it is also clear that additional conceptual elements would not provide the indispensable religious meaning of the concept.

It follows, therefore, that to say God (religiously defined) exists is equivalent to or at least dependent on saying that religious experience has evidential import. The existence of God is thus a religious matter of fact. There is no argument which could prove that God exists (in the religious sense) if the religious fact is illusory, if the religious dimension is not evidential. That is, there is no philosophical problem about God unless there is a religious warrant for saying that God—Source of Values—exists. If there is such a warrant, the philosophical problem is not the existence of God but the nature of God: What kind of reality would have this religious dimension? How are we to conceive or interpret this religious evidence? Answers to these questions are the province of systematic theology and/or metaphysics. It is important to realize that faith is both a matter of fact and a matter of interpretation. Evidence is not per se knowledge and the religious fact does not automatically validate any particular conception of God.

As a way of testing this view of the evidential import of religion, let me pose the question: What would one have to know to know that reality has no religious dimension? (or that no Source of Value–God–exists? or that religious experience has no evidential import?) One would have to know (a) that no actual fulfillment takes place, that no actual value occurs, and (b) if value is admitted, one would have to know that it was absolutely self-caused, that my being is, as it were, not dependent on anything for its well-being except its present being.

So far as the latter is concerned, it would seem exceedingly difficult to support a religious solipsism. Whatever the value or meaning, some environment or context or condition is presupposed. George Santayana makes the point unmistakably:

> Existence is a miracle, and morally considered, a free gift from moment to moment. ... Here the spirit has come upon one of the most important and radical of religious perceptions. It has perceived that though it is living, it is powerless to live; that though it may die, it is powerless to die; and that altogether, at every instant and in every particular, it is in the hands of some alien and inscrutable power. Of this felt power I profess to know nothing further. To me, as yet, it is merely the counterpart of my impotence. I should not venture, for instance, to call this power almighty, since I have no means of knowing how much it can do; but I should not hesitate, if I may coin a word, to call it *omnificent*: it is to me, by definition, the doer of everything that is done.[31]

In the development of a religious response, the whole spectrum from the preeminent fulfillment to the ultimate frustration is implicated, and with it the awareness that one's existence is in jeopardy at all times. The recognition of my dependence[32] on a world which now threatens and now supports is a virtually unavoidable feature of the human condition, one which leads Buber to speak of "the real God who is, to begin with, dreadful and incomprehensible."[33] The religious dialectic may go on to report a sense of commensurateness with reality, one affirming a positive sense of fulfilling relatedness even in the face of despair and evil.[34] The Psalmist testifies, "I sought the Lord, and he answered me, and delivered me from all my fears."[35]

This brings the recognition of dependence on objective conditions into conjunction with the valuational feature, the undermining of which was the first condition stated above for the elimination of the evidential import of religious experience. This aspect of man's nature is often alleged to be so subjective and even abnormal that, if the religious is keyed to values, it is already discredited. There are, of course, extremely complicated issues about man's psychological nature vis-à-vis religion. Here we can only indicate briefly the basis in religious exper· ience for saying that such experience is not merely subjective projection but is rather intentional (or referential and revelatory).

I would begin by acknowledging, indeed insisting, that religious experience is rooted in man's psychological nature, in the dynamics of desire. (It is, of course, also the case that religious experience reflects cultural conditions.) W. T. Stace goes so far as to assert that "religion is the hunger for the non-being which yet is."[36] Stace is right in recognizing the inner need and an objective correlate, though one which is sharply distinguished from temporal natural existence (hence, "the non-being which yet is"). But it would be better to say, not that religion *is* the hunger, but that it *arises* in the hunger for that which permanently or pervasively or preeminently satisfies the hunger. Religion arises in "a sense of lack," to use Sartrian idiom, or in the "chaos in oneself," to use a phrase of Nietzsche.[37] Jean Guettier writes:

> It is from within above all that creatures are incomplete. Lacking of themselves what would make them possible or even conceiv· able, need is woven into the very fabric of their being. A need so fundamental that there is none like it. They have need, not only of exterior nourishment, not only of an external complement, but of something that will distinguish them from nothingness.[38]

But the testimony of the religious experient is that there is a condition in which the hunger is satisfied, the lack overcome, the need met. William James puts it succinctly: "The warring gods and formulas of the various religions do indeed cancel each other, but there is a certain uniform deliverance in which religions all appear to meet. It consists of two parts: 1. an uneasiness, and 2. its solution."[39] The religious person reports after the fact that he or she has been fulfilled and therefore there is God. To say that God "is the only food which will appease (the soul's) hunger"[40] is thus analytic: God is the name for the fulfiller of the hunger.[41]

Now if we recognize value as satisfaction of desire or realization of need, we can understand how any concept of God would reflect a response to and interpretation of actual values or fulfillments. In a sense, to speak of God as a perfect being distills the essence of this story. On this basis we may be able to convert the traditional ontological argument from a speculative proof into the articulation of the intrinsic religious affirmation about relevance of reality to human fulfillment. Suppose that instead of saying that human beings have an *idea* of perfection, we say they have a *desire* for perfection; that is, they yearn for fulfillment, they seek meaning. The religious person avers that something existing actually meets his desire for fulfillment or perfection. He/she therefore calls that a perfect being which actually perfects his/her imperfection, satisfies his/her nature, makes whole, or the like. In this sense, "there is a supreme good requiring nothing else, which all other things require for their existence and well-being."[42] Taken strictly, this is not much more than that which we have been maintaining, namely, that if religious experience is evidential and actual fulfillment takes place, then some source of fulfillment (some perfecting being) exists.

Whether fortunately or unfortunately, the ontological argument is usually understood as giving much more metaphysical content to the notion of perfect being than the generic religious "argument" as I read it would authorize. It is at this point that highly normative factors become inescapable. Normative religion ("the best kind of religion") depends on judgments about what truly fulfills (theory of man) and what really grounds such fulfillment (theory of God). Conceptions of God have certainly mirrored the whole range of human values and have undergone development reflecting comparison, experimentation, and self-criticism. In concluding this section, let me mention two points which seem to me to show that the criteria operating in these normative judgments are not arbitrary or merely intuitive.

The first has to do with the notion of a necessary being; this idea has figured prominently in recent discussions of the ontological argument.[43] Suppose I argue: The only "thing" on which I can ground my existence and fulfillment is that whose existence does not depend on something else. If that is what "necessary being" means, then a normative definition of God is being proposed. That is, normatively God must be conceived as metaphysically ultimate; or only ultimate reality can be God. Hence, we have here a sophisticated formal criterion of "adequate object of religious attitude." Materially, this requires a judgment as to the nature of reality to know the nature of God. Whatever one may think of this argument in detail, it can scarcely be denied that its appeal is to the rationality it provides for the essential religious dimension.

The second point has to do with the criteria of value or fulfillment. It has been increasingly recognized that, as Whitehead puts it, "in human nature there is no such separate function as a special religious sense."[44] It does not follow from the fact that religion arises in need that there is an autonomous religious faculty or instinct. Rather, as Tillich says, "faith is a centered act,"[45] involving the whole person. Bouquet maintains that "the essential function of religion is to integrate life."[46] And according to Buber, "in religious reality the person has concentrated himself into a whole, for it is only as a unified being that he is able to live religiously."[47] The primacy of religious value thus seems to be predicated on the normative principle that maximum fulfillment is maximum wholeness and that such wholeness contributes to and is fostered by coherent relationship to reality. Internal coherence and external relevance are coordinates for the religious life.

Careful examination of the language of the mystics from this point of view might be most illuminating. What often seem like extreme statements about "undifferentiated unity"[48] may express a sense of wholeness and closeness to reality so intense that the mystic can only say, "Rejoice with me for I have become God." The sense of the dissolution of individuality can be given a similar exegesis: if being an individual means feeling cut off and I no longer feel cut off, then I am no longer an individual in that sense: "The I had ceased to exist," as one person described it.[49]

If I am right, the claim of uniqueness for the religious dimension reflects (a) an operative criterion of wholeness as the measure of fulfillment and (b) a sense that such fulfillment is unintelligible except as a function of transaction with reality.

We come finally to the emphasis on the immediacy of religious experience. We have space barely to identify some key features. The claim about immediacy is highly ambiguous. The least that one can say about it is that it reinforces a point we have already noted: we are talking about an actual occurrence, a matter of religious fact. That is, in religious experience, something happens obdurately, irreducibly. Religious experience is, as is often said, nonconceptual, not a logical inference. Nor is religious experience merely psychologically induced. It cannot be conjured up no matter how much one wishes or wants. And religious experience is not just a sociological function either. No one can have religious experience for someone else, and membership in a group does not automatically produce it.

The emphasis on immediacy sometimes carries a stronger meaning: to say that religious experience is immediate is to say that it provides direct access to reality. If this means that incorrigible knowledge is gained thereby, the claim is highly debatable. If it means that the religious experient is engaged with reality or that reality is directly impinging on the religious person, the issue is different.

Perhaps we can interpret the latter reading in the following way. Religious experience has two aspects. We are not now talking about the (objective) relationship between the human and the divine. We are concerned about the evidence in religious experience of such relationship. When the religious person claims an immediate experience of God, he/she is at least saying: My experience contains something which is at the time given and my experience also includes my taking it as given. That is, the recalcitrant aspect of my experience is taken as being what it is because God is impinging on me at the time. Something happens in my experience which reveals or points to something beyond my experience. As Tillich says, "if nothing happens objectively, nothing is revealed. If no one receives what happens subjectively, the event fails to reveal anything."[50] For religion, therefore, God is an existing perfect being.

There are, to be sure, serious epistemological problems regarding the relation of religious experience to its referent and to the claims made about it. We cannot hope to unravel them here. Enough has been said, however, to show that the issues are not so esoteric or opaque as to preclude critical inquiry.

I am aware that further clarification and elaboration is needed at many points. The ascription of ineffability, uniqueness, and immediacy to religious experience carries a heavy load. Although my inventory of this load is doubtless not sufficiently careful or complete, I hope I have shown that religious experience is not intrinsically inscrutable, inaccessible, or unintelligible.

I have tried to do this by making the case (1) that religious experience has evidential import and that reality has, therefore, a religious dimension of which some account must be given. I also conclude (2) that religious experience is inextricably involved in the total context of experience; hence, the problem of God is not merely the existence of God (the religious question) but also the nature of God (the metaphysical issue). I further conclude (3) that religious experience is subject to interpretation on the same principles that are applicable to all experience. Otherwise it is a travesty to speak of religious knowledge.

NOTES

1.   Peter A. Bertocci, *Introduction to the Philosophy of Religion* (New York: Prentice-Hall, 1951), chap. 4.

2.   Ibid., pp. 90-91.

3.   Ibid., p. 108.

4.   Ibid., p. 97.

5.   Ibid., p. 98.

6.   Ibid., p. 107.

7.   Ibid., p. 90.

8.   Ibid., p. 108.

9.   Ibid., pp. 9-12.

10.   Ibid., pp. 85-89.

11.   William James, *The Varieties of Religious Experience* (New York: Random House, 1902), p. xiii.

12.   The history of W. T. Stace's philosophical opinions provides an interesting illustration: initially a robust naturalist, he came to accept the deliverances of the mystics and with it the reality of non-being, an order incommensurate with (natural) being. He seems to accept the ultimacy of both orders. See W. T. Stace, *Time and Eternity* (Princeton: Princeton University Press, 1952).

13.   Martin Buber, *Eclipse of God* (New York: Harper and Bros., 1957), p. 35.

14.   E. A. Burtt, ed., *The Teachings of the Compassionate Buddha* (New York: Mentor Books, 1955), p. 204.

15.   Jacobus D. J. Waardenburg, "Objective Facts and Subjective Meanings," a lecture in the Franklin J. Matchette Lecture Series at Boston University on November 6, 1973.

16.   Fung Yu-lan, *A Short History of Chinese Philosophy,* edited by Derk Bodde (New York: Free Press, 1966), p. 257.

17.   William Ernest Hocking, *The Meaning of God in Human Experience* (New Haven: Yale University Press, 1912), p. 363.

18.   Quoted in A. C. Bouquet, *Comparative Religion,* 5th ed. (Baltimore: Penguin Books, 1956), p. 15.

19.   Alfred North Whitehead, *Religion in the Making* (New York: Meridian Books, 1960), p. 127.

20.   Paul Tillich, *Systematic Theology*, 3 vols. (Chicago: University of Chicago Press, 1951-1963), I, 14.

21.   John N. Findlay, "Can God's Existence Be Disproved?" in *Philosophy of Religion*, edited by George L. Abernethy and Thomas A. Langford, 2d ed. (New York: Macmillan, 1968), p. 213.

22.   I use this awkward locution as a substitute for an indefinite pronoun.

23.   Edgar Sheffield Brightman, *A Philosophy of Religion* (New York: Prentice-Hall, 1940), especially chap. 5. This book thoroughly documents the reference of religious concepts to the value dimension of human experience.

24.   For example, A. C. Bouquet, ed., *Sacred Books of the World* (Baltimore: Penguin Books, 1954) is a good source book on which to perform this exercise.

25.   Ibid., pp. 81-82.

26.   John 8:51 (RSV)

27.   Brightman, *A Philosophy of Religion*, p. 131.

28.   Buber, *Eclipse of God*, pp. 32-33.

29.   Whitehead, *Religion in the Making*, p. 120.

30.   But compare Charles Sanders Peirce, "Knowledge of God," in Abernethy and Langford, *Philosophy of Religion*, pp. 205-211, on the value of vagueness in religious belief.

31.   George Santayana, "Ultimate Religion," in *Obiter Scripta*, edited by Justus Buchler and Benjamin Schwartz (New York: Scribner's, 1936), pp. 284-285.

32.   Friedrich Schleiermacher's conception of religion as "the feeling of absolute dependence" carries this too far.

33.   Buber, *Eclipse of God*, pp. 36-37.

34.   The well-known "O Love that wilt not let me go" by George Matheson (1842-1906), who through blindness came to faith, is an illustration.

35.   Psalm 34:4 (RSV).

36.   Stace, *Time and Eternity*, p. 5.

37.   Friedrich Nietzsche, *Thus Spake Zarathustra*, in *The Portable Nietzsche*, edited by Walter Kaufmann (New York: Viking Press, 1954), p. 129.

38.   Translation of Jean Guettier, "Le Spectre de Prométhée," in *La Pensée Catholique*, No. 43 (1956), p. 16.

39.   James, *Varieties of Religious Experience*, p. 498.

40.   Stace, *Time and Eternity*, p. 7.

41.   It hardly needs to be pointed out that the use of the metaphor of hunger and thirst abounds in religious literature. Graphic examples which come at once to mind in the Bible are found in Psalm 42:1-2, Isaiah 55:1-3, and John 4:3-15.

42.   Anselm, *Proslogium*, Preface, in *Saint Anselm: Basic Writings*, translated by S. N. Deane, 2d ed. (La Salle, Ill: Open Court, 1962), p. 1.

43.   See, for example, Norman Malcolm, "Anselm's Ontological Arguments," in *The Existence of God*, edited by John Hick (New York: Macmillan, 1964), pp. 48-70.

44.   Whitehead, *Religion in the Making*, p. 119.

45.   Paul Tillich, *Dynamics of Faith* (New York: Harper and Bros., 1958), p. 4.

46.   Bouquet, *Comparative Religion*, p. 13.

47.   Buber, *Eclipse of God*, p. 74.

48.   W. T. Stace, ed., *The Teachings of the Mystics* (New York: Mentor Books, 1960), p. 23.

49.   Ibid., p. 233.

50.   Tillich, *Systematic Theology*, 1:111.

The Rationality of Mysticism

John N. Findlay

THIS ESSAY IS CONCERNED with two questions: (a) the meaning of the adjective "mystical" as applied to experiences, practices and utterances, and (b) the question of the objective relevance of mystical experiences or the objective validity of mystical utterances.

We all use the word "mystical" in many contexts, both in praise and in dispraise, but it is far from clear what characteristic we wish to cover by it. Thus it is desirable that we should delimit or fix its actual or ideal use more clearly in order that we may say something definite and interesting by it, not merely something vague and emotive. Do mystical experiences reveal any important features of the world, or can such utterances be held to say anything that may, on some interpretation or mode of treatment, be classified as true or false? Mystical experiences certainly have, as William James pointed out long ago, a noetic quality. They seem to dig beneath the surface of common appearance and reveal the inmost secrets of being; they do not appear to be merely extra-ordinary attitudes or feelings that *we* have towards things, which reveal nothing about the way things are. Mystical utterances, likewise, claim to state the deepest truth about the world, even if they do so in words and syntactical combinations that violate grammar or logic or common usage. Validity, the revelation of truth, is part of the phenomenology of mysticism, and we have to decide either in what sense mystical experiences and utterances can be valid or truth-stating or, on the other hand, how, being devoid of even the possibility of validity, they none-theless make a vivid and often persuasive claim to the latter.

I think it plain, in the first place, that the concept of the mystical is not an invented or philosopher's concept, involving a putting together of traits that we do not often encounter together in the world of experience, or which we do not readily *notice* as belonging together and frequently going together. Mysticism is not a recondite concept like the tip-point in interracial ecology or the differential threshold for intensity of sensations, etc. It is a phenomenon which "leaps to the eyes" in certain forms of human speech, behavior and experience. Although it is not common, and in fact is somewhat rare, it nonetheless has its own curious uniformity, differentiated at most into a few salient species, and it recurs again and again in practically selfsame forms over the whole canvas of history and geography without our being able to account for its widespread diffusion by means of any process of spreading from a central source. To have mystical moods and to talk mystically in them seems something that some men fall into no matter to what culture they belong, just as men have erotic or venatorial or decorative or organizing or exploratory urges. There is, moreover, an inherent coherence in the various traits of mysticism, a naturalness in the way they hang together, that stamps them as a basic human syndrome, something that distinguishes man as does laughter or reasoning or two-footed featherlessness or any other traditional differentia. Some people are of course incapable of mysticism, but so are some people incapable of decoration or calculation, and some hate mysticism and speak of it slightingly as confused, obscurantist, unmeaning, emotive and what not, but some likewise hate decorative or calculative activities and speak of them with a sneer in their voice. I myself cannot do sums, and never fail to speak of them or of those who can do them without deep, envious contempt. But this does not mean that there is anything disgraceful about these essential human activities, activities which, in the case of mysticism, occur again and again in the noblest of human products and utterances. Thus, while there are many unmystical poets, for example, Pope and Racine and perhaps even Shakespeare, there are equally great or greater poets in whom there are well-known mystical passages: we need only instance Wordsworth, Shelley and Dante. And while there are great unmystical painters such as Veronese and Rubens, there are painters in whom mysticism is an essential of their art: Botticelli, one of whose Venuses looks like a Mater Dolorosa and which is thought to represent the Absolute Beauty of the Florentine Academy, and Fra Angelico, every one of whose paintings has mystical, transcendental touches. There are unmystical operas like *Cosi fan Tutte* or the *Meistersinger*, but the men who composed them also composed the superbly mystical *Magic Flute* and *Tristan and Isolde*. And, of course, there are unmystical philosophers like Ockham or Locke or Kant, but there are the greater, essentially mystical philosophers Plato and Plotinus and Aquinas, Spinoza and, above all, Hegel. And even men of science have their mystical perceptions, and it is doubtful whether without such mysticism any man of science would make fundamental discoveries. The tree of science is not made to grow through the ashen irrigation of the philosophy of science.

What we have said does not, however, suffice to pin down or describe mysticism. Mysticism can be characterized as a tendency to see and feel absolute unity either in or behind all things in the world. This is a unity which sweeps the self and other selves into its net together with inanimate natural things and which is, moreover, a unity of the deepest and closest kind. We tend to speak of it in terms of universal identity and also in terms of the profoundest mutual dependence and logical coherence, so that nothing retains its isolated being but becomes like a bucket of water immersed in a vast ocean (to quote St. Teresa). The foremost mystics (including Dante, Meister Eckhart, Wordsworth and Plotinus) all confirm the existence of this unity. Dante writes:

> O grace abounding, wherein I presumed to fix my gaze on the eternal light so long that I consumed my sight thereon! Within its depths I saw ingathered, bound by love in one volume, the scattered leaves of all the universe, substance and accidents and their relations as though together fused, and after such fashion that what I speak of was but one single flame.

"All that a man has here externally in multiplicity," Meister Eckhart insists, "is intrinsically one. Here all blades of grass, wood and stone, all things are one. This is the deepest depth." Wordsworth says, "The sense sublime, of something far more deeply interfused, whose dwelling is the light of setting suns, and the round ocean and the living air, and the blue sky and in the mind of man." Plotinus states, "And (there) everything holds all within itself, and again sees all in each other thing, so that everything is everywhere and all is all, and each all, and the glory infinite." Or to quote the *Upanishads*: "Now as a man, when embraced by a beloved wife, knows nothing that is without, nothing that is within, thus this person when embraced by the intelligent Atman, knows nothing that is without, nothing that is within." I am credibly informed that this message of mystical fusion or interpenetration reaches its culmination in a Mahayana Buddhist scripture called the *Avatamsaka-sutra*, but, as this has not been translated, I cannot quote from it. Enough has, however, been said to establish the mystical as a state in which things lose their firm contours and are taken up and, as it were, lost in a more comprehensive unity and identity.

With this sweeping of all things into an absolute unity and this loss by them of their independence and apparent self-sufficiency goes an affective atmosphere of the most exaltedly hedonic kind. We enjoy the vanishing of all into the One with the most indescribable, truly ineffable bliss, joy, or ecstasy. Mystical experiences and utterances will further differ as to the extent to which distinct and independent things are felt to vanish in the ultimate unity. In some cases they are allowed to remain in a marvellous, transformed fashion, retaining their regional distinctness but with no clear demarcation from the encompassing whole. In other cases they are rather swept aside, and in some cases seen to be empty, insubstantial and illusory, while the ultimate unity is in no respect like them, nor retains any trace of them, and can in fact only be spoken of in negative terms. We can pin the Ultimate Unity down only by its utter exclusion of the things of our common acquaintance, of their properties and their mode of being. Mysticism is therefore an intellectual-affective state characterized by the suggested fusion or vanishing of the diverse things that we ordinarily acknowledge. In this state this vanishing or fusion is accompanied by an indescribable access or satisfaction, as if the piebald, disconnected character of ordinary existence were something that we above all things hated and wished to set aside. As many people like the piebald, disconnected face of our ordinary existence, and feel that it is the only existence that they know of or want to know of, it is understandable that they should feel rather repelled by the transports of mystics. They feel as a "sensible" matron would feel whose daughter talks of nothing but love or women's liberation or some other exalted but, to her mind, empty cause. It is, however, a strange fact that self-identification with an absolute, ultimate unity should be productive of bliss, but I can vouch that it is so. For five years as an adolescent I performed daily meditations on the theme of a unity beyond parcelled, separate existence, and was elated as I never subsequently have been. I was also frequently very depressed in the aftermath of such elation, and this is why I have become a *karma-yogi*, one who seeks satisfaction only in hard, rewarding work rather than in an ecstatic self-transcendence that cannot be sustained.

The mystical stress on unity and the sweeping away of disunity operates over all the gulfs of our experience: the separations involved in time and space, the separations involved in distinct individuality, the separations involved in clear-cut sensory elaboration, the separations between the conscious self and the world of objects and the separation of one conscious self from another, and the great separation, lastly, of what is from what ought to be. There are, accordingly, partial mysticisms, widely experienced by persons who are not mystics in the special sense, which are nevertheless sufficiently like total mysticism to be called "mystical." Thus the belief in the magical influence of X on a remote Y deserves to be called "mystical," and so does the sense of entering into the minds of other people which is experienced by those who love, and so is the sense of rational patterns beneath natural appearances which inspires scientists, and so on. To the early Greeks magnetic phenomena were mystical and led them to believe that all things were full of gods. Mysticism, therefore, involves a blissful lowering of barriers between segments of being: partial mysticisms involve partial lowerings whereas total mysticism involves a total lowering. The lowering of barriers characteristic of the mystical state is, however, profoundly at odds with our ordinary view of the world as consisting of divers, independent, mutually irrelevant things, and hence mystical utterances tend to be paradoxical and to glory in paradox: what is utterly different is also the same, everything is nothing and nothing everything, and so on. The appearance of logical contradiction in these utterances scares away the men of understanding, but men of sense know that logic will do whatever one really wants it to do. Moreover, the use of self-contradictory language does not necessarily indicate the self-nullification that it ordinarily indicates, but rather, for the mystic, the inability to adjust to the novel demands of some completely transformed situation. Some mystics, impressed with the difficulty of adjusting a talk based on absolute barriers to a talk which acknowledges no such barriers, take refuge in a pose of silence: what they have to declare is held to be unutterable, ineffable. Thus Plato in his Second Letter adjures Dionysius not to try to sum up the character of the first, superexistent Principle. But as mystics generally manage to utter torrents of words to express why the supreme unity *is* ineffable, it would seem that there is a higher-order, negative language in which mystical objects are, above all others, the most readily spoken of.

Mystical views of the world tend, further, to be accompanied by the notion or picture of a series of states leading from the extreme separation and disconnection which obtains in our normal experience to an interpenetration and convergence which terminates in a point of unity. There is a mystical geography as well as a terrestrial geography, and it leads from ordinary this-world difference to the extreme of unity, where all parallels come together in a common mystical pole. Buddhism has a whole series of levels through which one may ascend to the unshaded light of Nirvāna: The lower ones are quasimaterial and sensuous, and involve many simulacra of the bodily and the spatio-temporal and many visions of carnal passion, but as one goes upwards all this corporeality, all name and form vanishes, till one arrives at the Dharmadhatu, the world of pure meanings, of gist without illustration, where every essence interpenetrates every other. Essences which are separate in their exemplification are not separate *qua* essences. Beyond the Dharmadhatu are worlds of great abstraction, where there is only an awareness of the infinity of space, and then of the infinity of consciousness, till one arrives at a state which transcends consciousness and unconsciousness and then heads straight for the undifferentiated light of Nirvāna. The Buddha went up and down this scala mystica more than once when he was passing away at Kusinārā. Neoplatonism has a precisely similar spectrum of states, ranging from that of souls whose more or less spectral bodies have a close approximation to their gross physical appearance, to their state in the upper heavens where it is thought likely that they are manifest to one another in luminous spherical bodies and reveal personality only in their behavior. Don Juan in the books of Carlos Castaneda has a similar spherical vision of men. Above these heavens is, then, the completely immaterial noetic world of pure gist in which nothing is far from anything, nothing excludes anything, and everything is wholly perspicuous to everything else. And above all this is the limiting state where the soul brings its center into coincidence with the center of all being. Plotinus achieved this ecstatic coincidence three or four times in his lifetime. I shall not document my picture with quotations from St. Teresa or from St. John of the Cross, whose self-preparation for the supreme encounter where the beloved transformed into the beloved has many touches of supreme poetry. Nor shall I mention the visions of Swedenborg who seems to have travelled indefatigably in the lower regions of heaven and hell. And Dante is, of course, a supreme observer in this field who combines a nose for the mystical necessities with incomparable poetic expression. Even if, as might seem possible in these psychedelic days, one thinks of all these soaring journeys as hallucinatory trips, they are yet trips in which an *a priori* structure makes itself evident, trips in which necessities show through the luxuriance of imagery. I speak of such mystical necessities since it is plainly not at all absurd that those who believe in a mystical point of convergence should also believe in continuous pathways along which one may progress towards this point and which also lead down from it into this diversified world. It is by integrating mystical centrality with dispersed peripheral being through a whole series of transitional states that the unity and the dispersion are made parts of a single total geography and constitute a conceptual scheme that can throw light on the state of men and the world in which they live. Without the transitional spectrum, mysticism would merely substitute a unitive vision for our dispersed ordinary one. There would be little meaning in a point of unity set apart from the diffused system of which it is the focus, and no sense at all in declaring it to be more "real" than that system. Only if the mystical and the non-mystical are mutually complementary and bridged in a perfectly continuous manner can the one be said to throw light on the other.

This brings me to the differentiation among mysticisms on which I have already touched. There is, as I have said, a form of mysticism which merely sweeps away the sundered detail of the world, perhaps declares it to be an empty delusion, and then loses itself in the ultimate unity; or, if it admits a spectrum of states leading to the mystical consummation, it considers it rather low-grade to dally among these. One must try to get to the point of complete coincidence and indistinction as quickly as possible. This type of mysticism tends, further, to take a rather low view not merely of corporeal sensuous being in space and time, but also of the consciousness that we have of inferior and higher things. Consciousness may be a desirable state, but it involves a spice of duality. It stands opposed to its objects; it sees these objects in ever varying perspectives, and all *that* has to be laid aside as one goes on to one's mystical goal. One must at least try to reach a state where consciousness has no object other than itself, where it becomes a transparent jewel: a pure empty consciousness of a pure empty consciousness. This is the inferior *kaivalyam* (goal) of *samprajñata samādhi* (conscious rapture), but the supreme *kaivalyam* of *asamprajñata samādhi* (unconscious rapture) lies further: in this enviable condition one so overcomes the restlessness and need for content of the thinking principle that he ceases to be conscious of anything at all. I must confess that I am somewhat disappointed by this supreme consummation. If that is what the highest *samādhi* is, an utterly dreamless sleep, then it has no doubt an attractiveness after life's fitful fever, but there is nothing uniquely mystical and transcendental about it. Only if the supreme consummation is an awakeness more absolute than any conscious state that leads up to it am I prepared to be enthusiastic about it.

There is, however, another type of mysticism which does not unmystically set apart the mystical consummation from existence and experience in this world. It allows the mystical consummation wholly to irradiate the latter, and to make it wholly pervious to the light that shines beyond it. This, if I understand it correctly, was more or less the mysticism of Jesus who believed in making himself so pervious to the unifying, redemptive forces that streamed through him that he became in the end indistinguishable from them. And for this type of mysticism the self-differentiation of the absolute unity into forms which only seem independent and unrelated, and the whole creation of the spectrum of states leading from the point of unity to our troubled experience, is essential to its being the absolute unity that it is. It is the absolute unity only because it departs from itself in various finite, separated existences and returns to itself in mystical unity. In this view, the mystical consummation is something to be worked up to, but it is also something to be departed from, and it is its transforming, stabilizing effect on the whole of existence that is important, not the mere moment of union or some permanent prolongation of the same.

There are traces of this dynamic, self-departing, self-returning mysticism in the *Upanishads* where Brahman, without incurring guilt, says "Let me be many," and perhaps even in the Indian veneration of everything earthly and even sensual. In Neoplatonism, too, there are traces of this dynamic mysticism. In it the One, though utterly self-sufficient, cannot help giving birth to the pluralizing and distinguishing Mind, which sees unity reflected in a multitude of ideas, and the distinguishing Mind likewise has to give birth to the Soul which works out in time, and ultimately in matter, what is pure, simultaneous gist to the Divine Mind. The unique urge upwards which causes the Soul to imitate the Mind, and the Mind to aspire to the supreme unity, is only possible in virtue of the self-externalization of the One in the Mind and the Soul. Plotinus, however, only half-says that the One *must* externalize itself in this way in order to be the supreme unity that it is. It was left to certain German medieval thinkers, among them Meister Eckhart, to say just this, and for a German modern philosopher, Hegel, to make it the whole principle of his system. In Hegel's view of the world, the self-identical unity which underlies everything, and whose supreme expression lies in conscious, subjective life, is also essentially a self-othering unity. Paradoxically it can only be the same as itself by being other than itself, and by returning to itself out of otherness. All this does not mean that for Hegel differents are confounded in a common identity. It means that deeper identities are always revealing themselves in and through difference, the identity of things with other things that influence them, of the mind with the world which it manipulates and understands, of rational man who, in understanding and recognizing his neighbor, also recognizes and understands himself. Hegel's ultimate unity may be mystical: throughout it overleaps the gulfs deemed absolute by the analytic understanding, but it is a fruitful unity which illuminates the differences as well as the communities of things rather than sweeping them all aside. And Hegel's mystical consummations lie not in an *asamprajñata samādhi* but in the utter awakeness of aesthetic appreciation, of religious consecration, and of philosophical illumination. Hegel has not a spectrum of otherworldly states leading up to his mystical consummation, for this consummation, being entirely a thing of this world, requires no such spectrum. But even if we concede the importance of an ecstasy more mystically unitive than the aesthetic or the religious or the philosophical, and believe in a spectrum of semi-mystical states that leads up to it, we may still hold that it is only in the whole spectrum, including its often sorry earthly periphery, and in the going towards and away from this periphery, that the mystical point of unity has any significance. One cannot, after all, be a center or a unity unless one is a unifying center of something.

I have, however, still two major tasks to accomplish: the first, to establish that mystical discourse is meaningful, says something which might in some sense be true of the world, and the second, to establish that it is valid and that what it says is to be regarded as deeply true of the world. As regards the first, many objections might be raised, for it might be held to be self-contradictory to identify things set apart from one another precisely because their properties are incompatible. How can this wood be mystically identical with this stone, à la Meister Eckhart, when this wood is here and fairly soft, and that stone is not here and is not soft at all? Or how can I be mystically identical with my neighbors, when I am British and live on Beacon Street and my neighbors are American and live on Commonwealth Avenue? The criticisms thus raised are parts of an old dialectic which is prepared to fabricate countless unnecessary entities in order to salvage conceptions of identity and negation which are so absolutely rigorous as to be of no use at all. It is a dialectic which resolves the long life of a continuously aging man into a long series of vanishing moment-men, or dirempts our world into innumerable possible worlds each differing from every other by an iota. Needless to say, it is this dialectic which makes the scientist try to break phenomena up into wholly separate and uniformly operative factors and to presume that such factors are there even when he is quite unable to find them. It is this logic, moreover, which regularly confuses contraries, which are positive and not exhaustive and which often reside in tension in the same thing or situation, with the artificial contradictories which obey the laws of contradiction and excluded middle, and which are fatally ensnaring in all developing, open, imperfectly tilled conceptual fields. The answer to a rigidly differentiating logic is another logic of the sort that Spinoza to some extent constructed in his *Ethics*. In Spinoza's logic one does not have one thing that is thus, and another thing that is thus, but something that is thus *qua* thus, and thus *qua* thus, and so on. Or one may build a logic like Hegel's where otherness always presupposes identity, though not necessarily identity at the same level as the otherness, and in which otherness is to be conceived in terms of the notion of a self-othering or self-repulsion. This Hegelian self-othering is not a violation but a precondition of a return to self in identity. Above all, one is not committed to resist the forces of conceptual revision which, in a sufficiently profound treatment, force one to change one's stance, not necessarily in an undisciplined or irresponsible manner, almost from sentence to sentence. Plainly ordinary people do not use such a notion as identity in the way rigorous logicians want them to use it, so that when a man lives through many successive stages in which he does not stay as he was, they are forced either to break him into a large number of unmodifiable minute-men or to compound these into a large chunk of history which is similarily unmodifiable. Ordinary people, likewise, see no difficulty in the notion of entities which from being many become one and the same, or vice versa, or which are the same thing in different roles or guises. Particularly in a philosophy which thinks in terms of universals instead of surd particulars, it is quite legitimate to say that the same thing, a universal, is both here and not here, now and not now, eternally set apart from its instances, and yet also in them, and lending them whatever sense and substance they may possess.

There is no reason, then, why mystical speakers should not affirm the reality of a deeper unity and identity in all things. What they affirm is not absurd, and it need not be self-contradictory in the trivial formal sense. Is it, however, a profitable way of talking about things? Has it any point? Is there any illumination that stems from it? To sink back with a seraphic smile, as the sadhu did during the Indian Mutiny, and say to the British soldier about to transfix him, "Even you are He," may have its uses as a sedative or an anesthetic, but has it any positive meaning? Is there any sense in regarding the policeman or the tax-collector or the drill-sergeant who plagues one within an inch of his life as in some deep sense identical with oneself? Is the world deprived of its unprincipled randomness, its senseless monotony, its essential inconsequentialness, by our affirming that it is all the manifestation of a single principle with which we ourselves are one? The answer to these questions is complex. It only begins to appear when we consider the essential insights of philosophy, almost all of which spring from the attempt to draw more rigorous distinctions than are possible in ordinary life and from the plain conflicts that attend the attempt to do so. We may say that the world throughout bears witness to a deep gearing-in of part with part, and of aspect with aspect, which is quite incompatible with any thoroughgoing pluralism of philosophy of chance, and which points in the direction of an ultimate mystical unity, though it must be admitted that it does not do so convincingly within the limits of our present life and experience.

The features of the world to which I shall point will be exceedingly commonplace, so commonplace that they are readily taken for granted. They are not, however, readily understandable on the basis of a radically pluralistic philosophy and are, in fact, permanent surds in the proce-dures of such a philosophy. I shall refer first of all to the extraordinary, mystical unity and continuity of space and time, the two great media of our existence. We are inclined to think of them as mainly separative and divisive, as creating gulfs between things and as setting limits to the influence of one thing on another. They have this aspect, no doubt, and theoretically and practically it is of the greatest importance. However, they are also media which link all things unbrokenly with one another. In this regard they contain no perfectly definite limits at which their so-called parts pass into one another and which accordingly have no perfectly definite, separate parts. As Kant pointed out with superb insight in the *Transcendental Aesthetic*, they have to be accepted as totalities within which regional differentiations can be distinguished rather than as massed complexes of elements. Points, instants, lines, and surfaces are convenient fictions, but they are invented to make an unmystical treatment of the media work. In themselves these distinctions have no recommendation whatever. Not only are space and time astonishing in their unbroken unity, what is also astonishing is our awareness of this unity and our certainty regarding it. This certainty goes infinitely beyond the fragmentary materials of our experience. It is easy to take these majestic unities-in-difference for granted, as Carnap did when he simply suggested four coordinates for the pinning-down of everything. But how did Carnap know that these four coordinates would be sufficient for a total world-description? The further facts of the marking out of the purely quantitative diversity of the great media by qualities finite in number and continuously shading into one another in a number of well-defined modalities is another extraordinary provision. In default of that demarcation and grouping there would be no spatio-temporal world, however much certain scientists may think otherwise. So far we have merely considered quantity and quality, the categories of surface-description, but it is plain that such categories demand a completion by the categories which add explanation to descriptive surface. We require the categories which yield us an identifiability of permanent substantial nature, having alternative possibilities of manifestation, according as it encounters or does not encounter the manifestations of other cases of permanent substantial identity, without which the diversified contents of the great media would fail to give them the continuity of content which is essential to their being. I cannot give you a metaphysical deduction in a sentence. Plainly, however, the integrity of the great media demands the integrating action of those multiply dispositional, ingeniously geared, yet withal simply structured universals that we call the natures of various enduring natural units or substantial things. And we further require the integrating work of the natural species or kind, not necessarily given the rigidity that was once associated with it. This notion of species is one of superlatively mystical quality. To the scientist it is not at all mysterious, because he takes it absolutely for granted that the same "law" which regulates a molecule that he calls *nitrogen* or *neon* here will regulate the behavior of another molecule that exists or existed ten light years ago. Mysticism, it would appear, is respectable provided one uses the term "law," or speaks of a well-confirmed functional formula. I am not one for disputing about terms when the mystical facts are recognized.

If the refutation of atomistic pluralism is complete even at this lowly level, it becomes more complete when we proceed to consider life and mind. For in the organism insofar as it is organic and does not become the mere slave of its instruments or sunken in rigid ways, no part has an absolutely invariant function but is modified to suit the drift or trend of the whole, and the environment likewise is systematically used and transformed to suit organic drifts in a manner exemplified by civilized technology. Biologists, of course, do not like the mysticism of the organism. They can tolerate the channeled, stratified mysticism of inorganic substances, but in the case of the organic their whole experimentation is largely a rebellion against the organic idea as such, a desperate determination to reduce it to the ultimate nonexplanatoriness of factors operating vigorously upon other factors *ab extra*, and without end. Certainly they will find more and more of what alone they are prepared to find, but certainly also their remoteness from exhaustive success will point up the mystical character of at least this section of reality and, by its gearing in with the rest of reality, of reality as a whole.

It will not be necessary for me to say much of the mystical properties of conscious experience: its inherent mysticism is in fact the chief reason for its banishment from supposedly scientific discourse. In the phenomena of conscious life we have an outgrowth of material being betraying a most extraordinary accommodation to remote facts in the world, not only perceiving the environment in its true being and configurations, and guided by its remote rather than its immediately impinging characters, but also being influenced by remote resemblances of character, hidden affinities of logical form and connection which the neurologist, aided by the analogy of the most skillfully programmed computers, acknowledges with an idiotic faith in the unmystical character of the plainly mystical phenomena before him. The very fact that we hold the whole world and much more than the world in our thought, and that we know so much about it and can range so confidently in it, even far beyond the limits of our actual or possible experience, renders it meaningful to suppose that our thought represents an indispensable function of the universe. Indeed, in that thought the universe, as it were, becomes lucid to itself.

Even more remarkable are the cases of mystical transcendence required by our understanding of the experiences and aspirations of others and by our placing of the interests of conscious beings in general above the particular interests of this or that conscious being. From the point of view of ordinary logic and semantics the kind of self-transcendence here involved is absurd, no matter what specious formulae of "universalization" may be used to conceal this fact. For what sense can be assigned to saying what I, a particular, finite conscious individual would experience if I were quite another finite conscious individual, or even the dog which howls next door? It is about as significant as asking what a flagpole would do if it were a whale. And yet all ethics rests on being meaningfully able to conceive what we should feel if we were someone else, and without such, mystical meaning has no sense or sanction whatsoever. We have no duties towards merely behaving organisms. The fact that we have duties to others means very shockingly, therefore, that there is a stratum of our being that transcends the distinction of persons.

I have tried to give good reasons for postulating a mystical unity behind isolated objects, facts, and persons. Have I, however, given a reason that is good enough? It may be argued that I have not. It may be held that the world remains the same incongruous mixture of profoundly geared unity and inconsequent diversity that it always was, and that mystical experiences and utterances merely magnify and exaggerate the unity as extremely unmystical, atomistic views exaggerate the inconsequent diversity. Our world, it may be held, is a game played according to strict rules in a definite stadium, but apart from its rules and its location it is a free-for-all, which is always ready to degenerate into a melée or a fracas. Hegel tried to avoid this conclusion because he saw a master-plan working out in history, and many idealistic materialists and Marxists believe in a similar plan. It is, however, hard for a modern man to accept the rational optimism of the nineteenth century. I myself incline to believe that without the acceptance of an otherworldly extension of our this-world being, in which threads are drawn together, distances vanish, hard lines of separation become transparent, and the real comes into coincidence with what it ought to be, it is not more reasonable to look on the world mystically than unmystically. I wish, however, to present reasons for believing in that extension of experience which lies beyond our ordinary existence, and which we may perhaps hope to enjoy more perfectly when freed from the embarrassment of operating through the sort of body we now possess.

I should lay stress, first of all, on the fact that though our inner life of conscious experience undoubtedly involves the quite unconscious pressing down and pulling in and out of the stops and keys of a cerebral-neural organ, in virtue of which we perceive, imagine, symbolically refer to, or are made ready to perceive, imagine, or symbolically refer to whatever we have before us as an object and in virtue of which we unconsciously innervate our musculature or emotionally excite our sympathetic system, yet the conscious symphony played on this cerebral-neural organ has properties for which no precisely isomorphic cerebral-neural representation can meaningfully be found. Such properties as the guidance by what is remotely objective rather than immediate, or by what is highly generic rather than specific, or by what involves the gathering into a relevant whole of material culled from the most varied sources, or by what selects from an infinity of such material that which exactly fits some novel problem, or by what innovates in a manner novel in principle without being arrived at in some chance manner. Computers, our creatures, simulate these performances, but, being our creatures, necessarily lag behind their creators. They operate on our programs, often more skillfully than we can, whereas we transcend all our programs. We may further hold that even the silent symphony played on the cerebral-neural keys and stops in preparation for the full, conscious music has some of these transcendental properties. The cerebral-neural transformations prepare for but do not adequately reflect the illuminations, decisions, etc., for which they make us ready. But just as the cerebral-neural organ can be made silently ready for the full conscious symphony, so this symphony once established, or the enduring agency behind it, can arguably create for itself its own infinitely subtle, plastic, responsive corporeality when its grossly carnal corporeality has vanished. It can, then, in the manner more or less persuasively sketched by Dante, Swedenborg, St. Thomas Aquinas, the Tibetan Book of the Dead, and other reliable authorities make its début in an environment where distinctions between the physically real and the merely imagined lack all clarity, where the distinction between the public and the private is doubtful, where it is not always wholly clear what one man is experiencing and what another, and where meanings and values shine out in objects as they now only shine forth in the most finely arranged phrases and facial expressions. Such a world of liberated corporeality, such a veritable Kingdom of Heaven, may very well terminate in an upper Platonic region of pure gist, where everything will have become a matter of the sheerest understanding and nothing will any longer be spelled out in the redundant particularity of sense. What we are suggesting is rational because, arguably, it only carries further the process of decorporealization and departicularization. It extends the process of dying mentioned in Plato's *Phaedo*. It is rational because it only brings to clear consciousness our various obscure insights into the hidden nature of the things and persons around us which are always present in our experience, and it is rational because it explains why our admittedly rational enterprises are rational. And while in such decorporealization and departicularization we may move away from the objects of our common experience, we in a sense take them with us, since the pure gist to which we rise is their gist, as it is also the gist, and the ordered gist, of all other possibilities. It is at this point that one draws near to the mystical pole of unity, the central point in all this geography which is not so much a case of any particular kind of existence or insight as the boundless, unitary possibility of them all—in other words the absolutely One or Good, which we may, according to our cultural or theological preference, think of in negative or positive, in impersonally non-theistic or in warmingly theistic terms.

Can we, however, have assurance that the higher regions of this spectrum exist and are really experienced by some, and that the whole notion of the mystical spectrum and its culminating zenith is not a transcendental illusion? We can have no such assurance. For we inhabit an unmystical cave, where everything is split up into separate factors, and where only hints of such a higher unity are available. On mystical principles it is right that we should live in such a cave, since it is only in such a cave with its atmosphere of difficulty and obscurity that our higher experiences of scientific illumination, of revolutionary practical decision, of deep love and understanding of others, and so forth, become possible, experiences without which there would be nothing to be brought into and brought together at the mystical center. It is, then, wholly possible that mysticism is a transcendental illusion, a last fantasy in which the dreams of reason culminate. But whether real or fantastic, the mystical point of unity remains phenomenologically firm: it is the coordinating point of our reasoned thought and our life. Like the enlarged moon on the horizon in a well-known Kantian comparison, it remains an ineliminable appearance, one which gives sense and order to the whole firmament of our action and experience.

The Belief in Life after Death[1]

Hywel D. Lewis

THERE CAN BE LITTLE doubt that the greater part of mankind has believed, in some way or at some level, that they have a destiny beyond the fleeting transitory existence we have in the present life. This belief is deeply rooted in most of the great religions, and most persons in the past have subscribed to some kind of religion. Even Shinto, although a very secular religion in some respect, makes much of the worship of ancestors who are thought to be still "around" in some form. Theravada Buddhism, in spite of its skepticism, at least leaves the matter open and, while presenting special difficulties for any view of personal survival, has drifted into forms of belief and practice which involve at least some notion of a round of various existences; Mahayana Buddhism makes it very explicit. The so-called primitive religions seem also to center on the expectation of some kind of further existence. How profoundly religious allegiances have affected people's attitudes and how firmly religious persons have adhered to their professed beliefs is a more debatable matter. But few things have affected the general life and culture of people in the past more than religion: it has been a main determinant of attitudes, a shaper of major presuppositions; and it would not be incautious in the least to affirm on this basis that, at some level, by far the greater part of mankind has committed itself to the expectation of a life besides the present one and has shaped its activities accordingly.

Could the same be said today? There can be little doubt that most

communities today have become much more secular than at any previous time. How deep or permanent is this change may not be easy to
settle. Some, like myself, regard it as a phase in the profounder and
more intelligent recovery of religion, although this by no means
involves commendation of secular attitudes or the canonizing of them
as inevitable stages in some dialectic of religious progress. But without
going further into this particular question, I would hazard fairly
confidently the guess that, where the question of belief in life after
death is concerned, most persons, if a poll of some kind were taken,
would still return a fairly firm positive answer, even in countries where
vast material changes have brought about considerable secularization.
What importance we should ascribe to that I leave unanswered for
the moment.

Beliefs can be held in a variety of ways and at different levels. There
are at least two main ways in which this is true in respect to the present
theme. A belief can be held at one level only when we adhere to it in
spite of the fact that the evidence for it (or other reasons for holding it)
is not very strong. There are some beliefs which we can hold with much
more confidence than others. They need not be the most important
beliefs. If I believe that it is fine and sunny at the moment, I have only
to look up from my desk or step out into the garden to be sure of this,
and anyone who calls will confirm it. I am equally certain that I have a
pencil in my hand and am writing with it. I see and hold it, and that is
about the greatest certainty we could have. Philosophical questions
could be asked about the status of things like pencils or the nature of
perception. But for all normal purposes I am as certain as anyone could
wish to be that I am holding a pencil and that the sun is shining. I am
not so certain that the point of this pencil will not suddenly break or
that the weather will hold for my walk this evening. But the pencil
looks firm enough and the weather seems set for a glorious day. I make
plans accordingly. I am not quite so certain of what falls outside my
immediate purview, though in many cases as certain as makes no
difference. I am quite certain that King's College still stands in the
Strand. In principle there could have been some weakness in the
structure causing it to collapse this morning, but having heard no hint
or rumor of this, I do not give the possibility serious thought. But there
are a host of other matters, ascertainable in perception, of which I am
less certain. A road near my home in North Wales was closed recently,
but I only learned of this when I got there.

In more serious matters we are often a good deal more certain of some things than of others. Some of my acquaintances I trust absolutely, but I am cautious about others. Confidence is sometimes misplaced, and we must go on the strength of the evidence at the time. We likewise adhere with varying degrees of firmness to certain principles, socialism or pacifism for instance, and some are swayed more than others by evidence and rational reflection. But clearly, when a strong case can be made out for something and objections met, we are normally disposed to think favorably of it and try to put prejudice aside. One reason therefore for the weakness of a belief and oscillation in the firmness of our adherence to it is the difficulty of making out a simple overwhelming case, as I can for my belief that it is not raining in my garden at the moment. The belief in a future life cannot be established with that kind of conclusiveness. If it could only idiots would doubt it.

This is what has set many persons searching for some foolproof way of ascertaining that the dead do in fact live again. The most obvious approach here is parapsychology and mediumistic evidence. Some religious people are very contemptuous of this. It will not, so they say, prove the resurrection but only the survival or immortality of the soul, of which some religious people take a curiously dim view. But this is, in my view, a very great mistake. The evidence may not give us all that we want to establish in a religious context—it certainly cannot provide all that the Christian means by "the life eternal." But if it did the trick it would certainly give us a great deal. It might not prove that we live for ever; but if some kind of mediumistic or kindred evidence could be found which made it tolerably certain (as certain as we are about conditions in some of the planets we can more easily study, for example) that someone whose lifeless corpse we had seen put in its coffin and buried or cremated was now all the same unmistakably in communication with us, in whatever trivial a way, this would be momentous.

I can in fact think of nothing that would startle people more, or have greater news value. A journalist who failed to report it would obviously be falling down on his job. The trouble is that there is much to dispute about mediumistic evidence, and most people take the line that, while "there may be something in it," it is all too uncertain to be taken seriously—and in the meantime there is much to tell against it, including the lifeless corpse. I repeat therefore that if confidence could be established in the psychical approach to the question of survival, it would be a matter of enormous importance. The issue is not, of course, the straightforward one of finding conclusive or very impressive evidence; there are peculiar difficulties about the interpretation of the evidence available, as critics are not slow to point out. Some views about the nature of persons would rule out from the start the interpretation of any evidence in terms of actual survival, and those who defend the possibility of survival must reckon with such views as a vital part of their undertaking. But apart from this, and even allowing for some psychical phenomena, there are differing ways in which it is proposed to interpret the available evidence. Clairvoyance and tele-pathy among the living might cover much of it. I myself find much of the evidence impressive, and I am even more impressed by the fact that very clearsighted investigators with the highest philosophical competence like C. D. Broad and H. H. Price have thought it worth taking very seriously, the latter being fully convinced of its adequacy to establish at least some form of survival.

There are, admittedly, some people who would prefer the evidence to be negative, and Broad is perhaps the most notable example. There are indeed disconcerting aspects to the possibility of another life. It may not by any means be all that we expect now; but even so, and allowing fully for the somber side of those possibilities, my own expectation would be that most poeple would be immensely relieved and excited if they had firm assurance comparable to that which we may have about ordinary matters of fact that the friends they had lost were alive "somewhere" and might even be contacted, and that their own existence would not come finally to its end at the close of their earthly life. This assurance could in fact make a vast difference to the way we think of ourselves and our lives at present. We do not have to think of morality in terms of rewards and punishments to appreciate what a change it would make to our present attitudes and restlessness if we were certain that this life is "not all."

For these reasons I do not think that religious people should be as contemptuous or suspicious as many seem to be of the investigation of the alleged paranormal evidence for survival. They are indeed entitled to insist that this will not give them any of the essentials of a Christian faith or the reasons for holding it, and we need thus to be warned not to confuse major issues or draw attention away from the sort of assurance on which the Christian faith depends. All the same, an assurance that men do live after they are dead (even if it extends to only a limited period) would make a very considerable breach in the hard wall of skepticism which confronts us now and open men's minds to further possibilities which come closer to the profounder and more exhilarating insights which the Christian claims. It has been said in a classical context that philosophy can "make room for faith." This has sometimes been understood in a way that implies that philosophy has no place in faith as such, and it is, alas, this travesty that appeals most to those who invoke the distinction most often today, thus maintaining an unholy alliance between religious dogmatism or uncritical relativism and philosophical skepticism. This was certainly not Kant's idea, and without pretending to follow him further in how he thought of faith, we can insist that there are rational ingredients capable of philosophical refinement at the center of a religious faith. Nonetheless, philosophical and other secular assurances which do not affect the core of a Christian commitment can help to open men's minds to possibilities which prepare the way for a deeper religious understanding.

There are a great many ways in which this holds today, and there are many important and exciting tasks for religious philosophers who rightly understand their prospects and have the energy and courage to persist. But I cannot investigate these now; I must content myself with the insistence that philosophical and scientific investigation of the religious implications and possibilities of psychical research is a respectable and important part of seeking a better understanding and acceptance of Christian beliefs. The pitfalls are many, but that is no reason for avoiding the subject as many religious thinkers do today. If the results prove negative no harm is done, for this is not what faith turns upon; if positive, a great deal is gained. In any case, our first concern is with the truth, disconcerting or otherwise.

I come now to the second main way in which a belief may be held "at one level" of our minds only, namely when we believe, as it is sometimes put, with "one side of our minds" or "one part of us." To some extent, this is true of all of us, and it needs to be reckoned with more than is commonly the case in matters of belief. In extreme cases we have the situation memorably described by Plato in his account of what he called "the democratic man:"

> Day after day he gratifies the pleasures as they come—now fluting down the primrose path of wine, now given over to teetotalism and banting; one day in hard training, the next slacking and idling, and the third playing the philosopher. Often he will take to politics, leap to his feet and do or say whatever comes into his head; or he conceives an admiration for a general, and his interests are in war; or for a man of business, and straight-

way that is his line. He knows no order or necessity in life; but he calls life as he conceives it pleasant and free and divinely blessed, and is ever faithful to it.

This is not, in the main at least, a case of insincerity or hypocrisy. In certain moods men genuinely do believe what they do not believe at all at other times. This is how some well-known public figures leave the impression of a deep insincerity of which they may not really be guilty. They really do believe, perhaps quite fervently at times, what they also seem to reject or disregard, though there may be insincerity as well. We are, all of us, more of a mixture than we care to admit.

There has, on occasion, been serious commendation of this frame of mind, as in some doctrines of a dual standard or in the nineteenth century notion of a "truth of the heart" which could ease the intellectual strain for us by being entertained alongside an incompatible "truth of the mind." I hope no one today encourages this kind of intellectual schizophrenia. But we must all be on our guard against the insidiousness of our temptation to lapse into it in subtle ways.

It is here also that we may find the element of truth in John Baillie's famous account of believing something "at the bottom of our hearts" which we deny "at the top of our minds." Baillie's mistake was to suppose that this must be true of all unbelief. That is certainly not the way to take the measure of unbelief or the magnitude of our task in resisting it. But it may well cover many cases; and even notable atheists, like Bertrand Russell, come sometimes very close to the substance of what we profess.

The sum of this, for our purpose (it is a theme of great importance which needs to be treated more fully on its own account), is that our beliefs need to be cultivated. That is not a commendation of wishful thinking or of naive refusal to look serious difficulties in the face. But profound and precious beliefs about spiritual matters can neither be achieved nor maintained in a casual way. This is again what we learn from Plato, who spoke eloquently about "the long and toilsome route" out of the cave and how easy it is to lose a true belief or to substitute for it a merely superficial opinion. We have to be like athletes, a comparison to which St. Paul was also very prone, resisting "the softer influence of pleasure" and "the sterner influence of fear."

The saints have indeed been well aware of this: they are constantly wrestling with doubt and despair; the pilgrim sinks deep in the Slough of Despond; our hymns are full of varieties of mood, from triumphant certainties to deep despair, from the hilltops to the valleys and the shadows; and this is as it should be—we have to win our way through doubt to firm belief and the renewal of belief. But this is no mere intellectual matter; it is more a maintaining of the set of our thoughts and dispositions, of living with the evidence which leads to spiritual discernment; and for this reason we should welcome the importance that is accorded today to contemplation. Meditation has its discipline, and there are those who can guide us. This is often travestied and sometimes almost equated with physical exercises or mechanical stimuli. We need to understand much better what contemplation means, for it is in the fullness of meditation, which extends to thought and practice alike, that faith is renewed. This will have rational ingredients among which philosophical thought has a prominent place.

The belief in life after death is not an easy one. There is much to induce us to identify ourselves with our bodies, and philosophers today find it hard to avoid that. This is not the place to put the case against them—I have tried to do that elsewhere. But we all know what will happen soon to our bodies. They will rot or be burned. To believe seriously that we can survive this needs some very clear thinking, and I do not discount in this context the oddity we all feel, I imagine, of the notion of our own total extinction. But what I most wish to stress at the moment is the strenuousness at the intellectual level, and at the level of committed religious living, of maintaining a genuine belief. Belief in life after death is a momentous one, and the burden of our witness to it has come to be taken too lightly.

In the sophisticated thinking relevant to a belief in afterlife, there is one item of exceptional importance to which I wish to draw attention and which will be my chief concern for the remainder of this discussion. It is at this point that I find myself sharply at odds with Plato and with the vast range of philosophical thinking for which he has been largely responsible. Plato, you will recall, maintained that genuine reality consisted of certain general principles, the ideas or the forms, as we call them. These are not concepts, though the best way for us to begin to understand them is in terms of universals; they are in his view real, indeed the only true reality. They are also closely interrelated, and in the progress of Plato's own thought there is a deepening insistence on the essential interrelatedness of the forms. At the center and transcending all is the form of the Good; and it is in our glimpse or vision of this at the end of our toilsome route that we find our clue to the ultimate necessity of all the rest.

Particular things, it is thus affirmed, "the choir of heaven and the furniture of earth" (in the words of a kindred but more down-to-earth spirit), in the rush and travail of our own lives derive such reality as they have from the forms themselves; they have a questionable borrowed reality. The wise man will seek to draw away from the insubstantial fleeting world of particulars and center his thought not on "shadows" but on the only true realities, the forms. He will in this sense seek what is "above." It is significant that, in spite of this denigration of the particular and the seeming exclusiveness of the bifurcation into the world of particulars and the world of forms, Plato continues to think of the soul as essentially individual. Exactly where it fits is not clear, but it is certain that Plato never wavers on this—the soul is the individual, now and always; and it is also for Plato immortal because it is essentially indestructible, and it is indestructible because it has an essential affinity with the forms; the eternal world of forms is its home.

It is this affinity with the world of forms that Plato stresses most of all in claiming the immortality of the soul. The inadequacy of his other argumentation has often been exposed, but his main considerations provide a not unimpressive view of the immortality of the soul. It has many of the ingredients we would also stress: the sense of the inevitable transitoriness of our present existence, the urgency with which we are pressed to look to the things "above" (almost as the Bible tells us to "lay up treasures for yourselves in heaven, where neither moth nor rust doth corrupt"), the abiding conviction that at the heart of all is the absolute transcendent Good, the source of our being and our home. We must not despise this understanding; it is never monistic, "soul is soul" whatever else we say, and it has helped extensively to shape Christian understanding at various times. But it has one radical weakness. It does not take proper account of the here and now. This is not because Plato adopts an unmitigated otherworldly view as in extreme monism. He set the course, on the contrary, for the effective rebuttal of the arguments of Parmenides, whose force he well appreciated. The philosopher, in some ways like the *avatar*, has to return to succor and provide for others. In the world of forms there is an essential variety. Nonetheless the particular, whether in the world of nature or in our own lives, tends to count solely as a reflection of the true reality of eternal verities. The persistence of this view is the source of the main points of disagreement one would have with Plato.

This is seen to good advantage in Plato's treatment of the family and personal relations. He did not think physical enjoyment in any form an evil thing, but he rated it very lowly, not appreciating how physical enjoyment enters into a fuller experience to make it more meaningful. The intimacy of full personal encounter and a rounded friendship seems to give way before the idea of the blueprint and the pattern laid up in heaven (which is surprising in view of Plato's own enjoyment of excellent friendships and his great regard for Socrates). Appetite tends to remain brute appetite; it does not become an ingredient in a richer experience. For the same reasons, the morally or physically handicapped receive very harsh treatment. If they do not play their proper part in the fulfillment of "the pattern," they are dispensable. The same clues yield us the secret of Plato's famous perversity about poetry and the arts. A very great literary artist himself, and very consciously attracted to poetry, he would have none of it officially. This is because he understood well that poetry does not deal in essences or universal notions—a point about which our late and gifted friend Dr. Austin Farrer was peculiarly confused.[2] Art is some illumination of the particular, even in its rarefied and abstract forms, and it is for this reason that literature, music, painting and all the other arts are accorded such a very lowly place in a scheme of things which puts all its premium on the impersonal and eternal aspect of things.[3]

This is where true religion provides its corrective, and that is why Plato can never set the model for a truly religious philosophy. For religion, as I understand it, has always an element of revelation at the core of it; and in revelation the transcendent discloses and shapes itself for our illumination in a peculiar involvement of itself with a particular situation, a time and place at which the revelation happens notwithstanding that it may not always be precisely specifiable. The disclosure is to someone, and may well include some transmutation of what is presented immediately in his environment. It speaks of the "beyond," but it is also altogether of the here and now. Others may appropriate it, and it takes its place in the exchanges of committed religious living as the gradual refinement of our understanding of God and the sense of his presence.

This puts immeasurable worth on particular things, on an essentially created world in which the divine splendor shines, and on the lives of all. All the earth is holy, a "sacramental universe" as it has been boldly put, and personal existence as the peculiar center of divine involvement acquires a significance which nothing can efface, a place at the heart of the life of God. This is what the mystic perceives and this is why he speaks of an absorption in which God is all in all. This is a travesty if, as often happens, it is taken neat. God is God, but the point of true religion is the discovery of our place in the life of God himself, and as the disclosure deepens and the essentially self-giving character of it reveals itself, as the bond tightens, we know that we are "of God" and have no home but God. The inestimable worth that is placed on each, even "weak things" and "things that are despised," puts the question of the elimination of anything out of the question. This is in some ways a terrible truth for us to realize, for whatever is evil in our lives or persons is present there in this holy relationship. It is no wonder, therefore, that outstandingly saintly persons have been so peculiarly tormented by the sense of sin as to seem to others obsessed and unbalanced. We may much resent the words "sinners in the hands of an angry God," and indeed few things have been more travestied and misdirected, in theory or experience, than the sense of sin and the fear of God. But there is a certain horror, and an abysmal consuming wretchedness—the worm that does not die—in the spectacle of one's own life aglow in all its forms in the life of God. That is where the costliness of redeeming love begins to be seen.

In the peculiar claims of the Christian religion, the unfolding of divine love in history and the manifold experiences of men is alleged to come to a finality of fulfillment in Christ. Here God himself comes as a man to put the seal of his redeeming activity on the indissoluble bond of our own lives in his. Of the way we must understand this, and of the infinite sadness of the many travesties of it, we cannot speak here. But the Christian should have no doubt about "the price that was paid." Christianity without sacrifice does not begin to get off the ground, and it is in the sacrifice we celebrate in a holy communion that we find the ultimate seal on our own abiding destiny as sons of God. There can be no elimination of what is so completely of God himself.

These assurances in no way dispense with the need for thought; they have thought at the core of them. The wise Christian will come to terms with this, most of all in a developing culture. Insight is not random, and faith is not blind. Both are at the opposite poles to unreason. There is much work also in preparing the ground: in dealing, for example, with problems about the nature of persons, as indicated earlier, in sifting the evidence of psychical research, and in hard thought about the peculiarly tantalizing problem presented by extensive evil in a world governed by divine love. The latter problem does in fact find some easement in the present case in the very substance of what faith affirms; for, in the affirmation of a life beyond, we do have a broader canvas on which to view the various ills men endure now. Compensation in after life could afford a partial solution at least to the problem of evil, and some of the most impressive writers on the subject of late, such as C. A. Campbell, A. C. Ewing and John Hick, give it particular prominence. I go more cautiously with it, as indeed do Campbell and Ewing, because I wish to stand firmly on our present assurances. In these the feeling we have that it would be strange for personal existence to be eclipsed for reasons incidental to what our natures properly are and what we do deserves more prominence than is often accorded to it; and here the study of other religions could be very relevant. But the main weight has still to be placed on the peculiar assurance of faith through divine disclosure.

This lends particular urgency at the present time to the proclamation of Christian truth and our witness to it. This should include at center the affirmation of a life beyond, and if we fail in this we shall place a serious limitation on any renewal of faith in our time. The relevance of our proclamation to present ills will be much weakened. This is not because the new problems of today spring directly from irreligion; they come about largely through the complexities of a changed situation and marked advances in our understanding of ourselves and our environment. At the same time the limiting of our horizons to the here and now is not without profound effect, and, on the positive side, the transformation in attitude and expectation which could be induced by a detached and objective sense of illimitable possibilities of richer experience would be hard to calculate. The palliatives and substitutes would easily dwindle beside it.

It is in the context of this expectation and the renewal of faith in its fullness that the Christian should consider the question of a life after death. The hope we have in this precise sense is not a luxury, a secondary consideration to be investigated on its own account; it belongs to the essence of a Christian commitment. To tie that to some isolated doctrine of the Resurrection, or make the Resurrection stories pivotal on their own account, is a bad mistake. The work and person of Christ must be taken in its fullness, but it seems to be unthinkable that it should not be thought to include, in explicit word and in implication, the affirmation of our abiding place at the heart of God's love. We can form little conception of what this will be; the new dimensions of it go far beyond our present limitations and boldest speculation, involving transformations of the quality of life as much as its formal scope. It does not yet "appear what we shall be" but we shall be "like him," and that, to any who consider the matter seriously, is about as remarkable an expectation as that we shall exist without our present bodies. Indeed, it is in many ways the most bewildering item of our faith, as sober realistic theologians appreciated earlier in this century, however muddled in other ways. This is nonetheless the bold truth the Christian must proclaim, and in the long run we do better with the daunting character of the full Christian assurance than with half-hearted humanist travesties of it. That is one reason why narrowly dogmatic Christians succeed better, for a time at least, than the rest of us. Other reasons are less estimable. An enduring faith must be open and reflective. But it must be *faith* and the fullness of it, and that unmistakably includes our own conservation, sanctified beyond our dimmest understanding and renewed in the knowledge of the price that was paid, at the heart of the life of God. "For God so loved the world, that he gave his only begotten Son, that whosoever believeth in him, should not perish but have everlasting life." There is no Christian faith without "everlasting life," and it is in the fullness of faith, as a rounded personal apprehension, that this life of "the world to come" becomes also our proper possession "in this time now." In essentials it is all a matter of the right kind of faith.

NOTES

1.   The Drew Lecture delivered at the Whitefield Memorial Church on October 20, 1973, and printed by permission of the Trustees, New College, London.

2.   See *The Glass of Vision* (Westminster: Dacre Press, 1948), chap. 7, pp. 113-131, and my comment in *Our Experience of God,* chap. 7, pp. 131-145.

3.   Cf. my paper "On Poetic Truth," in *Morals and Revelation* (London: Allen & Unwin, 1951), chap. 10, pp. 232-255.

Towards an Understanding
of the Self

W. Norman Pittenger

IN THIS ESSAY, written to honor my old and good friend Peter A. Bertocci, I shall make some suggestions towards an understanding of the self from the perspective adopted by process thought. This subject seems appropriate in this *festschrift*, because Bertocci has long been one of those philosophers, not too numerous in our day, whose major interest has been the concept of "person" and the development of a metaphysic whose point of departure is found in that concept. And I should say at the very beginning that I for one have always been impressed by his treatment of this subject, even though I have not always agreed with what he has had to say.

Indeed, in my judgment Peter Bertocci has been much more impressive in his treatment of the meaning of "person" than his own teacher and (as he would doubtless say) master, Edgar Sheffield Brightman. But that is another matter and I shall not dwell upon it. At least I can say, however, that in respect to his understanding and even partial use of the process-conceptuality, I believe that Bertocci has considerably advanced our awareness of the relationship between an evolutionary or processive view of the world, of human existence, and even of God's way in the world (perhaps, too, of God's own nature), and that he has offered a viable presentation of the self as person. Nowhere is this more obvious than in his book *The Person God Is*; but I have found particular help, for my own thinking, in his incidental comments in several of his writings dealing, on the face of it, with quite different topics, namely human sexuality and the creative tension known to us in our experience as men.

In beginning this discussion of a process understanding of self, I wish to quote some words from Dean Harold K. Schilling's recent (and wholly admirable) book *The New Consciousness in Science and Religion.*[1]

> When [man] arrived, evolutionary activity took on a new character. His extraordinary powers enabled him to bring forth a great variety of utterly new realities: tools and processes, abstractions and symbols, languages and logics, rational analyses and syntheses, measurement and experimentation, and many others equally unprecedented. In this way social rather than biological evolution came to dominate change. The arts and literatures emerged, and the religions, and philosophies, laws, the sciences and technologies—and thus man's cultures and civilizations, with new orders of good and evil, beauty and ugliness, truth and deception. Moreover, there came to this new being the capacity for self-analysis which was quite unprecedented. He learned to investigate himself, as well as his world, with both critical objectivity and discriminating introspection—and in depth. He discovered that his "self," his so-called "nature," and his tremendously varied potentialities are not "possessions" or innate attributes of his own but in large part the gift-consequences of his relationship with other entities and processes and with nature as a whole. Through this knowledge and understanding he has achieved a remarkable measure of self-determination. To a large extent he is now in a position to be both the architect and builder of his own future, which certainly could not be said about any of his evolutionary forbears.

In this fine passage, Dr. Schilling has stressed several points which seem to me of great importance in any attempt to make sense of what we mean when we speak of "our selves." He has noted the emergence of man from the evolutionary past; at the same time he has stressed that this is an "emergent" and not merely a resultant—for man has distinctive and specific qualities which distinguish him from anything else in the course of evolution. Perhaps we can sum these up by saying that man is able to engage in rational thought, to make and employ "tools and processes" for his own use, to observe and experiment and comprehend that which is not himself, to appreciate and value moral and aesthetic significance, to look introspectively into his own experience and see something of what it has to tell him, and to know himself *as* "himself." Furthermore, Schilling has stressed that all of this is made possible for man through his social relationships, in which through his continuing and inescapable contacts with other men, with the natural order, and with everything that goes on around him, each man becomes more than an individual (in the sense of one member of a given class or category)–he becomes a *person*, which (even so long ago as in the time of Thomas Aquinas) means a self in society, with the give-and-take or reciprocity that is so much part of his own selfhood that we may claim that to say "person" and "society" is to speak of the two sides of one coin. Finally, Schilling has indicated the importance of human decision: the capacity of the self for "a remarkable degree of self-determination" in such freedom as makes possible significant choices that count enormously "for his own future" and (we may properly add) for the future both of his society and of the entire creative advance in its wider and deeper sense.

If, as I believe to be the case, Schilling has thus admirably summed up what it means, what it feels like, what it suggests to be a self, we are at once obliged to say that denial of this reality is both experientially impossible and philosophically absurd. Yet there are those who have been prepared to make just that denial. Sometimes they are very crass behaviorists; more often, in our own day, at any rate, they are sophisticated thinkers who ought to know better.

I believe that one reason for this kind of denial of significant selfhood is that for many the reality of self is identified with the notion that to speak of self at all is to talk about some "soul substance" introduced into the evolved physiological stuff which is man's body– and introduced, so to say, from outside as an intrusion upon an otherwise orderly developmental process. Of course, in a highly complicated, technological society, it can be very difficult to maintain a keen sense of "my" selfhood; personal self-awareness is likely to be suppressed by the pressures of a mass-world. But more than this is often involved. Many feel that man can best be seen as a complex machine whose patterns of behavior (whether crude or sophisticated) can be observed, but whose supposed capacity for self-knowledge and self-awareness is at best epiphenomenal: it plays no real part in whatever a man does.

There is no time in this essay to refute such a reductionist position and to show how entirely inadequate it is to the facts. I say "the facts"; and I intend here not only the introspection which I am convinced is to be found in every man, in however minimal a degree, but also the plain deliverance of observation of others. After all, we see others acting as if they were conscious, more or less rational, appreciative, free selves; and I stress that we see them acting in that way, not simply fondly thinking themselves to be such. Nobody really behaves as if he were merely a complicated machine; and perhaps Bishop Butler's remark about freedom applies here in a wider sense: that since men do act this way, there is every reason to assume that they are what they act as if they were. However, I need not engage in any such detailed refutation, since at this point Peter Bertocci has himself given us as complete and adequate a rebuttal of such a view as we could ever hope to accomplish. For this we are most deeply in his debt.

In this essay I am concerned to set forth a way of understanding selfhood, of the order Schilling has sketched; and I am doing it from a double perspective. I write as a supporter of the process conceptuality, in the first place; and in the second, I write as a Christian. I do not claim for a moment that the process way of seeing things is *the* truth, in any absolute sense. Indeed I doubt that it is given to man to have any absolute truth with which he can deal. The best we can do is to try to develop a general view which will work with and account for as many of the facts as possible. The results will be tentative, of course; but insofar as they do include such facts and do make sense of them in some coherent pattern, those results (may we not say?) are so far forth the truth for us at this time. We have to do here with what Whitehead called "a vision of reality," not with a supposedly omni-competent and utterly final metaphysical scheme.

In the same way, I should not wish to claim that the Christian way of seeing things is demonstrably *the* truth, in some exclusive and narrow sense. Rather, I should say that it provides us with an insight that derives from what Whitehead styled, in another context, "the brief Galilean vision" of God's nature and agency in the world; and insofar as that insight also includes the facts as they are and makes some kind of sense of them, it too advances us toward the truth for us at this time. In other words, both in respect to "process" and to "love as the clue" to God, man, and their relationship, I should wish it to be understood that my acceptance is both whole-hearted and humble. There is something in each of them which I take to be true, which I believe does reckon with the facts, and which I am prepared to trust and use.

I presume that I need not here do more than mention the main motifs of process thought: its stress on an evolving and changing cosmos with what Whitehead called its "creative advance"; its recognition of the societal or interpenetrative quality of everything in that cosmos (including human existence, of course), by virtue of which there is a prehension by each entity of other and antecedent entities, in however great or small a degree; and above all, its insistence that the ingredients or "building blocks" (to use an inappropriate word since it suggests things) are not substances to which "events" happen but are in fact themselves events or occurrences, so that the universe is made up of foci of energy with routings or directions taken towards realizing potentialities. And the basic thrust in the cosmos is not so much coercive force, although in certain ways such force is operative to preserve an ordered or structured dynamic movement, but persuasion or love. This last point is often thought to be surprising in a metaphysical pattern; yet process thinkers are prepared to urge that from introspection and from observation it is indeed true that such persuasion is ultimately more effective and more basic than the more obvious coercion we assume to be in control.

As to Christian faith's contribution, let me say simply that so far as our present purpose is concerned this amounts to the affirmation that man is not entirely "alone" in the world but that there is a source of "comradeship and refreshment" (again to use Whitehead's words) whose character is "pure unbounded love," and that this Love is both the chief (yet not the only, since man and other creaturely entities have freedom and a causal efficacy) causative agency in the cosmos and also the ultimate recipient of that which is accomplished or achieved in the creative advance. In many different ways the nature and purpose of this cosmic Love is disclosed; but for Christian faith it is seen as made manifest supremely in the event which we name when we say Jesus Christ. In that event, through genuine human loving to the point of self-giving in death, cosmic Love is believed to be actively at work. This tells us, the Christian claims, that man too is being created through his response to the lure of the divine Love to become a creaturely and finite lover in society with his brethren and under the "sovereign rule" of the cosmic Love itself. At the same time, because of man's continuing defection from this goal and his frequent preference for more self-centered and partial "goods" (as he sees them), the disclosure in act of cosmic Love works to "redeem" human existence from triviality and frustration and from the wrongness of lovelessness with its hate, malice, arrogance, and easy self-concern.

I believe that these two—process and love—fit together and help us make sense of the world, not least in view of the presence and power within it of evil, against which a struggle is going on and to defeat which man is called to exercise his given freedom of decision and action—however limited by circumstance that freedom may be. I am well aware of objections which may be made against both process and love, but I shall not pause here to consider these and attempt to answer them. At the very least, the two do offer a possible slant on the cosmic process and more particularly (for our present concern) on man himself and on what it means to speak of the human self.

Like everything else in the cosmos, each man is a routing of events or occasions. It is not that things happen to something which exists in separation from such events, but that man is himself the series of happenings or occasions. Precisely here the problem becomes the very real one of how one can speak of a self when each man is precisely such a series of routings or occasions. Must there not be some "thing," call it if you wish "the soul," which is of a different order from those occasions and which is the quite separate (if related) subject of what happens to it? I believe that to think in this way is to return to the notion of an intrusive self and to open oneself to the charge made by Ryle that we can easily land thereby in the fallacy of "the ghost in the machine," or the Cartesian dichotomy of *res cognitans* and *res extensa.* There must be some way out of this situation; and I believe a useful approach to that way is through considering what we are talking about when we speak of human identity.

Every routing or series of occasions is a complex affair. It includes the past which has now "perished," in one sense, and which yet lives on in its efficacy in the present. In what we may style "memory" there is a continued presentness of that past, through what it has effected for each present occasion. There is also the immediacy of the contemporary moment, with its prehension of the past both remote and close at hand and with its reaching out to that which surrounds it and presses upon it. And there is the future possibility, which while not yet realized is in a real fashion effectual before such realization, since it lures the present instant to make decisions towards its fulfillment, even if there is also freedom to decide negatively and thus reject the potential fulfillment. Here is a richly complex event, then, with its past, its present, and its future. Nor is it chaotic, aimless, or anarchic; there is an indicated direction for the routing and there is a continuity in that the past works in the present and the present moves towards the future—the line is clear enough, however deviant may be the decisions and however short of fulfillment each entity may come.

Out of what has happened in the past that is thus in varying ways remembered—sometimes consciously, sometimes unconsciously (when the psychoanalyst, for instance, may be able to find effectual causes for many present choices), and sometimes viscerally or in the very "stuff and bones" of each man—there has been provided the material for relationships sustained in the give-and-take of the immediate present. Past and present provide the background and the "materials" which are in the future. That future lures the given entities in their routing; it is the "subjective aim" towards which they are moving if they are to make actual the potentialities which have been the constitutive "stuff" of the entities in their processive movement.

To speak of human identity, with such an analysis in mind, is to speak of the way in which there is precisely this continuity in routing, when the past, the present, and the future are thus held together. This sort of talk is possible in respect to any and every routing in the cosmos, at any and every level. But with the emergence of man and with those capacities and qualities which Schilling has so well sketched in the passage with which we began, there is also a difference. Schilling himself indicated the difference when he spoke of an "emergent," the appearance of a novelty within the broader continuity of the creative advance of the cosmic process.

If we had to do with a resultant, and not an emergent, the case for reductionism would be made—man would be nothing but a more complicated instance of the simian, perhaps only a complex machine. But there is ample evidence that such is not the case. For somewhere along the evolutionary line a novelty made its appearance, not by the introduction from outside (what could that mean, in any event?) of something that was alien to the world, but by a special variety of integration and ordering in an organic manner of the stuff of the world, of such a kind as to produce something different. Unlike the usual series of energy-events anterior to man, unlike a stick or a stone, unlike an insect or an animal, that emergent had, and in his descendants continues to have, the ability to know and to feel what is going on.[2] In other words, the distinctive quality of human routing, as different from other finite routings in the cosmos, is an awareness of the routing and a conscious sense of the identity along the line which is taken as the past moves into the present and towards the future. Whether there are other creatures (elsewhere in the creation, as perhaps on some planet not yet known to us) who are also possessed of this awareness and conscious sense of identity, we have no information. The point is that so far as this planet is concerned, we do have a distinctive emergent and we must take very seriously the fact of its emergence.

The physiologist and psychologist may attempt to determine how this quality emerged, what elements play their part in it, and the relationship of it to the psychological and physiological states which accompany it. But they cannot deny the fact of that awareness and conscious sense of identity. Why is this? For the simple reason that to deny it, and hence to deny also those implementations to which Schilling drew attention (such as intellectual capacity, logical thought, analysis, etc.), is to presuppose the very thing that is being denied. The reductionist presents the interesting spectacle of a man using his consciousness, his awareness, and with these his rationality, to argue that none of these does in fact exist. And as Whitehead once remarked, in another connection, "Scientists animated by the purpose of proving that they are purposeless constitute an interesting subject for study,"[3] so the person who employs his conscious reasoning powers to prove that such powers do not exist, and that with them the self-awareness on which they depend also does not exist, becomes not only "an interesting subject for study" but a ridiculously self-contradictory individual.

This awareness and conscious sense of identity is what we are talking about when we speak of the self. But we need also to see that because that self is not intruded from without but emerges from within the rich complex that constitutes the emergent, man, the physical as well as the mental is here involved. When the body is in pain, the self is also in pain; when the body enjoys some feeling of well-being, this feeling is enjoyed by the self. The psychosomatic constitution of selfhood, to use a phrase employed by the newer medicine, is never to be forgotten. I have often quoted in other writings Gabriel Marcel's insistence that "man does not have a body, he *is* a body"; so also, I urge, man does not have a mind but he *is* a mind. The self is the inclusive description of the totality of human existence as this is consciously apprehended in awareness, with all of its many implications and applications.

But it is equally true that the emergent, man, is not simply an individual; he is a person, as we have stated earlier. The social belonging which is man's is as much an ingredient in his totality as his physiology. He lives with others of his race; indeed, he lives from and by and in them, too. By this I am suggesting that what we might style man's sociality is as much an element of his human selfhood as his specific awareness of his particularity. "No man is an island entire unto himself," John Donne said in a famous sermon; on the contrary, he is so related with others that it might almost be argued, even with some exaggeration of the facts, that without that relationship he would neither be fully human nor genuinely a self at all. If he were submerged in the "mass" of manhood, conceived as something amorphous and undifferentiated, he would be no man; but equally, if he were merely individualistic, as an instance of some quite general class of creature, his specificity as man would also be lost.

Still another point needs to be made, however. Coupled with man's awareness and conscious sense of identity in the routing of occasions which constitutes him, there is what I like to call the aesthetic element. I am here referring to something more profound than the sense of beauty, although that is real enough. My meaning is that there is a profound feeling-tone, an emotional intensity, an enjoyment, an appreciative and valuational aspect in the experience of human awareness. The self is not only a thinking agency; it is also a deeply feeling one. With this, naturally, there is a desiring, yearning sensitivity and sensibility, and a striving to apprehend that which is thus desired, yearned for, and felt after. This has its bodily basis, of course; and no purpose is served by pretending that such a basis, with its own kind of sensitivity (and sensation), is incidental to selfhood. On the contrary, once more, we should see that bodily feelings and the whole "sensational" part of human existence provide the grounding of and the condition for the more fully conscious sense of enjoyment and appreciation.

Finally, when I speak of the self I am talking also of the human ability to decide—and to decide with awareness of what one is doing in making such decisions. At other levels, there is decision in the sense of "cutting off" certain possibilities by the very choice that is being made of this or that one—the word "decide" comes from the Latin *decidere* which means "to cut off." At the specifically human level, however, decisions are made, to greater or less degree depending upon the ends which are chosen and how much is at stake in the choice, with a conviction that they matter and with the knowledge that they will have results. Freedom thus to decide is not entirely unlimited, as we all know. If I live in Britain I cannot decide to walk along Fifth Avenue, New York City; and similarly my freedom is always within the bounds of the possibilities open at a given moment and place, in the situation where I am and with the inheritance which is mine. Yet the freedom is real enough; and it is at its maximum when I decide in such a way that my fullest possibilities are thereby brought closer to actualization.

This suggests to us that the self is moving towards, or away from, such completeness of integration in the direction of human purpose in general and of my own purpose in particular, as shall open up for it ever fuller and more satisfying (in an ultimate and not merely proximate sense) objectives. Increasing or decreasing integration is something everybody knows, as he lives day-by-day with his problems, seeks to act in accordance with some plan and towards some goal, and feels within himself satisfaction or dissatisfaction in terms of the possibilities which he envisages as open to him.

So far I have tried to indicate something of what I believe we may be intending when we speak of our self. We are speaking of the consciously sensed, more or less deeply felt, more or less rationally articulated, more or less freely decided routing which is specific to us. Here is no substantial selfhood, existing as a sort of extra to which things happen; rather, here is a known and felt experience of happening as constitutive of the *me*. In terms of a very different philosophy from the one to which I subscribe, I am suggesting that man is hylomorphic, in that his "form" is not intruded into but is integral to the "matter" of which he is made. The difference between that Aristotelian-Thomistic way of phrasing it and the one which I prefer is obvious: we should talk, not of "matter" which is thus "informed," but of routings of events or happenings which are identified for what they are, the awareness of which is an emergent in the cosmic order. This awareness is human in that it involves conscious knowledge, feeling, volition, and appreciation entertained as the routing goes forward. Here there is indeed what we may quite properly call "self-transcendence"; but that is a poor term to express the comprehensive awareness of past, present, and possible future, which I may grasp and understand. In other words, I am aware of the routing; and I am aware of my own awareness of it. But I am not outside it; I am in it and of it, because it is precisely that routing which makes me what I am.

I have said earlier that man is becoming: to be human is to be "on the way to manhood" in its realized sense. What, then, is the specificity about our human purpose? I now speak from my Christian stance and repeat what I urged at an earlier point in this essay: to become human is to become. a lover. I quite realize that the word "love" is highly ambiguous; it can, and often does, seem to suggest sentimentality in the cheaper sense, easy tolerance, and a rather sloppy and soft attitude. On the other hand, love can be a strong word; and it is in that strong sense that I am employing it. I am pointing towards conscious giving-and-receiving, mutuality, sharing, participation, and union which does not destroy either partner but brings each to his finest reach of development. Something of the sort, so far as union and sharing are in the picture, goes on elsewhere in the cosmos; so Teilhard de Chardin can speak of the world as the place where "amorization" is going on. At the human level, however, this amorization is a conscious enterprise; I am aware of love and of loving and I can interpret the world (as W. H. Auden has taught us) as the when and the where in which love is made possible and can become actual.

By introducing the word "lover," I am thus calling attention to an aspect of selfhood which has not received its full recognition in what has been said previously. In an interrelated or societal universe, each entity depends upon, as it receives from, every other; each entity, and each routing of entities, influences and is influenced by every other. At the human level, I urge, this mutuality is given a peculiar focus, since now it is a matter of conscious awareness, known in our feeling-tones, understood as a challenge and opportunity, and effectual (positively or negatively) in our several decisions. To put it in a sentence, man is a conscious routing of occasions in which his awareness of continuity of direction is to be interpreted as towards his living "in love": towards his becoming a lover of other men, a lover of the natural and animal creation from which he has emerged and of which he is yet a part, and a lover of the source of enrichment and empowering that religion calls "God." This is what Christian theologians, beginning with St. Paul and suggested before his time in what the Jewish tradition believed, are getting at when they speak of man "in the image of God." I prefer to phrase it this way: "man is being created, by his own creative activity in decision as he responds to the lure of cosmic Love, towards the image of God who is Love."

To say this is at the same time to say that no self can or does exist in and to itself; always it is in relationship with other selves, with the created order, and with God who in his "secular function" is the agency towards amorization, bringing into actuality the love which he purposes for his whole creation. The self is then set in a profoundly organic situation. Above all, it is this which enables us to see why "person" is so central; and also to understand how we are brought to such personal selfhood through the personalizing effects of loving relationship—a relationship not with some idea of manhood-in-general, but with this or that other who is integrally part of the community of men yet has his own inalienable selfhood which is to be cared for and hence personalized too.

I content myself with one final comment; and this brings me to mention my particular delight in Peter Bertocci's discussion of human sexuality in several of his books. In the kind of understanding which I have urged, human sexuality must be utterly central, although I have not touched upon it in this brief essay. That sexuality of man, in its physiological-psychological-volitional-emotional-spiritual reality (and I have linked the adjectives to show that I am talking about one complex aspect of manhood), provides the ground or basis for the sharing in relationship which is the meaning of love. I am convinced that until and unless we take full account of what might well be styled the "ontological status of sexuality" (using "ontology" as a term to indicate a comprehensive world view), we shall never be able properly to grasp the point of our selfhood. We shall never know what it means to be a human self. Peter Bertocci has done much to help us in this matter; but more work needs to be done if we hope to deal faithfully and fully with the question of the self, the human person, and the distinctiveness of man the emergent lover.

NOTES

1. *The New Consciousness in Science and Religion* (Philadelphia: United Church Press, 1973), pp. 148-149.

2. Cf. A. N. Whitehead, *Adventures of Ideas* (New York: Macmillan, 1933), p. 167.

3. *The Function of Reason* (Princeton: Princeton University Press, 1929), p. 12.

The Riddles of Behaviorism

John Howie

IF HE COULD READ our books, a visitor from outer space might be surprised in a number of ways. He would doubtless discover that the animal known as the human being gives more thought than any other animal to himself. He would discover that these beings keep diaries (even travel logs, embellished with slides at the slightest hint of a request), use mirrors, write autobiographies and histories, and develop such sciences as psychology and sociology. He would find that such beings probe curiously into the origin of their species on earth, with every newly uncovered ancient skull arousing additional interest, and even speculate, apparently without end, on what happens to the individual after death, and on what is to be the destiny of the species in the future of "space-ship earth."

Most surprising of all to this visitor from outer space would be what man has thought himself to be. Perusing human history he would be amazed to discover what weird things human beings have been willing to take themselves to be. Man is breath, atoms, force, fire, logos, clumps of habits, bundles of instincts or of conditioned responses; he is consciousness, subconsciousness, a group of complexes, a censor, an inner tug of war. In recent decades another view of man, not altogether new, has achieved considerable prominence and acclaim. This view, espoused by John B. Watson and, more recently by B. F. Skinner and others, is behaviorism. The purpose of this essay is to explore some of the riddles of this view of man, especially the behavioristic view of consciousness, and to suggest a perspective that may be more adequate to its referent.

Generally speaking, behaviorism may be characterized as a methodology and as a metaphysics. As a methodology it approaches man on the assumption that for scientific purposes the mind must be observable; and that what we observe of each other, in an objective and public way, is physical conduct. Often critics insist that they have no objections to this approach as a methodology.[1] Such an insistence is too lenient with behavioristic methodology for at least three reasons. First, in the hands of the most prominent behaviorists, Watson and B. F. Skinner, the behavioristic method is exclusive. It is not simply one way, among many, to study the human organism; rather, it is *the* way or *the* approach to understand correctly the human organism. It claims that the human organism can be viewed accurately as a creature whose behavior can be determined entirely by its environment. To change or to control human beings one need only control their environment. This claim to exclusiveness in the behavioristic methodology must be rejected for reasons that will be made clear shortly. Second, the behavioristic methodology can hardly be considered non-objectionable unless the purposes it purports to accomplish are themselves not objectionable. One purpose of his approach (as Skinner explains it) is to establish a planned community in which the achievements of man in government, education, and economics are all skillfully managed by positive reinforcements, especially pleasurable experiences. This sort of detailed planning, or, more accurately, managerial manipulation, to the extent that it is inextricably tied to behavioristic methodology, requires that the methodology itself be rejected or at the least significantly modified. If the purpose of the method is an integral part of it and the purpose is untenable, then the method is likewise untenable. Third, there is a sense in which the employment of the behavioristic approach itself precludes the attainment of the specific conclusions that the behaviorists embrace. The connections between behavioristic methodology and its conclusions have not been appropriately emphasized. In particular this is the case with regard to the nature of consciousness. If this claim is warranted (as the argument that follows will try to show), the critics who hesitate to attack the behavioristic methodology are mistaken.

Behaviorism may also be called a metaphysics since it does make claims concerning what is real or actual. It does set forth specific conclusions as to the nature of man, especially the nature of consciousness. Behaviorism holds that mental behavior is bodily behavior. In this assertion Skinner does not differ essentially from Watson. Not only does behaviorism insist that only bodily behavior exists, but also it affirms that organisms relate to their environment essentially by responding to stimuli. Moreover, stimulus and response stand to each other in much the same way as cause and effect. Skinner believes that events in the nervous system are all the results of conditioning by stimuli from outside. His program for psychology calls for the establishment of correlation between observable stimuli and observable bodily reactions and responses. If this program can be carried out, it will, so Skinner claims, explain all kinds of human behavior.

To disclose the riddles of behaviorism it is wise to consider Skinner's "neobehaviorism" as a development from the earlier behaviorism of John B. Watson. A few of the basic tenets of Watson's position which are elaborated and developed by Skinner may be mentioned. Watson, attempting to make a fresh start, proposed that psychology consider as its subject matter the objectively observable actions of organisms. Positively, this meant taking physics or chemistry as models for psychology, and negatively, it meant the discarding of introspection as a method. Doing away with introspection, for Watson at least, carried with it doing away with consciousness and its states. "The time seems to have come," Watson wrote in 1913, "when psychology must discard all reference to consciousness; when it need no longer delude itself into thinking that it is making mental states the object of observation."[2] Almost half a century later, in contrasting behaviorism with introspective psychology, he insists that "belief in the existence of consciousness goes back to the ancient days of superstition and magic."[3]

Often from a polemical stance Watson tries to show how phenomena formerly believed to require introspective study (such as thinking, imagery, emotions, feeling) can be explained in terms of stimulus and response. The major thesis underlying Watson's emphasis is the notion that the methods of animal psychology can be extended and applied to the study of man. This notion is the core theme of his early but influential volume, *Behavior: An Introduction to Comparative Psychology* (New York: Holt, Rinehart and Winston, 1914). Support for the extension and application of these methods of animal psychology Watson obtained from various quarters—the work of Pavlov, Loeb, Jennings and others, the stress on psychological continuities between animals and men in Darwin's theory of evolution, and selected elements from important philosophical developments in the late nineteenth century (Peirce, Dewey, James—the truth of a proposition can be assessed only by determining its consequences for action or behavior; realist and neorealist emphasis on objective aspects of consciousness as expressed by Woodbridge, Bush, R. B. Perry). Skinner does not disagree with Watson's focus on observable actions and his rejection of introspection.

Consider some aspects of Watson's behaviorism which are appropriated and modified in various ways by Skinner. Note first the stimulus-response model. "The goal of psychological study," Watson explains, "is the ascertaining of such data and laws that, given the stimulus, psychology can predict what the response will be; or ... given the response, it can specify the stimulus."[4] To grasp the full meaning of Watson's statement one needs to know what he means by prediction, stimulus, response, and the purpose of prediction. What Watson is seeking to predict is which stimuli cause which responses and which responses are the effects of which stimuli. In other words, he hopes to make reliable inferences from stimuli to responses as well as from responses to stimuli. He must then ascertain both necessary and sufficient grounds for such inferences. The terms "stimulus" and "response" are simply physiological terms with their meaning somewhat extended. For physiology a stimulus is a measurable physical energy which can excite the receptors of a sense organ (the eye, for example). A response is the contraction of muscles or the secretion of glands. The causal connection between stimulus and response is mediated by the passage of nerve impulses through the intricate structure of the nervous system. When the factors provoking a reaction by the organism are more complex, Watson called the stimuli "a situation"; Skinner uses the term "contingency" to refer to the same complexity of factors. Similarly, when the response is more complicated than, say, a patella reflex, Watson used the terms "act, or adjustment, or meaning," while Skinner seems to prefer the terms "forms of behavior," "behavior modification," or others. Regardless of terminology and whatever subtle shades of difference are implicit therein, a common assumption made by Watson and Skinner is that situations and adjustments, which are complex stimuli and responses, can be analyzed into simple stimulus-response conditions, and their hope is that laws holding for simple conditions will also hold for the more complex conditions.

The function of prediction, as elsewhere in science, is control. Watson has not hesitated to boast that from any healthy infant and a specified environment he can train any type of specialist—doctor, lawyer, artist, businessman, or even thief or beggar.[5] Skinner's proposals for "a technology of behavior" and "design of a culture"[6] are certainly not more modest, although they have greater urgency because of our failure to solve such crucial problems as the population explosion, the threat of nuclear holocaust, world famine, disease, and mounting pollution. What alone might enable us to avoid the catastrophe that could well result from any one of these problems taken by itself is a behavioral technology comparable in power and precision to physical technology. This he hopes psychological behaviorism may supply.

Second, consider peripheralism as a trait of the behavioristic perspective. It is the tendency to stress, in psychological explanations, events at or near the boundaries of the organism. Sensation and perception, for example, are not thought of as conscious states of mind (as the introspective psychologists would hold) but are rather located at the edges of consciousness. They are no longer thought of as mediating processes between stimulus and response. In the main this is an extension to human beings of the study of sensory acuity in animals. Consider a typical example. A psychologist is conducting an experiment with a rat to test for a differential response to lights. He puts the animal in a situation in which, by punishing one response (running down an alley toward a light of one wave length) and rewarding another response (running down an alternate alley toward a light of a different wave length), he finds whether the differential response can be learned. If so, it adds nothing, Watson would insist, to say that the animal "sees" two different colors. All that can be observed is that the animal responds differently. Now this same method may be used, it is reasoned, in studying human sensory capacity. Whether the subject manifests the differential response by movements (running, walking, or in other ways) or by spoken words ("verbal behavior") does not matter essentially. All that is important is that one not attribute to the animal or subject a state of consciousness called "seeing." Watson and Skinner simply extend this approach and claim for it equal reliability in application to other so-called mental states (for example, imagery and thinking). Thinking and imagery, these psychologists insist, are equated with "faint reinstatements" of the original muscular responses involved in speech and other motor behavior. All learning, Watson insists and Skinner seems to concur, can be characterized in terms of stimulus-response, a conditioning process.

Another emphasis is the stress these psychologists place on environmental modification of human behavior. Watson tends to stress the environmental modifiability of human behavior as contrasted with determination by constitutional structure. "There is no such thing as an inheritance of *capacity*, *talent*, *temperament*, *mental constitution*, and *characteristics*,"[7] Watson noted. Emphasis on practical control and the extent to which behavior may be shaped by environment are characteristic emphases of behaviorist writers. Neither of these emphases is absent from Skinner's approach with its stress on "design of culture" and "a technology of behavior."

Skinner did alter certain aspects of Watson's approach but did not essentially change it. Two alterations may be noted: the Skinner box and operant conditioning. Skinner built a box to serve as an experimental device to reinforce or shape a specific behavior that he could measure with precision. His best known experiments with this device were conducted with pigeons as the subjects. A pigeon, for instance, learned to peck at a lever that would cause food pellets to drop into a box. With this device and its modifications, hundreds of researchers have produced volumes of data on learning, on the effects of regular or intermittent rewards, on brain impairment in specific areas, and on the behavioral effects of drugs. In a playful moment, he even managed to teach pigeons to play ping-pong.

"Whether from narcissism or scientific curiosity, I have been as much interested *in myself* as in rats and pigeons," Skinner once remarked. "I have applied the same formulations. I have looked for the same kinds of causal relations, and I have manipulated behavior in the same way and sometimes with comparable success." Although he recognizes that the human environment is vastly more complicated than any box, he does now propose to redesign all of culture—government, education, economics. It is his conviction that this redesigning can be accomplished if sufficient control by behavior-shaping methods is exercised. This behavior-shaping process he calls "operant conditioning."

As a supplement to Pavlov's view, Skinner recognizes two primary types of conditioning, each with its own laws. Respondent conditioning (type S) is similar to the Pavlovian case, depending only upon temporal nearness of stimuli. Operant conditioning (Type R) is instrumental behavior that is strengthened by the presence of what is called a reinforcing stimulus. In very general terms, it is the organism acting upon the environment so that the environment in turn acts upon the organism. Or, to state the matter slightly differently, it is what man can make of man by a judicious alteration of his environment.

Has this environmental approach been applied? Yes, it has been applied on a limited scale in various places and institutions. Token economies, for example, in mental hospitals often produce gratifying results. Patients who do not respond to drugs or psychoanalysis or staff authority tend to become alert and healthier when each good behavior wins a token that can be spent for candy or pleasurable freedom. This practice has spread to other institutions, including schools (a smiling face on a child's paper, or candy as a reward for doing one's mathematics assignment correctly).

Upon reading Skinner's recent book, *Beyond Freedom and Dignity,* one's initial reaction is the feeling of being insulted or outraged by his approach. One pictures to himself the entire world as a Skinner box. In such a situation the vast achievements of man in government, education and economic systems are skillfully managed by positive reinforcements, especially pleasurable experiences. A sense of revulsion floods one's consciousness and all of Skinner's talk of the saving of time or reserving time for "creativity" (defined in his own way) and leisure activities begins to appear as a contrived illusion. Reading Skinner's earlier work, *Walden Two*, hardly dispels the sense of depression. In that novel Skinner depicts a "planned utopia" under the direction of an unobtrusive and self-effacing old Indian named Frazier. In the "planned utopia" there are ways of modifying the cruder forms of selfishness. Every woman and man in this ideal community has enough, a light share of the dirty work as well as of the children, and time to be "creative." Any tendency towards conspicious consumption gets engineered out. People learn never to want special rewards or honors. Skinner, complaining that his novel was subjected to all sorts of malicious and misguided attacks, suggests that the basis for these attacks was his insistence that the entire community be a planned one.[8] One suspects, however, that such is surely not the sole reason, perchance not even the main reason, and that other reasons, lying at deeper levels, are far more important.

Unearthing these underlying problems or riddles is the task of this essay. As it has been noted, Skinner proposes not only a method of approach but also specific conclusions concerning the nature of man and in particular human consciousness. Skinner and Watson are agreed that mental behavior is bodily behavior. For Skinner, events in the nervous system are all the results of conditioning by stimuli from outside. Correlations between observable stimuli and observable bodily reactions need to be established. The purpose or use to which these correlations will be put is the control of human development. For Skinner, references to feelings, motives, attitudes, ideas (if these be considered "nonphysical events") as effective factors in either determining conduct or explaining it is an appeal to a "fictional explanation" unworthy of a scientist and perhaps rooted in an anachronistic animism. For him there is no consciousness or mind that cannot be reduced to some bodily behavior.

Implicit in Skinner's behaviorism are riddles with which the philosopher cannot be content. Let us consider them in detail. First, there is the puzzle or conundrum that no behaviorist actually behaves as though his own theory were true. Suppose we consider one by one the contents of consciousness from a behavioristic perspective and note how a behaviorist might be expected to act in terms of each. In common sense parlance these contents or ingredients of mind have been labelled sensations, ideas, feelings, and volitions. Each of these terms may be employed by the behaviorist but each one must have its meaning radically altered. These ingredients are to be understood by the behaviorist in the same way as the ingredients of physical nature. If physical nature is a vast system of material particles moving in space, then the human mind (since it is identical with human behavior) is, in the final analysis, nothing more than an intricate and rapidly moving swirl of these particles. Seeing, as an instance of sensation, is observable at least in theory, and it can be explained without remainder in terms of light rays, optic nerves and physiological accessories. In theory, then, I can see your seeing. The sensation which we call seeing has no private aspects and no non-quantifiable aspects. But, of course, in fact behaviorists don't act as if this were the case. Suppose a behaviorist is watching a pigeon peck a lever to obtain food. What does he think he is himself doing when he makes such an observation? Is he just receiving optical stimuli and responding to them by making ink marks in his notebook? Is he not aware of the jaunty motion of the pigeon's head, the turning of the pigeon's neck, etc.?

What of volitions? Does the behaviorist act as though his own volitions were instances of matter in motion? Does he not assume that he has jurisdiction over which of, let us say, two choices he will make? I can only think that he does, and I think correctly so. His own execution of an experimental procedure seems to make a lie of his theory. The behaviorist cannot and does not in fact behave as though his own theory were true. Consider an idea. Does the behaviorist act as though his idea were simply an instance of matter in motion? Again it seems that he does not. Take the idea that consciousness is behavior. Is this idea simply an instance of matter in motion? The behaviorist cannot so claim because to do so puts his idea exactly on a par with the ideas of introspective psychologists which he so detests. Or consider feeling. The behaviorist does not act as if his feelings (particularly if painful) are just one among millions of physical changes and no more objectionable than many others to which reference may be made. If his feelings be pleasurable, he is no more likely to be wholly neutral in relation to them than the staunchiest non-behaviorist. His behavior, for example, after he hits his thumb with the hammer is not likely to differ from that of the non-behaviorist. He will not be neutral toward the pain he feels. The riddle that the behaviorist acts in ways to belie his theory remains unsolved.

Second, there is the puzzle or riddle that the experimental practices of the behaviorist presuppose the reality of the consciousness he claims to supplant. The behaviorist acknowledges that as a psychologist he is concerned with sorrow, feeling pain, seeing colors, anger, love and the like. What he insists upon (in a manner reminiscent of James) is that we bestow these names solely upon physical responses rather than con-scious experiences. But, even to label the behavior in this fashion implies a recognition of the distinction between the conscious experi-ence and the behavior to which the term is newly assigned. But no such distinction is indeed possible if the behaviorist adheres strictly to his theory. Here is an instance of behavior; shall we call it anger or sorrow? Now, the issue here is more than verbal. What we are concerned about is the referent of the terms "anger" and "sorrow." To answer this sort of question requires us to consider what is the usual expression of anger and sorrow and to compare the two in some way. If it is a destructive mode of behavior, we are likely to ascribe it to anger. And it is only by reference to this conscious experience of anger that we come to label the behavior in Skinner's fashion. Skinner's labels, then, far from being a substitute for the state of consciousness, continually presuppose it.

But perhaps the real basis for this riddle lies at a deeper level. As a behaviorist, Skinner, in agreement with Watson, rejects introspection. Now, there doubtless are certain peculiarities about introspection and certain extravagant claims have been made on its behalf. One such extravagant claim is that information mined by introspection is always pure and never tainted with error. This is simply a mistake; intro-specting provides no infallible cognition. The attempt to scrutinize one's own experiences, to formulate the judgments into concepts and statements, to distinguish between these types of experience, and to relate the types of experiences to each other—all of these processes involve cognition. But to say that one is infallible in carrying out these processes seems to belie that one has ever made a real effort to do some introspecting himself. Introspection is difficult. It requires skill and, perhaps most of all, rigorous honesty. It is not easy to describe one's experiences and to distinguish the different components.

Introspection does have certain peculiarities. Two of these may be noted. First, the object of the scrutiny is not something that can be directly perceived by anyone else. The business of observing one's own mind and its various states has the awkward characteristic of being non-public or private. What one says about his own states of consciousness, then, cannot be directly verified by any other observer. Nor can it be directly denied. To one who is trying to make public observations and measurements this peculiarity is a distinct handicap. It may be for this very reason, in large measure, that Skinner is especially eager to downgrade introspection. His program calls for the establishment of a science of psychology and its application ("a technology of human behavior").

Second, introspection, as a cognitive endeavor, is often a process that occurs only after an experience has been undergone. In this respect introspection is not simultaneous with the experience critically observed. It is almost invariably retrospective. That being the case it depends upon memory for its object. The object of the introspective scrutiny is an experience as recollected and now present to consciousness. This need not mean, as some critics have hinted, that introspection is always in error. It does mean that the unreliability of a short-span memory could call into question any introspective findings.

There is a sense in which a primary or primordial introspection occurs simultaneously with the awareness of any object. But, this introspection is virtually devoid of cognitive import. The only cognition that this primordial or residual awareness bestows is that the awareness is one's own. This minimal self-awareness accompanies any and every observation or awareness of an object. To say that this residual awareness occurs is not to say that it is always in the forefront of consciousness. One may be largely unconscious of this self-awareness to the extent that he is "absorbed" (in the popular sense) into the object. Of course, it is possible that, under the influence of alcoholic beverages or drugs, one may not have even this self-awareness. He may not remember that he was the one who did so-and-so while intoxicated or under the influence of drugs. This failure to recall what happened is usually ascribed to an aberration or distortion of memory, but it could be that the alcoholic beverage distorts self-awareness at the time of the experiences themselves. However that may be, what does this mean for introspection? It may mean that introspection is certainly dependent upon effective physiological functioning. It need not mean that physiological functioning and introspection are identical. If it does not mean this, however, the behaviorist has not given us a convincing argument.

The behaviorist argues in objecting to introspection that there is no "private experience" or exclusive "mental occurrence." The words "private" and "mental" do not make sense. But this is a puzzling view because the word "public," in which the behaviorist delights, seems to garner its meaning through contrast with what it is not. We know, indeed, what is public because we can contrast it with what is private. It may be that this is simply a verbal aspect of the conundrum. If the term "private" loses its meaning, then the term "public" also loses its meaning.

Two frequent objections to introspection may be briefly noted. First, it is often insisted that introspection cannot occur simultaneously with the undergoing of an experience. Whether this claim is true or false depends upon what is meant by it. There is a respect in which whenever any experience occurs I am aware that I am the agent or individual who is undergoing that experience. This primordial introspection is almost non-cognitive, even though it occurs as an accompaniment to any experience. If one is referring to this primordial experience, introspection does occur simultaneously with any experience. If, however, one means by introspection the careful and skillful scrutiny of one's experience with the essential aim of discovering knowledge, then this appears not to occur simultaneously with the undergoing of the experience. One can call this sort of introspection secondary introspection. It generally if not invariably occurs after we have undergone an experience.

A second objection requires only brief consideration. It is sometimes urged that introspection is a kind of infallible cognition. This claim is, of course, mistaken regardless of which sort of introspection one has in mind. If one is referring to primordial introspection then it must be insisted that there is no infallible cognition. In fact, it is only by stretching the meaning of cognition that one can say there is any knowledge at all. Essentially, this sort of introspection merely involves the awareness that the experience through which one lives is one's own. To say that secondary introspection provides infallible cognition is also a mistake. It is difficult to consider critically one's own experiences, to make judgments about them, and to bring them within the scope of concepts. Error may occur at any of the three stages: one's scrutiny of his own experience may be myopic; one's judgments may be biased; one's choice of concepts to express the judgments may be inadequate or faulty. In no respect, then, can secondary introspection be a source of infallible knowledge. In summary, then, whether one is thinking of primary or secondary introspection, it is an error to consider the knowledge derived therefrom infallible.

To claim that knowledge acquired through introspection may be in error and to claim that introspection is a completely deceptive process with nothing at all for its object are two entirely different and incompatible claims. At times the behaviorists seem unaware of this. Suppose, it is contended, that an experience (let us say a feeling) is changed by secondary introspection. Granted that this is a fact. How does one know that the feeling is less intense or different in tone? There may or may not be behavioral indications of that intensity or tone. If there are no such indications, how does one know the feeling is different? The answer, it seems to me, is by more careful introspection. The claim that knowledge gained through secondary introspection may be in error presupposes that a more carefully conducted introspection can discern the error. And this assertion is incompatible with the notion that introspection is a completely deceptive process.

A third riddle should be noted. Skinner repeatedly appeals to "survival value" and calls it "the only value." This appeal is paradoxical because it presupposes the reality of the consciousness whose existence he has denied. What Skinner proclaims as the only value depends for its valuableness upon the being of a consciousness which he denies. He apparently believes a "technology of behavior" is required to keep man from destroying himself through overpopulation or through the affluent pursuit of happiness resulting in uncontrolled pollution. Survival value is for Skinner the only value because it is the prerequisite without which other values are not possible.

Leaving aside the exclusiveness claimed for survival as a value, one may ask: What specifically must be present if there is to be any human value at all? The answer, it seems to be, is that the existence of any value presupposes the reality of consciousness. Survival can have no meaning, much less value, apart from consciousness. Is not consciousness, then, the sine qua non of all goods and evils, of all values of all kinds?

Although far from providing a proof, two examples may be suggestive. Most of us would agree with Aristotle and Epicurus that friendship is a value. What is it that makes friendship valuable? What is the locus of its value? Where is it to be found? Is it to be found in what the friend has? Is it to be found in what a friend does (that is, how he behaves), or is it to be found essentially in the experience or consciousness of friendship? To my way of thinking, it is the experience of friendship that we prize. Without consciousness there is no friendship and consequently no value to it. But isn't this true of all values? Consider love. Isn't it the conscious experience of loving and being loved that we consider of worth? Surely without consciousness there is no value. Accordingly, when Skinner speaks of survival value as the sine qua non of all value and at the same time denies the existence of consciousness, he is unwittingly speaking in a paradoxical manner.

Turn now to a fourth riddle. The appeal to a technology of behavior with its emphasis on control is likely to be ineffectual, because as soon as the individual to whom it is applied learns of the manipulation, he will not submit to it. Its effectiveness, then, will depend on its being carried out surreptitiously. Granted the value of a democratic system with its openness to public scrutiny, it does seem likely that a technology of behavior will be ineffectual because to the extent that the public is informed of the control exercised over them they will not submit to it.

To offer a causal account of human behavior and to insist on a technology that will control the contingencies that act as causes is surely misguided. It is misguided because it cannot result in the "independence" and "creativity" Skinner intends. The causal account of human behavior is inaccurate because it is not the whole picture. It is precisely because man can choose when to act or to respond that his deliberative and choosing process fall outside the causal network in which his behavior actually occurs. Human consciousness modifies the cause-effect chain at its threshold.

In *Beyond Freedom and Dignity* Skinner almost seems aware of the problem. "When a person changes his physical or social environment 'intentionally'—that is, in order to change human behavior, possibly including his own [Skinner writes] he plays two roles: one as a controller, as the designer of a controlling culture, and another as the controlled, as the product of a culture."[9]

But Skinner's entire conception of "a technology of behavior" mitigates against anyone ever performing as a designer or creator. If I am simply a product or result of causal forces operating in the environment, how can I also function as a designer or creator? To the extent that it is rigorous and consistent in its approach, behavioristic theory can provide no account for creativity. A more adequate scheme is provided if we conceive of the physical world as simply a causal network into which human excursions make their forays. Skinner's view seems to have caught half the truth and enlarged it. It is, of course, true that the self builds itself indirectly by altering those conditions it must confront in the physical world. Man's rearrangement and alteration of the world lead him to alter his own habits. Thus, indirectly, man does become his own architect. Even in this interaction with his environment, however, it is erroneous to say that man is controlled. It is not the case that man is entirely molded by the causal network of physical nature in which he finds himself. Rather the human agent can decide, and the decision is a process that radically differs from the cause-effect process. W. E. Hocking, in a perceptive analysis, suggests that human decision differs from causal process because it is capable of hesitation or postponement (while the causal process is not) and of inventing alternatives which could not be defined beforehand.[10] Each of these differences is crucially important. The ability to hesitate means that man can control the time factor in his approach to action. The human agent can withhold action until the alternatives and their meanings are carefully considered. With the cause-effect process the alternatives are definable in advance. What will happen can be anticipated and, at least in principle, nothing new can happen. With the human agent, however, new alternatives can come into being. These new alternatives are not simply reactions by the human agent to alterations that occur in the environment. They are the inventions of the agent, and they owe their being to his initiative and decisions.

The behaviorism of Skinner, it has been shown, contains at least four riddles that bring into serious doubt its adequacy and its practicality. It is one of Skinner's central theses that the technology of behavior provided by his approach offers practical solutions to the almost overwhelming problems confronting modern man. He repeatedly insists upon its practicality in the planning essential to solving the problems of overpopulation and pollution. If the riddles that have been disclosed may serve as the basis for a conclusion it follows that behaviorism fails decisively at the place where it has boasted of success—the crucial point where theory issues into practice.

NOTES

1.   See H. H. Price, "Some Objections to Behaviorism," in *Dimensions of Mind,* ed. by S. Hook (New York: Crowell-Collier, 1961), p. 79.

2.   "Psychology as the Behaviorist Views It," *Psychological Review* 20 (1913): 163.

3.   John B. Watson, *Behaviorism* (Chicago: University of Chicago Press, 1959), p. 2.

4.   *Psychology from the Standpoint of the Behaviorist* (Philadelphia and London: Lippincott, 1919, 1924), p. 10.

5.   *Behavior: An Introduction to Comparative Psychology*, "Introduction" by R. J. Herrnstein (New York: Holt, Rinehart & Winston, 1967), p. xxii.

6.   The terms are taken from Skinner's recent book, *Beyond Freedom and Dignity* (New York: Knopf, 1971).

7.   *Behaviorism*, p. 94.

8.   Richard I. Evans, *B. F. Skinner: The Man and His Ideas* (New York: Dutton, 1968), p. 47.

9.   *Beyond Freedom and Dignity*, p. 197.

10.   "What is Man?" in *Preface to Philosophy: Textbook* (New York: Macmillan, 1947), p. 70.

Will

Robert N. Beck

FOR THE PAST quarter century, philosophical discussions of the phenomenon or concept of will have been dominated by Gilbert Ryle's *The Concept of Mind*. Influenced both by his method ("linguistic behaviorism") and his conclusion (there is no faculty or immaterial organ of will), many philosophers have continued to hold and argue for similar positions. During the same period, however, a more modestly sized group of philosophers, including some idealists, phenomenologists, and existentialists, have argued against the negations of *The Concept of Mind*. They have asserted that there are such realities as minds, mental acts, and acts of will; and they have argued that, not only does Ryle fail to make his case, but that interpretations of experience are distorted and partial if these realities are not accepted for what they are.

Bertocci belongs to this latter group. Over the whole of his professional career, he has reflected on the special nature of consciousness and the uniqueness of our experience of will. It is the purpose of this paper to state and assess his contribution to our understanding of that experience.

But first it may be well to review the official Rylean doctrine. In direct terms, Ryle rejects the notion of will, finding it "just an inevitable extension of the myth of the ghost in the machine."[1] The doctrine assumes, he says, both that there are mental states and processes having existence in contrast to bodily states, and that there is a causal relation between a bodily act and the mental act of willing the bodily act. But both these assumptions are wrong, and their error is shown by the fact that in daily life we do not use the concept of will, and do not even know how to apply it. The concept, in fact, is a technical one manufactured by past philosophy but now having no utility.

Ryle offers four brief objections to the notion of "counterpart hidden operations of willing." The first is that no one, except to save a theory, ever describes human conduct in the idiom of willing. In fact, such description is nearly impossible because there are no classes of predicates through which to make the description—which, Ryle seems to imply, is the reason ordinary men never report the occurrence of will acts. The second is that, since willing as a mental act can never be witnessed, no one can praise or blame another, because it can never be determined whether an act was willed; nor even could an agent himself know that his own action was the effect of a given volition. The third objection is that the supposed connection between mind and body is not only a mystery but a mystery of the impossible kind, involving as it does transactions and links between mind and body where no links can be. Finally, Ryle argues that to admit one voluntary volition, say to pull the trigger, is to admit an infinite series of them, for that volition must issue from a prior volition, and so on ad infinitum.

That these objections to the notion of willing carry any argumentative weight is now doubtful, or at least very debatable.[2] The reason volitions are not normally spoken of is that they are not acts which rival other (physical) acts but are essential ingredients of all acts. The objection that acts of will cannot be witnessed reflects a behaviorism cruder than Ryle himself, I think, would admit.[3] The argument that admission of mental will acts involves the mystery of mind-body interaction must be made out more as a conclusion than as a premise for rejecting mental acts. Finally, the infinite series argument depends on the assumption that an act of will is a discrete initial episode rather than a continuing intention holding throughout an act.

These detailed arguments, though, are less important than the general approach Ryle brings to his discussion of will. What Ryle generally wants to do is to make will words (or whatever is left of them when they are related to ordinary language) fit under the meaning-is-use doctrine. The consequence of this effort is that words evaporate from their status as referring to first-personal and inner experience to become roughly[4] third-personal and outer. But, as Findlay has pointed out,[5] the doctrine of use has its own special difficulties—difficulties which are reflected in philosophical conclusions such as Ryle's which are drawn from it. Findlay argues that however subtle our analyses of meaning become, intentionality, denotation, and connotation must remain basic in them. And he goes on to observe that however public our language learning may have been—and children's games suggest that it is in fact not all public—there is as well a private anteroom attached to the public square. Indeed, Findlay says, ordinary language, if looked at really concretely rather than aprioristically to support some slogan, shows that the move from "I" to "he" is made easily, effortlessly, and usually errorlessly. In sum, appeals to ordinary language, or meaning doctrines based on them, do not support a denial of mental acts but in fact tend to justify belief in their existence.

But I cannot really defend here the thesis that there are mental acts— I only assume it, though I do believe that it is a most defensible thesis. With it I accept the notion that there are mental or conscious acts of willing. Complicated as the phenomenon of willing is, it is surely not just behaving or being disposed to behave in certain ways, not even behaving linguistically in certain ways. Rather it is, at the least, the conscious act of accepting, of projecting or committing oneself to a meaning proposed for personal action.

Given a nonbehavioristic stance relative to consciousness, there remains the critical philosophical task of identifying, describing, perhaps defining, such distinctive experiences as that of will—in sum, that is, of providing something of a phenomenological account of them. In numerous places,[6] Bertocci has sought to provide and develop such a phenomenology. It will be convenient for expository purposes to present his views in four parts.

1) *Will agency*. The primary experience denoted by the word will, Bertocci insists, is effort. With William James, he agrees to call the experience *fiat*, meaning thereby the particular act of the self which can be formulated or translated as "let it come into being." In this experience of effort, the self comes to itself as agent rather than as being a mere process, "for it is at this point in my experience that I *try* to take a hand in effecting the shape of my emerging future."

Furthermore, Bertocci says, this conscious experience of effort is qualitatively unique. That is, activities of willing are not—and are not experienced as—activities of desire, want or emotion. "I will" denotes an experience distinct from and irreducible to such experiences as "I want," "I must," "I feel that," and so on. When "I will" is experienced or uttered, more is involved than desire; rather, "I seem to be asserting myself as an agent over against aspects of my own being or the environment which I do not at that time approve." Thus, so to speak, the self pulls itself together, and asserts itself in favor of an approved objective. It initiates a process and thus proposes to influence future development.

But what is the status of this end or objective willed by the self? An objective, Bertocci says, can be present to the self only as a thought, an intended goal, an idea. While, to be sure, willing is not reducible to thinking, the latter is one of the conditions making willing possible. Thinking does this by allowing the self to contemplate, that is, to rise above the causal forces in and around it and to have in mind that which is not simply present to it. "We can will only if we think. For we can will only the *object in mind*. We will an end which exists only as a thought or idea." Reciprocally, though, one can also will to think, in the sense not simply of having ideas, but as ordering and connecting them in relation to ideals such as coherence and truth.

2) *Will power.* Willing, then, is initiative relative to an approved objective. But, Bertocci observes, the very same examination of experience which reveals the unique agency of willing also shows that willing is often—even usually—confronted with factors which limit it. Whether external ones like natural phenomena or internal ones like habits and drives, these factors constitute a nexus of causal processes which are not within the will's own control and which can constrict its expression. Therefore, it is necessary to distinguish will power from will agency, and to define will power as "the measure of control determined by [the will's] interplay with other factors in the total choice situation."

So understood, will power turns out to be a variable, depending as it does on the power—supportive as well as inhibitive, to be sure—of factors in the individual's nature and in the environment. But once identified, the notion of will power clarifies a number of points about volitional activity. Practically, it provides us with a concept to account for the failures, even impotencies, of willing: the inability to achieve a posited ideal, to carry through on a personal resolve, or to live by a proposed change in values. Theoretically, and perhaps more importantly for philosophy, the notion of will power prevents the concept of willing from being conceived as a merely arbitrary, even chaotic, set of activities. A human being, after all, is a relatively ordered and structured being; much of his activities are predictable by a scientific observer; and stabilities of habit, character, and attitude affect his actions and his willing. While no "mechanics" of will agency is possible, one of human action is. Willing is but one factor in the total development of personality, and it "is empowered (or weakened) in effecting its goals by the constellation of habits, emotions and feelings, attitudes, sentiments, traits" of the individual person. It does pay to teach our children honesty, and it is possible to make scientific predictions of behavior; but neither is a fatalistic determinant of personality development. Will agency uses order as well as establishes new orders, and the givenness of many orders is recognized in the concept of will power.

3) *Freedom*. At the very heart of Bertocci's theory of will is the concept of freedom: will agency is always understood by him to be free initiative, and freedom of the will is a correlative of the act of willing itself. Like will agency and will power, this freedom, Bertocci says, is first discovered in the phenomenological examination of experience, particularly choice experiences. While the experience of freedom can be had rather generally, it is most clearly present in those moments "when something is happening to me which (a) I do not wish or want to happen, (b) which I could terminate, but (c) *will* not terminate for the sake of some other approved objective." Hence, we find freedom in our acts of willful choice.

The freedom thus found, Bertocci believes, is critically important for two other concepts, namely those of thought and human creativity. As has been noted above, thinking and willing in Bertocci's theory stand in close interconnection: our ability to think, and thus to contemplate foreseeable possibilities, helps to make willing possible; and we will to think when we seek to judge thoughts in reference to epistemic ideals. But now thinking too is—and must be—a free activity, for thinking which seeks truth (for truth to have meaning at all) is directed by the person in the light of an acknowledged criterion. Quoting C. I. Lewis's *The Ground and Nature of the Right*, Bertocci concludes that in thinking we are experiencing passages of consciousness not dominated by anything beyond the person himself.

The essential meaning of the doctrine of human creativity is also tied to the reality of freedom. The problem of creativity, of course, is not simply that of what a man can do given his needs and capacities; rather it is what a man does with the capacities and endowment he has.

"The crucial, creative point in a man's life, then, is what he will make of himself. . . . Here is the creative root of his being, and here is his responsibility." Our futures, to be sure, are not in our hands alone, but the paths we take among presented possibilities mark out the creative moments in our lives.

Much of Bertocci's exposition of these notions of choice, freedom, and creativity is made in phenomenological terms. But he is not unaware of a kind of transcendental argument for freedom, and he has in fact referred to it. With Kant, Bowne, and many others, he urges that freedom is the necessary presupposition of thinking and willing, and that apart from this presupposition no assertion, even the one rejecting freedom, can be accepted as true. *"Deny freedom and you deny a universal ground for trusting the very truth or the falsity of the statement by which you assert it."*

4) *Obligation.* A fourth experience clustered with the preceding three is that of obligation. Like willing, "oughting" is found to be a qualitatively unique and therefore irreducible experience. "I ought" never feels like "I must" or "I want," however much the latter may accompany it. Nor is oughting simply willing: rather, oughting is experienced when, in a choice situation, a decision is made with reference to values. When A is believed better than B, an imperative quality enters experience, and one is cast into the new situation of oughting A whether one wants or likes A or not.

Furthermore, Bertocci says, the experience of oughting, this obligation to the best, pervades the conscious choice situation. There is no conscious choice without an ought becoming involved. To be sure, final choices are not always correct ones, and persons differ widely in what they conceive to be the best. But these observations do not deny the structured presence of obligation in human personality; they rather indicate that the experience of obligation does not define the best but is simply the imperative to a conceived best. The task of defining the best must be assigned to ethics.

This exposition of Bertocci's views on will, brief as it must be, reveals a number of significant philosophical points. Throughout his theory, Bertocci has resisted the easy reductionism of so many other views. Willing, oughting, and choosing are not analyzable exhaustively either by reference to behavior (however much willing is expressed in behavior) or to other elements of personality structure such as desire and emotion. These experiences are and must be retained throughout a philosophical analysis as unique and basic elements of personal experience. Bertocci's exploration into the correlations of willing, oughting, freedom, and creativity reveals both theoretical and practical insights of great value. Especially significant is his distinction between will agency and will power—a distinction which not only clarifies elements of the total will experience but also undercuts many of the positions which have denied personal freedom and creativity.

One of the dangers—or problems, at any rate—of a phenomenological approach, however, is that initial descriptive terms may tend to limit the range and adequacy of subsequent analysis. Though his theory transcends many potential limitations of this kind, Bertocci has, I think, adopted such a narrowing term in his use of James's *fiat* to refer to the basic will experience. To be sure, there is in willing an experience of effort, and this can never properly be denied; but I think the better and broader term is expression, particularly if used with some of the connotations it has been given by estheticians.

That is, willing is not just, or primarily, effort. It is essentially and first the proposing by the self to itself of a structure of practical meaning to be accomplished or realized in action. The self in willing thus comes to be (practically), in-forms itself, and through this informing seeks to express in action (Hegel would say objectively) the meaning or meaningfulness it subjectively intends. This structure of practical meaning may, with Pfänder,[7] also be called a "project," and willing may be likened to a "mental stroke" in that action is proposed though not yet executed—provided, of course, that these terms are read as connoting the expressive activity of the self. In any case, willing is not just striving, though it does involve a structure to be accomplished; and this because of a phenomenological reason pointed out by Pfänder, that will, but not striving, includes an immediate consciousness of self.

If such a descriptive account of willing is found acceptable, some modification in Bertocci's views seems necessary. The first is that willing and choosing, closely related as they are, must be distinguished, with choosing being seen as a subcase or special case of willing. Some care must be taken in making this point, for the one word *choice* may be used to cover two very different phenomena. Choice, it seems, is properly used to indicate selection from among two or more possible and presented meaning structures; it is not saying yes or no to one structure—which is just what willing or not willing is. It follows that there may be willing where there is no choosing, and that therefore it is not paradoxical to say literally that "I have no choice but to will or commit myself to this action." Will is thus an act of self-expression or self-determination, with the self as both subject and object of the act, whether or not there is choice involved.

In turn, this relationship of will and choice implies a slight amplification of Bertocci's statement of the case for human freedom. There is strong phenomenological evidence, I believe, for the reality of freedom, but it is primarily a freedom of willing and only more specially a freedom of choosing. It is also a freedom which, I believe, can be exercised without contradiction when there is no choice experience. The older phrase, self-determination, conveys this notion, for the self "comes to be"—expresses itself—as surely when one project is possible as when alternative projects are open to it. Choosing may sometimes uncover the self's freedom more dramatically than other cases of willing, but freedom surely is found in the latter as well.

Yet another deviation from Bertocci's view seems necessary in regard to the experience of obligation. I have agreed with him that this experience is a unique and irreducible one, and as well that in willing a practical meaning structure the self has the experience that the proposed structure is in some sense valuable. Bertocci has gone beyond this, however, to suggest that the experience of oughting pervades the conscious choice situation. I am not sure whether he would accept the distinction I have made between willing and choosing at all. In place of his almost universal statement about obligation, I would prefer to say that at times willing may be accompanied by an additional consciousness of oughtness. Particularly is this necessary, I think, if obligation is understood in a basically moral sense (as distinct from, say, logical, technological or hypothetical obligation). Willing the only open possibility may involve simply a sense of selfhood; and willing one of many possibilities may refer to ideals of economy or logical elegance rather than to the better or best in the moral sense. Bertocci may, to be sure, mean only that some sense of ought accompanies all willing, though if this is the case, the relation of willing to the specifically moral ought needs further clarification.

Finally, Bertocci has insisted that while willing is not reducible to thinking, thought is one of the conditions making willing possible. As noted earlier, he says that an objective can be present to the self only as a thought, intended goal, or idea. Now the difficulty here, I think, is either that we may tend toward an outmoded faculty psychology in talking about what the will does, or what thought does (and I in no way ascribe this view to Bertocci, though some of his readers may infer it); or we may tend to overrationalize the experience of willing. It is, of course, the self who wills, thinks, feels, and so on; and I should prefer, therefore, to say that it is self-consciousness with its capacities of self-transcendence that makes willing possible or is the necessary condition of willing. Thinking is the self's capacity to judge, to form propositions, to infer; to envisage a project, one or one out of many, is not helpfully ascribed to thought. Such envisagement is rather a distinguishing capacity of self-consciousness itself. Neither, it may be added, should theoretical assent to a judgment be classified as an act of willing, nor should contemplation of possibilities for willing be seen as an act of thought.

In suggesting these modest developments of Bertocci's theory, I have been aware of the proximity of their outcome to the spirit of his position. But I believe that even modest proposals, if they help increase our understanding, must be made. Even more is this true, I think, of our efforts to understand human selfhood, for in the problem of the self we find the whole amplitude of the philosophic enterprise.

NOTES

1.   Ryle's treatment of will is found in chap. 3 of *The Concept of Mind* (New York: Barnes and Noble, 1949), pp. 62-82.

2.   See especially the extended treatment of them in H. D. Lewis, *The Elusive Mind* (London: Allen and Unwin, 1969), pp. 56-67. My observations here are heavily indebted to Lewis.

3.   The early Wittgenstein, it may be noted, did not use his ontology of facts to deny the will, though he did argue that the (transcendental) will is not in the world but is the world's limit. See Jeremy Walker, "Wittgenstein's Early Theory of the Will: An Analysis," *Idealistic Studies*, 3 (1973):179-205. This ontology did, however, constrict (aprioristically?) what Wittgenstein could conclude about the will.

4.   Because "I" would be interpreted as relating to my body. The subtleties here I leave undeveloped.

5.   In his contribution to the symposium on "Use, Usage and Meaning," *Proc. Arist. Soc.*, Supp. Vol. 35 (1961):223-242.   Reprinted in G. H. R. Parkinson, ed., *The Theory of Meaning* (Oxford: Oxford University Press, 1968), pp. 116-27.

6.   In addition to some class notes, I am relying particularly on *Free Will, Responsibility, and Grace* (New York: Abingdon Press, 1957), chaps.1 and 2, and "The Moral Structure of the Person," *Rev. Meta.*, 14 (1961):369-388, reprinted in *The Person God Is* (London: Allen and Unwin, 1970), chap. 4.

7.   Alexander Pfänder, *Phenomenology of Willing and Motivation,* trans. by Herbert Spiegelberg (Evanston, Ill.: Northwestern University Press, 1967), p. 22.

Creativity in Royce's Philosophical Idealism

John E. Smith

IT MAY SEEM STRANGE to be considering the sources of creativity and novelty in Royce's metaphysics in view of the long-standing belief, largely established by the critical attitude of William James, that Royce believed in a "block universe" presided over by an Absolute which leaves no room for finite freedom and creativity. While there is no need to deny that in the earliest expressions of his position Royce could speak of the Absolute as possessed of "*totum simul*" knowledge and of individuals as "drops" in an ocean of Being, the fact remains that Royce's theory of reality is first, last, and always a voluntarism embracing the primacy of individual will and purpose. This feature of his thought has often been missed entirely or has been dropped from sight by those who, correctly noting that the form of his philosophy belongs to the systematic strain in modern rational idealism, have nevertheless failed to take seriously the central place accorded to the individual will in his scheme of things. Royce's is not an idealism of knowledge and logical determination alone; it is an ethical idealism in which being is defined in terms of purpose and the resolve to be, or the desire to shape life in accordance with a chosen plan. Moreover, in his view, the world disclosed by theoretical knowledge—the world of description—though perfectly real, is abstract in the sense that the full scope of reality includes as well the world of free individuals and the social relations in which they stand. Whatever necessity attaches to the world of nature expressing itself in lawful form is seen by him as both

abstract and relative vis-à-vis freedom and individuality.[1] I mention
these considerations at the outset lest distorted views of Royce's
position have established the presumption that creativity and freedom
are alien to his thought.

Before proceeding directly to Royce's own position, I would like to
cite several important features characterizing what I would consider a
viable conception of creativity under any circumstances. And since for
want of space I shall be concentrating in my treatment of Royce on
creativity in relation to the self, I shall frame my own conception
accordingly. A fuller treatment would, of course, have to include an
account of creativity in all natural processes as is done, for example, in
Whitehead's thought; and while I do not say that Royce left nature out
of account,[2] the fact that he frequently understood it exclusively in
terms of what it would have to be in order to be known or to be the
expression of the divine knowledge and will led to the neglect of other
features.

Creativity in relation to persons should be understood primarily as a
constructive response. I purposely use the term "response" in order to
distinguish the activity from that of a "reaction" which is provoked or
evoked in situations where a preceding action determines in large part
what that reaction will be. By contrast, response entails acknowledgment of a situation as having a certain pervasive quality; it involves
appraisal, appreciation and judgment. Response, in short, is a critical
affair involving logical, ethical, esthetic and other factors which guide
and structure the activity. To this extent, creativity as constructive
response is quite different from habitual reaction which, when it is
successful, is almost exclusively repetitive of past patterns of behavior.
Creativity in response means the realizing of novelty in the form of a
relevant contribution to some projected aim or goal. Kant saw this
point very clearly in his *Critique of Judgment* where he connected
purposive behavior in man, artistic expression, and organic development
in nature with judgment, itself a creative process which cannot be
entirely reduced to rule, even if some rules are required for critical
judgment. The point is that the judgment of a singular case requires
appeal to a general rule, but the actual application of that rule to the
case at hand is not to be uniquely determined by an endless hierarchy
of interpolated rules. Judgment is impossible without a creative
element, and that is precisely why we think of "good" judgment as a
worthy talent.

Creativity must be distinguished from certain phenomena which are frequently associated with it in the popular mind but which are really quite antithetical to it. Creativity excludes bare repetition both in fact and in intent, because repetition involves no constructive contribution on the part of the one who responds, and therefore no novelty. Creativity excludes chaotic novelty unrelated to either form or plan. A mere succession of the different, as in a series of changing colors presented one after the other, no matter how striking, shocking, arresting these different items may be, does not of itself constitute creativity. Creativity excludes irrelevant innovation unrelated to a plan or form; the merely novel is not by itself an embodiment of creative response. Creativity, by contrast, requires the *significant novel*, which always means a constructive contribution to the realization of a good. Royce, in my view, fulfills all these conditions in his conception of the free individual whose task it is to create his will, find a life plan, and then seek to realize it in his own unique way.

In order to present Royce's views as clearly as possible, I shall select from his many writings three topics which seem to me best to represent the creativity theme. First, there is the concept of imitation, which figures largely in ethics and social philosophy and leads to the conception of the creative act which transcends its model. Second, there is the metaphysical concept of the individual who, as creative will, is called upon to fill his place in the social order of persons in his own unique and induplicable way. Third, there is the logic of interpretation, embracing the will to interpret, which expresses itself in creative activity aimed at establishing communities of understanding for mediating conflicts inimical to human welfare. Thus the spheres of ethics, metaphysics and logic serve to exemplify the creative aim at the center of Royce's thought. As was previously mentioned, creative action is essentially connected with will and with the voluntaristic cast of Royce's idealistic theory of being.

Since each of our three topics directs attention to a particular manifestation of will, it will be helpful to specify what Royce meant by the term. He understood will in a sense broader than that made familiar by the traditional faculty psychology. For Royce, will is virtually synonymous with the individual himself—it means his life-plan, his interest or involvement with that life-plan, the finite purposes and series of acts which realize these lesser purposes within the life-plan, and the *nisus* toward self-realization characteristic of a free individual. The scope of will in Royce's view is well illustrated in the following:

> I am a will, a will which is not there for the sake of something else, but which exists solely because it desires to exist.[3]

> My whole inner life is, namely essentially, my will, I long, I desire, I move, I act, I feel, I strive, I lament, I assert myself. The common name for all this is my will.[4]

The ultimacy of will for Royce is seen in his insistence that it finds justification in itself and, consequently, that it may serve ultimately as the justification of everything that is. Royce's constructive idealism—in his language, the Fourth Conception of Being—clearly expresses the point. According to this view, *to be* is *to be the fulfillment of a purpose*; whatever is finds its being in manifesting the will of a divine self such that all finite individuality has its uniqueness in the fact that this or that being and no other represents the realization of the divine purpose. As we shall see, there is a certain tension in Royce's thought centering on the relation between *what I was meant to be* in accordance with the divine purpose and *what I mean to be* in accordance with my own will. Royce was not unaware of the problem, and sought to deal with it in his account of the human person and his place in the world of being. For the moment it is sufficient that the breadth of his concept of will be understood.

SELF-CONSCIOUSNESS, IMITATION AND CREATIVITY

Regardless of the attempts that have been made to subordinate Royce's metaphysics and to deal with his views on this or that topic by omitting his theory of being, the fact remains that such attempts run counter to Royce's own frequently expressed intention. What Royce has to say about the self, its nature and knowledge of itself, its moral tasks, its freedom and its destiny cannot be made intelligible apart from his fundamental contention that the self is not a substance, that it is not "any single and unambiguous fact of consciousness"[5] such as might be apprehended in one perception, but is to be understood primarily as an ethical concept, a time-spanning intended purpose or life-plan in seeking to realize which we are at once distinct from our fellow human beings and related to them at the same time. The dual relational character here involved stems from Royce's social theory of self-consciousness which explains how the empirical, individual ego comes into view.[6] According to this theory, we come to an awareness of ourselves as realities distinct from other selves precisely through the process of contrasting our ideas, our deeds, and our plans with the ideas, deeds, and plans of others. In an early paper, "Some Remarks on the Anomalies of Self-Consciousness,"[7] Royce declared:

> If a man regards himself, as this individual Ego, he always sets over against his Ego something else, viz.: some particular object represented by a portion of his conscious states, and known to him as his then present and interesting non-Ego.[8]

Considered as alone and apart from such contrasts I do not grasp myself; my own self as this individual comes into view only as I find myself in some contrast relationship involving another who listens to me, who contradicts me, who interrupts me or approves of what I have done: in short, all the familiar relations of social intercourse. Later in *The World and the Individual*, Royce expressed the point thus:

> I affirm that our empirical self-consciousness, from moment to moment, depends upon a series of contrast-effects, whose psychological origin lies in our literal social life, and whose continuance in our present conscious life, whenever we are alone, is due to habit, to our memory of literal social relations, and to an imaginative idealization of these relations.[9]

Here Royce is speaking of the fully developed, emergent self-consciousness which is the product of social training and interaction with the non-ego. We must, however, attend to his account of the details manifest in the process through which this consciousness comes to be, for among those details is the concept of imitation which plays a major role in understanding the creative act.

Royce begins by distinguishing acts which may be regarded as essentially instinctual—eating, sleeping, crying, and the enjoyment of "physical well-being"—from acts which are essentially imitative in character. When the child plays at being a horse or a doctor, or when he acts in the fantasy of some interesting hero, he is seeking to follow a model presented to him from beyond himself. He is more or less vividly aware of shaping first his conduct and later his ideas in accordance with those of another person. Such shaping Royce regards as the initial move in the direction of self-consciousness in contrast with being simply a creature of natural impulses and passions. The special significance of imitation in this initial stage is that the child acquires ideas about the meaning and intent of the acts he imitates, and comes to view this meaning and intent as belonging to the mind and consciousness of the person he imitates. He perceives what the other person does, and he listens to directions, explanations, suggestions as to how to follow the other in what he does—speaking, using implements, performing physical exercises, or whatever—and as the process advances and imitation becomes a reality, the child finds itself now aware of a basic contrast marking a boundary between two sets of contents. On the one hand, there are the perceptions of the acts performed by the model, together with the gradually discovered meanings which they have for the one who performs them; these contents appear as uncontrollable and as belonging to the other person so that the child has to wait for them to be performed. On the other hand, there is the set of perceptions of the imitative acts themselves which the child has been able to perform, and these perceptions are accompanied not only by enjoyment but also by the discovery of new powers, the sense that he can do the imitative deeds, that they are controllable and do not emanate from a source beyond himself. Thus arises the contrast between ego and non-ego, drawn, in this instance, on the basis of the discovery of one's capability or capacity to perform; the non-ego appears in the form of the presented which is merely accepted and cannot be controlled. In whatever terms the disclosed ego may come to be understood, one point remains firm: in Royce's view, the social character of self-consciousness, far from entailing any merging or submerging of the individual into an impersonal or alien other, serves the function of awakening individual consciousness in the form of an awareness of skills, talents and powers which we ourselves can express. As he put it later in *The Philosophy of Loyalty*, through imitation we learn how to possess and carry out our own self-will; "we learn speech first by imitation; but henceforth we love to hear ourselves talk."[10]

Imitation, however, though a primary channel leading to the marking of a boundary between ego and non-ego, does not of itself account for the forms of creative self-expression which, for Royce, constitute the life of the free individual. Imitation, in the form in which it leads us to reproduce an act or some feature of our model, places us in a position where we can distinguish our reproductive act from the model given to us; by itself, however, imitation means no more than conformity and habitual adjustment to the customs and conventions of society.

Obviously such habitual activity always forms some part of our self-conscious life, both in thought and action; however, in Royce's view, social conformity fails to solve the problem faced by the morally autonomous individual of finding unity and directionality in realizing himself, and it also cannot account for the creative response in which I do not merely repeat myself but surpass my former state in a novel act.

With regard to the first of these problems, I can do no more than indicate the bare outline of Royce's proposed solution; I want chiefly to emphasize the second topic, the creative act in relation to the model. Royce envisaged the task of answering such questions as, For what do we live? What is our duty? What are we to value and what to reject? in terms of a paradox expressing an impasse which no one can avoid. On the one hand, following Kant, Royce held that we are morally autonomous beings who must have our own plan of life and who cannot accept as the reason for our duty any external authority such as is represented by social conformity.[11] On the other hand, his claim is that no one can discover a life-plan if he confines his quest merely to his own individual consciousness. "I have," he says, "no inborn ideal naturally present within myself,"[12] and the conclusion drawn is that, apart from social training of the sort discussed in connection with the process of imitation, we do not know our own will. The problem is that the will we can discover through social training frequently represents no more than routine conformity, something which Royce describes as quite different from "ideal life." Social training, moreover, heightens the sense of the importance of having one's own way and of rebelliousness, all of which may result in nothing more significant than the discovery of clever ways for an individual to outwit others and obstruct the social process without any corresponding self-fulfillment. And yet, Royce insists, it is only through such social training that we learn of our own will, or rather that we become aware of having a will of our own. "To learn your own will,—yes, to create your own will, is one of the largest of our human undertakings."[13] This assertion brings us to the heart of our concern. Our own will is not "given," as it were, apart from ourselves; it does not already exist, needing only to be discovered. That will must, in some sense, be created by each of us, and yet it will not be "created" *de novo* out of nothing since it will be a function both of our own powers, talents, and capabilities and of the social causes and opportunities that may present themselves in our situation. There is here a tension similar to one we shall meet in the next section: we are faced with the problem of "finding" our wills and we are also called upon to "create" them. The first suggests a discovery and acceptance of something already given; the second suggests a bringing forth of something novel. The two come together for finite, that is, human freedom, in the awareness that creativity in finding our purpose in life is a creative synthesis of both features; we discover our actual capabilities and capacities through the self-knowledge that arises from social intercourse, and we form our life-plan as that which is to unify these talents so as to perform the creative acts aimed at carrying out that plan.

I turn now to the account Royce gives of the creative or free act in relation to its model. This account takes us back to the idea of imitation, and requires in addition a second concept not previously mentioned in our discussion, the concept "between." This concept, as Royce reminds us, had been given quite extensive logical treatment in the chapter entitled "The Linkage of Facts" in *The World and the Individual*,[14] though not every part of the concept is relevant for describing the activity of the self. In order to help in understanding Royce's position, two preliminary comments are in order. First, Royce had a faith in the direct application to metaphysics of such logical concepts as "between," "self-representative system," "least upper bound," etc., which was no less infinite in extent than the unending system of interpretation with which his philosophy comes to completion. In principle, there can be no objection to this attempt to achieve clarity and precision of thought vis-à-vis notoriously difficult problems. But there is a liability involved: in applying these generalized concepts to the concrete, to the self, for example, Royce frequently modified this meaning and the result is often confusing. Second, and more important, Royce had an annoying tendency to restate, summarize, and reformulate what he had said before. Again, this practice is unobjectionable, or rather would be if he had not so frequently made changes both in meaning and emphasis in the course of the restatements. The use, for example, of such logical concepts as "between" and "well-ordered series" for elucidating the activity of the self appears in at least four distinct places in *The World and The Individual*, each time with modifications which make it difficult to be sure that one has grasped his meaning. Therefore, in order to focus the issues for our discussion, I shall pass over the restatements and express in my own way what I take to be Royce's view in accordance with the following chapters of the Gifford Lectures: "The Linkage of Facts," "The Human Self" and "The Place of the Self in Being."

To begin with, Royce sets out to distinguish clearly between the world as it is disclosed from the standpoint of science—the world of description—and the world of purposive and creative individuals who express themselves in novel acts—the world of appreciation. Science begins with discrimination involving comparison and differentiation. Every discrimination requires the specification of a difference which holds the discriminated items apart; comparison is thus not dyadic but triadic because "between any two objects of the world there is always another to be found."[15] The function of intermediaries is itself dual because intermediaries both link items and hold them apart. A red object and a green object differ with respect to their color, but are the same in being colored. For Royce, the entire procedure of science is to be understood as the process of finding series of terms such that every discrimination means finding what is "between" the discriminated items and thus indicating the sort, degree and direction of their difference. In short, the relation "between" establishes directionality in the world because we come to see the between as a stage to be passed through in a process of development. The series thus generated by discrimination is not well-ordered as is the natural number series, for example, because in them there is no immediate "next" but always a third to be discovered "between" the discriminated items. We need to preserve this concept of "between" for the later analysis of imitation and creative activity. At this juncture, Royce wants simply to employ the distinction between (a) well-ordered series in which there is an immediate "next" and (b) the series of discriminations in which there is no "next" but always a "between," for distinguishing the activity of scientific knowing from the apprehension of the world as it is experienced by the self which has a unique life of its own.

The decisive difference between the worlds is that in the world of description there is nothing about its objects that requires us to investigate them in one order rather than another, whereas in the world of purposive activity, there is a necessary order. We may begin with physics or anthropology as far as the objective world is concerned, since it is "anybody's world"; the only requirement for science is that we employ methods which result in a convergence of one scientific truth. But if we introduce the concept of purposive activity, all is changed. A purpose and its realization require a determinate succession of events which has an irreversible direction; no plan can be realized unless we know what is to come next in the order of activity. The world of description is but one aspect of a larger reality; there is in addition the knowledge which we as individuals have of the world—the meaning which it has for us as persons–and the volitional processes which we initiate in it. For Royce there is, in addition to the discriminatory processes resulting in facts and their serial arrangement–discoveries which might have been made as readily by anyone as by anyone else–a world of creative activity. In expressing ourselves in purposive deeds, we no longer have the sense that another might have done the same thing. On the contrary, when we project a plan and set out to realize it through action, we have the vivid sense of bringing forth something individual and unique, something not to be duplicated elsewhere by anyone else. Royce was prepared to interpret science itself as a purposive activity when viewed from the standpoint of the scientist himself. To link facts in objective series is to describe the world, but the activity of doing this is, for the individual thinker, an activity which occupies a particular place in that order which is the expression of himself. Stated in logical terms, the world of purpose and of persons is a world of self-expression taking the form of a discrete series in which each act is followed by a *next* without intermediaries. In Royce's view, I repeatedly proceed from one act to the next, and thus, through a recurrent operation, produce novelty because I always proceed to a new act. Insofar as the process of discrimination is my own activity and belongs to my own life, then, I am aware of my conceptual acts as succeeding without intermediaries, even though the logical process of discrimination as I carry it on requires the finding of intermediaries.

On the basis of the two distinct types of series, Royce believed that he had found a clear way of discerning the world of impersonal, universal knowledge on the one hand and the world of unique, creative persons on the other. A word of caution is, however, in order at this point. In the initial discussion of the difference between the worlds of description and appreciation to be found in "The Linkage of Facts" and in the treatment of purposive self-expression in the "Supplementary Essay," the impression is given that the well-ordered series formed by a recurrent operation is alone required for understanding purposive activity, while the series formed by discrimination and the "between" relationship belongs uniquely to the process of gaining scientific knowledge of nature. This impression is not in fact correct; further on in his account of the self and its place in the system of reality, Royce makes it clear that both types of series are involved in purposive action and that the between relationship figures essentially in a certain type of creative act which has imitation at its base. I shall not consider what is behind this apparent shift beyond pointing out that in the later treatment Royce was attempting to connect the two types of series in the interest of showing that reality has the character of selfhood.[16] To that analysis we may now turn.

Royce begins with a distinction between two kinds of activity possible for finite beings; for the sake of convenience, we may call them *direct* and *exploratory*. When we are in possession of a purpose and feel that our knowledge of the situation is adequate, we proceed to act directly and in a determinate way. This type of activity, though recurrent, has its own element of novelty and it marks the life of the self who knows what his life-plan is. On the other hand, there are those who are as yet unable to act in a direct way and who therefore are experimenting or exploring, a process which Royce describes as the search for a new object "between" any pair of objects that have already been discriminated. The search for the between, itself a kind of activity which may be recurrent, is connected by Royce with the phenomenon of imitation. As we saw, imitation was described in the paper on self-consciousness as an essentially reproductive affair in which the child repeats the activity of the model. Here two new features are added which at once introduce the possibility of creative novelty. Imitation is now seen to depend, first, on discriminating between acts performed by another and one's own acts, and second, on an interest in modifying what one has done in the past in the direction of what is done by the model. In short, to imitate is to construct an act which stands between my previous acts and the acts of the model, and this standing between is precisely what holds the new act apart from both my former conduct and the conduct of the model. "I never merely repeat his act,"[17] says Royce, and this means that imitation is "a kind of experimental origination, a trial of a new plan, the imitation of a trial series of acts."[18] The process of finding new intermediaries is seen by Royce as identical with the growth of the self. The results of imitative activity themselves become established and lead in turn to recurrence or repetition, the sign that the will has found its purpose. But we must distinguish between the will on the lookout, so to speak, and the will that has discovered itself. The latter acts directly in well-ordered fashion, while the former is engaged in a process of trial and error, seeking by mediation to discover what one has to do. For Royce, both processes have novel results, although it is clear that he regarded the discovery of the act which lies between my past behavior and my model as "the principal source of the novel forms of self-expression."[19] Action which is a direct and definite form of self-expression, and which has become habitual or recurrent, nevertheless brings forth novel results in accordance with the nature of the circumstances. Royce was fond of comparing this sort of activity with the recurrent operation of counting which leads to the number series and to an endless wealth of new theorems about that series. The activity which is indirect, tentative, and aimed at discovery is non-recurrent with respect to any given experiment, and it is essentially a process of adaptation through novel forms of response which are not "given" in advance but must be discovered and embodied in what is essentially a creative act.

BEING MYSELF AS A TASK

The second topic I have selected for its bearing on the creativity theme, although it involves Royce's metaphysics, is actually more concrete than the preceding discussion, and in addition it has the advantage of familiarity. That Royce's purposive idealism represents a type of absolutism is well known, as are also the difficulties, real or alleged, which an absolute idealism must face when the question of the reality of the finite individual is posed. It was precisely these difficulties which William James, himself an indefatigable defender of the individual, had in mind when he uttered his famous challenge—"I say, Royce, damn the Absolute!" I cannot undertake to set forth in any detail either Royce's conception of the Absolute Self or his theory of individuality. It is possible, however, to explain what he meant by the claim that the self is an ethical category carrying with it a task, and to show how he proposed to characterize the uniqueness of the individual in an idealistically conceived world where that individual is already understood as in some sense the expression of the divine will. As was suggested previously, the problem is to relate what an individual "was meant to be" from the standpoint of the Absolute Self to what that individual "means to be" from the standpoint of his own purposive will.

In accordance with Royce's conception of Being as that which fulfills a purpose, the world and all its contents, selves and things, must be viewed as "the expression of one determinate and absolute purpose, the fulfillment of the divine will."[20] The world in its wholeness is therefore unique, and every one of its proper parts is unique in virtue of its being distinguished from all the rest. Thus far we have the familiar doctrine that given one unique individual, an infinity of others can be defined through relations to that given individual. The question that interests us is: What does this doctrine mean in the case of the individual self or person? For an answer, we must return to Royce's conception of the self.

The crucial feature of that conception is that the self is not a substance and is not a single, unambiguous fact of consciousness; the self is a complex unity of life extended over a temporal interval and unified by a purpose which serves to identify that self in distinction from all the others. Such a fixed and finished characterization, though correct in outline, is nevertheless misleading because it leaves out of account the distinctively ethical dimension of what Royce means by a self. In any present we can become aware of some portion of ourselves—thoughts, feelings, hopes, fears, plans, deeds—and in so doing we become further aware of a past through which we have lived and a future through which we expect to live. In short, the present is but a fragment of a larger self which we feel that we ought to be able to identify as enduring and as distinctively ourselves in contrast to all other individual selves and to the Absolute Self. This principle of identification or time-spanning unity is not simply "given" to us from without, but appears to us as something which we *ought* to be and which, in the end, we must create. After a man has discovered that the self is not exhausted in the present or passing experience, he will seek to identify himself in some other way. He will have, says Royce,

> ... the really deep and important persuasion that he *ought to possess* or create for himself, ... some one principle, some finally significant contrast, whereby he should be able, with an unified and permanent meaning, to identify that portion of the world's life which is to be, in the larger sense, his own, and whereby he should be able to contrast with this, his larger self, all the rest of the world of life.[21]

My being as a self, then, comes to me as a task to be performed, as a purpose to be fulfilled such that in fulfilling it I am at the same time expressing the divine will in human form. My task, in the end, is to be an individual and unique self in contrast both to other selves and to God. Here Royce resolves the tension between what I was meant to be and what I mean to be. I was meant to be a unique, individual self, and I ought to mean to become that self by finding a life-plan or ideal for myself which remains as my steady intention throughout my temporal span. Reference to God or the Absolute Self, far from leading, as has often been thought, to a dissolution of finite selves or to their mystical blending in one Individual, actually has the opposite effect. The divine purpose is realized only to the extent that an individual becomes a unique self by finding his own purpose in a life-plan. Each self, to be sure, remains in relation to all other finite selves and to God, but it belongs to each individual's intent, says Royce, "always to remain other than" his fellows in virtue of a plan which no other can realize.

The question now arising is this: Has Royce forgotten, in this strong emphasis on unique individuality and the otherness of selves to each other, all that was previously said about the social origin of self-consciousness, about social training, and about the linkage of persons brought into being through the myriad social interactions of daily life? Royce's answer takes the form of admitting that we are all dependent on the world surrounding us insofar as we are defined in general terms. "Your temperament," he says, "you derived from your ancestors, your training from your social order."[22] Indeed all opinions as definable ideas can be shared with other selves. What cannot be derived from other lives, however, is the unique character of the individual, that character which represents his own way of expressing his will to be a self. Referring to the individual's purpose, Royce writes:

> Now this purpose, I maintain, is indeed your own. As nobody else can share it, so nobody else can create it; and from no source external to yourself have you derived it.[23]

In his explanation of man's relation as a self to the world of description, Royce goes even further and maintains that all causal explanation is confined to types and to describable, general characters of events, so that the self as an individual eludes such explanation. The individual is said to be "the indefinable aspect of Being"[24] and this means that my being as this individual who is nobody else in God's world is causally inexplicable. This inexplicability, however, is not that of any given fact or event, because being this individual is never divorced from my intent and resolve to be this individual, which means that it is ultimately my *will* that transcends the world of description. In short, being a self remains a task given to my creative will. I am this individual insofar as I mean to be so and see my purpose as my own. Ultimately, however, this purpose is not only my own, because it is also God's purpose for me; nevertheless, only I and no other can carry it out.

INTERPRETING AND MEDIATING
AS CREATIVE ENDEAVOR

Our third topic, though it has prefigurations in Royce's earlier works, properly belongs to the last phase of his work—the philosophy of interpretation and community. I shall attempt to make clear what I take to be the creative and constructive features of the interpretative enterprise both as it figures in the realm of logic and knowledge and in an endless number of practical, social situations where some form of mediation is called for. As we shall see, we are once again concerned with the will, but now with the will to understand, to mediate and overcome conflict, and ultimately with the will either to create community between multiple individuals or to bring to clear consciousness already existing bases for community which have become obscured or forgotten.

The background for Royce's theory of interpretation is to be found in Peirce's theory of signs[25] and in his account of the triadic relations involved in all sign-reading activity. In accordance with the philosophical discussions taking place in the early decades of this century concerning the respective nature of and connections between perception and conception, Royce liked to set interpretation off against both as a distinctive process which is not reducible to either, nor to their bare conjunction. We may clarify this point by citing Royce's own example of the weather vane and its function as a sign. His main contention is that someone may perceive a weather vane and note that it consists of a certain arrangement of pieces of metal rotating on a vertical axis about a pair of crossed horizontal axes, and he may set about conceiving or describing this object by means of the most exact concepts you please, but that in neither activity has he yet encountered the weather vane as a sign which must be read. To read it he must know that the weather vane is a purposeful device, that the positions of its arrow have a meaning and that he must assign the appropriate meaning to the positions he observes. This example is, of course, a simple and obvious one, but it illustrates the fundamental fact that the being of a sign is to be read or interpreted. For Royce, all signs are signs of minds and are addressed to minds which alone are capable of reading them. The signs may be spoken words in conversation, they may be the behavior of persons to be understood, they may be texts to be deciphered, interpreted, or translated from one language into another, or they may be deeds to be interpreted; in all cases, however, the logical structure of the process remains the same. Three terms are always involved: there is the interpreter,[26] the object or sign to be interpreted, and the person to whom the interpretation is addressed. The interpreter always says, in effect, to the one he addresses, What I say to you is what the sign said to me, i.e. what it means, and the process is, in principle, endless, since the interpretation is itself expressed as a sign which needs to be read and so the process continues. The process, moreover, is a creative one in the sense that in reading signs I am attempting to pass beyond the enclosed circle of my own ideas and experience in order to enter into the thought and experience of another mind. In reading a passage from Homer, for example, I must have the will to understand what he meant with the aid of an essentially living reason. To do so requires sympathy, insight, and ingenuity. I may have to consider in some cases what he might have meant, or could have meant, in the light of other knowledge concerning him and the period in which he lived. While interpretation aims at grasping and expressing the same meaning expressed in the original signs, the process is more subtle than that of finding synonymous expressions in a dictionary. Interpretation is not in fact reducible to the application of strict rule. Rules of grammar and syntax will, of course, be assumed, but beyond that I must be guided by my will to understand and by my desire to enter into the experience of another.

Royce saw the process of interpretation as especially fitted for the attainment of self-knowledge and the understanding of others. Wherever interpreting succeeds, a community of understanding is created; two distinct minds are now brought into a unity in virtue of their becoming related to the same third term. Royce's extensive analyses of communities based upon memory, or the acknowledgment by many distinct selves of common items which belong to their respective pasts, and upon hope based on the anticipation of some goal to be realized and with which all members identify themselves, depend on processes of interpretation where the many members all come to attach the same meanings to the signs involved.

Royce also understood the process of comparison, which he regarded as fundamental for the extension of knowledge, as akin to that of interpretation because it is essentially a triadic affair requiring creative ingenuity on the part of the thinker in supplying the missing third terms. To make instructive comparisons, for example, between two biological forms, two paintings or symphonic compositions, two economic systems, two pieces of creative writing, it is necessary to find relevant and interesting "thirds" or respects by means of which the two forms can be compared. The finding of these respects represents a creative activity. Comparisons do not make themselves nor are they made, as seems so often to be assumed, merely by making an exhaustive description of each form to be compared. What is required is the proposal of a significant common term as in the following example: If we show a person an ordinary ring strip made of paper and also a Moebius strip and ask him to compare them, he will have to introduce some idea, however vague, of a feature in accordance with which the comparison can be made. Let us suppose that he is not a mathematician and is forced to rely on direct perception; he will almost certainly concentrate on the shape. One is "round" he will say, and the other has a "twist" in it, and surely they differ in this respect at least. Such an answer is so far correct, but it is not very precise or particularly instructive. But now suppose that we ask him to introduce a more interesting, less obvious, and perhaps more fruitful respect for comparison. Perhaps he can say more exactly what he meant by the vague idea of shape. If he is able to translate this idea into, for example, the number of sides or edges determining a figure's shape, he will have a new basis for comparison. With this idea on the ground, he can now make a more precise comparison: one strip has two sides and two edges and the other has but one side and one edge. A more exact comparison has resulted, but only because the thinker has hit upon a significant respect which was not "given" but had to be introduced as a creative act. All comparison requires the same ingenuity, and thinking in this view is an endlessly creative process.

Interpreting or mediating was for Royce not only a matter of knowledge in the narrower sense but also a highly practical activity aimed at the overcoming of conflict and the harmonizing of competing claims. The mediating function involved is an offshoot of Royce's concept of community, and it represents an attempt to unify the diverse in some specific and practical way. In a curious little book entitled *War and Insurance*, Royce called attention to certain situations in which individuals are related in a merely dyadic way so that they constitute what he described as "dangerous pairs" because of the possibilities for conflict latent in their relationship. Examples of such pairs are buyer and seller, plaintiff and defendant, insured and beneficiary, employer and employee, and all the familiar examples of related individuals whose interests are to some degree opposed such that the advantage of one means the disadvantage of the other. In Royce's view, these dyads must be transformed into triads or rudimentary communities of interpretation. Mediation of some kind is required, whether in the form of an actual mediating individual or in the form of a containing system which will make it possible for each member of the pair to have access to the means of understanding the other, his rights and obligations in the particular situation. The task of the mediator is to interpret one member of the pair to the other. In some cases the tensions resulting from misunderstanding will be overcome through further knowledge and insight which dispel illusion and prejudice. In others, the conflict may be more severe, requiring mediation going far beyond any mutual understanding. In those cases, the mediator must appeal to a system of law established for the purpose of determining the nature and extent of just claims and their satisfaction. In Royce's view, all forms of mediation exhibit essentially the same phenomenon, namely, the transformation of a dyadic relationship—the claim of A, for example, merely counterbalanced by the opposed claim of B—which is a source of conflict, into a triadic one where a third term is interpolated between A and B for the purpose of containing their potentially dangerous clash of interests.

Mediating of the practical sort here in question is a creative affair in at least two respects. First, the mediator must have the will to interpret, and he must express it in the form of a penetration into two distinct selves; and if he is to succeed he will need whatever measure of creative imagination he has at his disposal. Second, the mediator is attempting to create a community of understanding where none existed before, by bringing into a new relationship two individuals, interests, claims, etc., previously related in an external and dyadic way. Royce frequently saw the interpreter as filling the role of a peacemaker who aims at linking together what would otherwise pose a constant threat of conflict if left unreconciled.

There are other facets to Royce's philosophy which have been left largely untouched. I believe, however, that the topics I have selected provide some insight into the creative freedom of the individual which played so large a part in his thought from the early papers to *The Problem of Christianity*.

NOTES

1.   Royce, *The World and the Individual* (New York: Macmillan, 1901), II, 72.

2. Royce, "The Interpretation of Nature," in *The World and the Individual*, vol. II. Royce's account is remarkable for its emphasis on the factor of time-span in the analysis of natural processes.

3. Royce, *The Spirit of Modern Philosophy* (New York: Houghton, Mifflin & Co., 1892), p. 253.

4. Ibid., p. 252.

5. Royce, *The World and the Individual*, II, 265.

6. See Royce, "The Contemporary Significance of Royce's Theory of the Self" in *Themes in American Philosophy* (New York: Harper & Row, 1970), pp. 109-121. In what follows, I shall not stress the relations to other selves because here I want to stress the *rise* of self-consciousness. The social relations are, of course, of paramount importance in Royce's thought, and they are an ingredient in the imitational process precisely when the child understands the act to be imitated as having meaningful intent for the mind of the other self.

7. Royce, *Studies of Good and Evil* (New York: D. Appleton, 1898), p. 169ff.

8. Ibid., p. 180.

9. Royce, *The World and the Individual*, II, 260.

10. Royce, *The Philosophy of Loyalty* (New York: Macmillan, 1908), p. 34.

11. See *The Philosophy of Loyalty*, chap. 2, esp. p. 30ff. I believe that in this analysis Royce did not sufficiently attend to the difference between finding a life-plan and justifying it or discovering a reason or ground for its claim upon us. The discussion in the text, however, can be carried on without making a special issue of the distinction.

12. Ibid., p. 31.

13. Ibid.

14. Royce, *The World and the Individual*, II, 76ff.

15. Ibid., p. 88.

16. I further abstract from Royce's ultimate metaphysical thesis that according to the true view of reality which transcends our ignorance, the two worlds of description and appreciation become one, and what there is must be viewed as one well-ordered series expressing the absolute self.

17. Royce, *The World and the Individual*, II, 311.

18. Ibid.

19. Ibid., p. 314.

20. Ibid., p. 292.

21. Ibid., p. 274.

22. Ibid., p. 293.

23. Ibid., p. 294.

24. Ibid., p. 325.

25. See John E. Smith, *Royce's Social Infinite* (New York: Liberal Arts Press, 1950) for a full account.

26. To avoid confusion, it is essential to notice that the "interpreter" here means both the one who interprets and the idea or meaning through which he interprets.

Personal and Cultural Autonomy in "Third World" Ideologies of Development

Walter G. Muelder

THE PLURALISM OF THE so-called "Third World" is evident to all but the least informed persons. Yet the idea of *development* casts its shadow of uniformity and of Western stereotypes on a complex and dynamic phenomenon. What has transpired in the course of independence, decolonialization, national consolidation, and development has shocked and shaken both the "First" world and the "Second" world. The subject of this essay on cultural and personal autonomy in the ideologies of development raises basic issues in the way development in the new nations is perceived and studied in the West, and it focuses also on self-perception and self-determination on the part of the developing nations of the "Third" world. Through their ideologies we may glimpse the paradoxes that confront all three worlds within the growing interdependence and cultural conflicts of the present time. Do personal and cultural autonomy, as appeals, give us any insights into the prospect of universal values or perspectives on values which will contribute to the unity of mankind as a truly human community? This brief overview is only a small part of a vaster problem in the philosophy and theology of development.

As a starting point I shall, for the moment, bypass the economic aspects of development and begin with a significant question raised by Ernst Troeltsch whose thought is now undergoing a renaissance.

Fifty years ago Troeltsch wrestled with cultural pluralism in his books, *The Absolute Validity of Christianity* and *Der Historismus und*

Seine Probleme. His mature reflection on the relativism to which he was driven is expressed not only in these books, but also in the lectures published under the title *Christian Thought* in 1923. I am not aware that those who are seeking to grasp the empirical realities and the complexity of the economic and political situations in the developing countries have availed themselves of the contribution which Troeltsch made at that time to the study of historically rooted values, nor of the challenges which Troeltsch's work poses for those who are in quest of universally valid values. Our appeal to Troeltsch will be for assistance in appreciating cultural and personal autonomy as aspects of development.

Troeltsch would have seen each of the developing nations as an Individual Totality or, in other words, as a Historical Totality in each of which overlapping and concentric circles of meaning and value are to be found. The Individual Totality is his basic historical category. In history we find and have to do with these wholes or unities which are in each case syntheses of psychical processes and natural conditions. Each constitutes a life unity or totality. Typical totalities are the family, class, folk, state, cultural epoch, religious community, a particular revolution, war, or school of thought. Each such social whole has five essential characteristics: (1) common spirit or common mind; (2) originality and non-repeatableness; (3) unity of meaning and value; (4) an unconscious dimension and relations to material and historical realities of which it is unconscious; (5) creativity and freedom. Troeltsch stressed the uniqueness of historical or cultural wholes, each pervaded by a common spirit and focusing in a unity of meaning and value. Common spirit is, nevertheless, objectively real, a primary phenomenon in which individual personal consciousnesses participate. The competition and conflict of these plural historical wholes and their common spirits give rise to many of our moral and cultural predicaments.[1]

As the European colonies in the Third World came increasingly under the domination of the Western powers in technology, politics, and economics, their prior unities of meaning and value received a rude shock and were often distorted or suppressed by the governing elites made up of foreigners or of ex-patriots. Artificial combinations of cultural unities were often geographically grouped under coercive administrations. In the struggles for independence national and tribal feelings arose along with a resurgence of traditional religions and other value systems. With the effort to modernize through the introduction of technology and industry, a new agenda of meaning and value is presented to the various countries. The category and the problems of the Historical

Totality may illuminate the nature of these new agenda. Technology is never a neutral value; it is a bearer of values and power.

Troeltsch wrote:

> The subject to which I devoted most attention was that of the relation of individual historical facts to standards of value within the entire domain of history in connection with the development of political, social, ethical, aesthetic, and scientific ideas. I encountered the same difficulties in each of these provinces—they were not confined to religion. Indeed, even the validity of science and logic seemed to exhibit, under different skies and upon different soil, strong individual differences present even in their deepest and innermost rudiments. What was really common to mankind, and universally valid for it, seemed, in spite of a general kinship and capacity for mutual understanding, to be at bottom exceedingly little, and to belong more to the province of material goods than to the ideal values of civilization.[2]

If this is bound to be the case, we may add, it is not surprising that it is so difficult to construct a general philosophy and theology of development today and so easy to focus on science, technology, and economic growth to the neglect of a more coherent enterprise.

The relativistic and pluralistic outcome of Troeltsch's thought may be noted in his observations of the relations of world religions to each other and may prepare us for appeals to traditional values in the ideologies of the developing countries.

> We need to recognize that they are expressions of the religious consciousness corresponding to certain definite types of culture, and that it is their duty to increase in depth and purity by means of their own interior impulses, a task in which the contact with Christianity may prove helpful to them as to us in such processes of development from within.[3]

This emphasis on "development from within" is one of his central motifs, as it probably must be for any true development or cultural transformation today.

Troeltsch was reluctant to adopt the skeptical idea that there is nothing that is absolute in the objective sense of constituting a common standard for mankind as a whole. Yet, as we shall see, even in the idea of the worth of personality or personality as a category, we do not, according to him, achieve universality. This is a crucial question for both secularists and for Christians as they perceive the "Third World," and it is also a basic question for all persons who are to act responsibly in that world and have their cultural roots there. It is a no less crucial question for the United Nations whose Commission on Human Rights has developed a Universal Declaration of Rights and Freedoms. Where these personal or human rights have been placed in the political constitutions of developing countries, we must ask whether they have more than ritualistic significance?

One must therefore ask: Does the concept or the fact of personality provide the cross-cultural transcendence needed to arrive at some universally valid standards among the pluralism of cultural wholes? The question is so basic that we must face it squarely. Fifty years ago Troeltsch argued as follows:

> The conception of personality itself is . . . different in the east and in the west, hence arguments starting from it will lead to different conclusions in the two cases. Yet, there is no other concept which could furnish a basis for argument concerning political values and truths save this concept of personality, which is always itself already one of the fundamental positions of the several religions, and is determined by them according to these respective general attitudes of theirs.[4]

The relativity of the idea of personality for Troeltsch is evident not only in his treatment of religion but also in ethics and in history.

> No man is born a personality; everyone has first to make himself into a personality by obedience towards another instinct, which leads to unity and homogeneity. Freedom and creation constitute the secret of personality, but this self-creation of personality is, of course, no absolute creation in us finite creatures which takes place in obedience and in devotion to an attraction towards emancipation from merely natural and accidental determination...:[5]

After emphasizing this generic situation, he notes:

> The idea of Personality, which, in the form of Freedom, determines everything in the morality of conscience, and, in the form

of Object, everything in the ethic of values—this idea is, after all, a Western belief, unknown, in our sense, to the Far East, and preeminently and peculiarly the destiny of us Europeans. But in view of the whole of our history we cannot but believe that it is for the truth.[6]

The relevance of this excursus into the thought of Ernst Troeltsch will become apparent as we investigate certain of the ideologies in the "Third World" particularly as they deal with modernizing nationalism, with development, and with liberation, including its revolutionary aspects. The word ideology itself invites definition. In this essay I shall not follow the usage of Marx or Mannheim, but rather that of Paul E. Sigmund, Jr. whose book entitled *The Ideologies of Developing Nations* prompted my first investigations of these problems about ten years ago. In this book Sigmund presented and summarized extended statements from twenty-six leaders of Asia, Africa, and Latin America with a special selection of five ideological statements from the Islamic world. Beliefs, he said, are ideologies when they "elicit an emotional commitment by the leadership and their followers and are directed toward action—the development of a new society in a certain direction, in conformity with certain goals."[7] Ideology has a social function. It draws on various traditions and goals to carry the people through "the period of modernization of traditional society and to justify the ensuing sacrifices and dislocations."[8] Sigmund and many other scholars agree that these ideologies cluster around the goals of "modernizing nationalism." There are accents on "national independence; rapid economic development; the creation of a nation-state governed by a regime based on a populist identification of leader, party, and people; regional federation; and nonalignment in international affairs."[9] My special concern has been to note in these and other ideological statements an appeal to cultural and personal autonomy and the relation of these appeals to the other emphases.

Modernizing nationalism, of course, is not supranationalism or internationalism but focuses on national identity and in this appeal implies national pluralism. Sukarno of Indonesia may in this respect be an "ideal type" representative of others as recorded in the following ideological appeal in 1959 to the students of Hasanuddin University:

No, as I said before, we have to return to our own personality. We want to return to our own identity. Do not let us become a carbon-copy nation. We have had democracy since olden times. I do not imply that we should remain as we were then. But the things of former times are good material for us to refer to, because we are going to establish democracy in our own country. . . . Let us find a democracy which is suitable for our own identity. And use materials which are to be found in our own country.[10]

Here is an ideological call for a unity of meaning and value in the shaping of a new historical totality through a common spirit, as Troeltsch would call it, developing ancient themes and synthesizing them with modern aspirations. The significance of such a statement—along with scores of others from different nations—depends on and modifies the notion of modernization and of the very idea of development.

Development in Western countries has often meant primarily economic growth. More and more, however, development is understood as a total social process. As Gustavo Gutierrez says,

This humanistic approach attempts to place the notion of development in a wider context: a historical vision in which mankind assumes control of its own destiny. But this leads precisely to a change of perspective which—after certain additions and corrections—we prefer to call liberation.[11]

The theme of liberation presupposes the theme of revolution as more than just economic development. Development as commonly perceived in Europe and America is an evolutionary concept stressing penetration by updated technology and industry and gradually reshaping countries through new economic measures. But development is increasingly recognized by many Asians, Africans and Latin Americans as a profoundly disturbing experience, involving neo-colonial patterns of domination and dependence, and hence linked with revolutionary liberation as cultures are shaken to their foundations. Modernization often entails manifold revolutions. Troeltsch's category of personality is relevant to such revolutionary change if it is understood in a dynamic way, as self-consciousness leading to a "new man."

In dealing with national liberation Eric R. Wolf pleads for radical attention to man, for the "root is man."[12] The "primacy of the human factor" needs to be affirmed in a world increasingly emptied of human significance. Radical questions of morality and human values press forward in the face of "the unholy alliance of technocratic and bureaucratic elites."[13] In this same context Manfred Halpern finds the origin of revolution not only in social imbalances but also in substantial "incoherence" as an anomic result of persistent breaking and reconstructing of linkages between individuals, groups, and ideas. Capitalism on a world-wide basis liquidated age-old institutions, converted human groups into commodities, and violated the identities of persons. This triple crisis Wolf sees as the key to modern peasant rebellion and revolution.[14] These peasant rebellions have received inadequate attention in theories of revolution in the present century. Mao Tse-tung has made the cause of the peasant the most dynamic element in his leadership of the Cultural Revolution in China. It calls forth new action based on a new consciousness and creative participation with emphasis on egalitarian values.

The need for a new consciousness and the understanding of the appeal for cultural autonomy in the ideologies of many developing countries are illuminated by two general perspectives lifted up by Manfred Halpern:

(1)   Never before have we lived in an age marked in every society in the world by the continuous breaking of connections—connections between generations, between established ideas and their intended consequences, between talking and the possibility of being heard, between felt pain and perceived remedy.

(2)   The world is being molded neither by a conspiracy of world revolutionaries nor by counterrevolutionary forces, but primarily by unintended, incoherent change. This kind of incoherent transformation turns encounters into chaos, renders dialogue impossible, and obscures (and so also deepens) injustice.

To the extent that these perspectives are clarifying, it becomes evident that technology and modernizing industry cannot supply the key to "incoherent revolutionary change" nor achieve "transformation of such change conducive to justice."[15] The constructive responses take the form, in part, of various ideologies in which the appeals to nationalism, to cultural autonomy, and to transforming humanism—which form the focus of this essay—without denying the appeals to modernizing development, including technological and economic change, are crucial aspects. In these responses the political aspects of leadership are bound to play a decisive role.

The revival of traditional culture serves sometimes to raise group consciousness of a common heritage of values not only in nations but also in regions. For example, Senghor emphasized the rediscovery of an African culture by the symbol of "Negritude" and Nkrumah by the symbol of "African personality." These appeals strengthen common bonds, and in the midst of modernization they conserve elements of the traditional culture and the moral values which they represent.[16] Modernization separated from awareness of cultural rootage precipitates problems in new elites. Nehru has noted the "spiritual loneliness" of the Westernized elite who have rejected the values of traditional civilization and yet need it. In part, the appeal to ancient values balances the overwhelming force of technical, economic and military elements on modernization; in part, the appeal provides internal cohesion; and in part, it makes valid development from within the nation possible as it does in regions in search of dignity after the humiliation of imperial devaluation.

Many leaders contrast the moral, religious, or spiritual superiority of their cultural past with the materialism, utilitarianism, and the technology of the West. Moreover, they deliberately induce a new appreciation for the native music, literature, art, and poetry, and warn against "mental colonialism" whereby the intellectuals have often been separated from their roots and made subjects of alien values characteristic of Western society. For example, Ayub Khan, speaking of Islam in Pakistan, says: "Between the ideology of Communism and the materialist conceptions of the West, Islam is the only point of view that can prevent the spirit of humanity from being destroyed."[17] Haya de la Torre of Peru protested and fought against "mental colonialism" in Indo-America. In 1956 he wrote:

> Between the Communist anti-imperialism in the service of the Soviet empire, and *Aprista* anti-imperialism in defense of our countries, there is the firm separation between two economic and social scenes which cannot be compared—that of the Old World and that of the New World. They should not be confused....[18]

The culture of colonial or imperial powers, whether they be capitalistic or socialistic, is an enemy.

Sékou Touré of Guinea, writing on "African Emancipation" in 1959 argues against the education of the elite which under French domination set the intellectual elite in opposition to the peasants. He said:

The education that was given us was designed to assimilate us, to depersonalize us, to Westernize us—to present our civilization, our culture, our own sociological and philosophical conceptions, even our humanism as the expression of a savage and almost unconscious primitivism—in order to create a number of complexes in us which would drive us to become more French than the French themselves.[19]

By means of these illustrations the principal point has been presented, but attention to a few more appeals to the primacy of cultural autonomy in the process of development and modernization will supply an emphasis. Chou En-Lai made a major address at the Bandung Conference in 1955 and lifted up the value of Asian-African cultural exchange. Chou En-Lai said:

Our cultural exchange should have respect for the national culture of each country, and not ignore the characteristics and special merits of the culture of any country so that we may learn and benefit from each other.[20]

U Nu of Burma in 1958 in an address entitled "Toward a Socialist State" appealed to human rights and then added:

Those individuals who aim to create the socialist state will not dare to ignore or set aside the temperament, the heritage, the traditions, the culture, and the religious beliefs of the people. These elements of tradition, culture, and religion will have to be accepted as component elements of the socialist state. And this acceptance will ensure the cooperation and ardent support of the entire people of the country in the task of building the socialist state.[21]

Earlier, in 1946, Gandhi's argument for "Indian Home Rule" passionately contrasted Indian and Western civilization:

The tendency of Indian civilization is to elevate the moral being, that of Western civilization is to propagate immorality. The latter is godless, the former is based in belief in God. So understood and so believing, it behooves every lover of India to cling to the old Indian civilization, even as a child clings to its mother's breast....[22]

This kind of appeal was, of course, much stronger in Gandhi than in Nehru who was a great apostle of modernization and of democratic socialism.

Another illustration of the appeal to cultural autonomy is found in an interview with Ahmen Ben Bella in 1962 on the theme, "The Future of Algeria." He was asked about the Arab element in the Algerian revolt. He responded:

> When I say we are Arabs, I do not, even remotely, want to make any allusions to questions of race, blood, or color of skin. I do not know how much Arab or Roman blood is in my veins; this does not interest me. But it happens I have a way of acting and thinking in life, a certain ethic, a definite heritage of culture and civilization, a specific type of humanism and certain moral values.[23]

There seems, so we may conclude from this list of ideological appeals, to be a general agreement on a point which can well be summarized in the words of Sékou Touré:

> We can also say that the life of a society, of a social unit, or of a nation is not essentially governed by laws, decrees, or regulations. The life of a society is governed by habits, customs, historic traditions, and the necessity for its maintenance and development. Thus, the value of a government is determined by the balanced development it assures on the national level.[24]

This appeal in the process of development is obviously in contrast to the classical Marxist position and the predominant capitalistic pragmatism, both of which make the powers of production through evolving technology basic. On the changing powers of production, according to Marx, are developed new relations of production whether of classes in capitalism or of the state and party power as in Communism. For the Marxists, government is a superstructure, and the culture reflects the changing substructure. As in Marxism so in capitalism, technology is a basic factor; and the market mechanisms of production and distribution are key factors along with management. The humanism of the earlier Marx tends to be obscured in the productive materialism and the apparatus of state collectivism of later Marxists, but many "Third World" socialists note the inherent humanism.

Humanism, as the key concept of development by way of contrast to both Marxism and capitalism, is found brilliantly expounded by Kenneth D. Kaunda, President of Zambia. His case for a true humanism as the basis for development clearly transcends technological modernization as it also transcends the dualism of racial conflict and of independence embattled against colonialism and neo-colonialism. He is a cultural pluralist who stresses national identity within the perspective of the universalism of humanity. He writes:

> It is primarily through the evolution of a genuine culture that a people discover their national identity. But cultural growth may be inhibited by the reluctance of a government in straitened financial circumstances to devote some of its resources to the encouragement of activities—sculpture, visual arts, writing, music, and drama—which many of the people would regard as irrelevant to national development.

> Universities, too, tend to be strictly utilitarian in scope, turning out a stream of the technical, professional, and scientific people required in the central areas of nation-building, and having neither the resources nor the personnel to devote to such rarefied subjects as fine arts and theology. Yet, the nation which lacks a firm cultural substructure is jerry-built and though the people have title deeds to property and the key to the front door in their pockets, they are still homeless.[25]

The humanism here expressed reflects the personalism of which Ernst Troeltsch wrote, and it should not surprise anyone that Kaunda is a Christian and was invited to address the Fourth Assembly of the World Council of Churches in Uppsala. Indeed, his personalistic socialism raises the question whether the appeal to humanism differs qualitatively among the ideologies of the leaders of developing countries along lines of direct influence by Christianity, or Marxism, or Eastern or African religions. This question requires research beyond the limitations of this essay.

Appeal to culture involves, of course, a consideration of religion. The function of religion as both a powerful conservative force and the root of culture making fruitful development possible must be recognized. There are paradoxes in such a situation, and some of its facets must now be addressed.

Awareness of the past can provide a mantle for a planner and reformer like Nehru, but it can also be exploited by those who wish to clip his wings. There can be an idealization of the past and there can be the kind of appeal that urges the process of modernization by criticizing the past. The appeal may inhibit modern life and be an obstacle to patriotism in the new modern nation. Old religions like Hinduism, Buddhism, or Islam are not necessarily inimical to political and economic development. Sometimes changes are given a religious facade. Hinduism has never been explicitly egalitarian, but Islam and Buddhism have often been related to egalitarian appeals. In Burma the teachings of Buddha are presented as the explanation for modernization ideals. Both "Marxism" and "Non-Marxism" have in Burma been held up as in conformity with Buddhism. One Burmese stated: "Marxist theory is not antagonistic to Buddhist philosophy. The two are, frankly speaking, not merely similar; in fact they are the same concept."[26] Communists in Burma have been careful not to attack religion. Indeed, according to Gunnar Myrdal, Marx's declaration that religion is the opium of the people is never quoted in South Asian countries.[27]

What many intellectual leaders who support modernization do is to hold that religion should be relegated to private life. Any division of people according to religious creed is branded as "communalism" and as a danger to national consolidation. The official view which stresses the secular state is a legacy of the liberation movement, but this does not prevent political parties from exploiting religious communalism for their own purposes in elections, despite public condemnation of it.

In the case of Pakistan one must note that it was created as an independent state for Moslems. In Ceylon, the dominant Singhalese group identifies itself openly with Buddhism, while the Tamil minority stresses Hinduism. Buddhism was by gradual steps made the state religion in Burma. Indonesia and Burma have experienced a kind of religious revival. In the case of Indonesia this revival is a reversal of earlier tendencies toward religious skepticism among intellectuals.

Myrdal's study of Asian poverty emphasizes the conservative influence of religion. He notes that revivals of religion or resurgence of ancient faiths have not generally been associated with religious reformation. Myrdal states:

> In India there is a definite retreat from the Nineteenth Century movements to purify Hinduism; a hands-off attitude is observed by the intellectual elite, who do not even carry forward Gandhi's criticism of filth in the temples and of all the superstitions connected with popular religion.[28]

But to let sleeping dogs lie may not be, in the long run, a sound policy in national consolidation, for the role of popular religion as a force of inertia and irrationality that sanctifies the whole system of life and work, attitudes and institutions, should not be overlooked in connection with underdevelopment. For one thing, as Myrdal points out, "the irrational elements in a people's thinking about themselves and their society erect a wall of confusion that makes the very idea of planning difficult to disseminate rapidly and effectively."[29] Even the philosophical expressions of religion when practiced, apart from popular religion, comprise the emotional container of so-called "Asian values" which by their sanctions render the whole way of life and work rigid and resistant to change.[30]

The paradoxical and dilemmatic quality of ideologies that appeal both to modernizing nationalism and to cultural autonomy must now be evident. But we must highlight the tensional aspects even more by stressing the obvious differences in Western and Eastern assumptions about economic planning for development. Economic theory in Europe and America has a narrower intellectual base than is characteristic of developing countries. It is long since a highly specialized activity. More-over, it developed in a historical context of Western philosophies of natural law, of the Enlightenment, of hedonism and utilitarianism. Even Marx retained many of the assumptions of classical economic philosophy along with Hegelianism and Judaic humanism. What seems empirically grounded in the West may be inappropriately a priori when applied to South Asia or Africa. This difficulty may be extended, as we have already noted, to those Asian and African social scientists who have had their training in the West; and their elitist postures and positions may readily remove them from the realities of the social systems they are supposedly helping to develop.

The most general concepts of economic theory are loaded with biases: terms which divide realities into consumption, saving, production, unemployment, underemployment, investment, output. These and others that abstract from modes and levels of living and from attitudes and institutions do not readily make sense in the cultures of so-called underdeveloped nations. "A realistic analysis," says Myrdal, "must deal with the problems that are attitudinal and institutional and that take into account the very low levels of living and culture."[31] Indeed, abstractions from the existential living of these cultures as wholes created the very stereotypes that entered into the minds of the European colonial masters, even in their sophisticated reasonings. Consequently, the responses in both the "post-colonial ideologies and the ideologies of the liberation movements were deeply stamped by protest against that thinking."[32] Yet, paradoxical configurations also occur which intermingle Western biases and protests against them. Myrdal reports:

> We thus often find at the universities of South Asia economists who are strongly anti-Western in their sympathies and politically far to the left, even avowed Communists or fellow-travellers, but who are yet eager and proud to place the emphasis of their teaching on the latest abstract and formal growth models developed at Cambridge or Yale, and whose ambition is to write articles resembling those in Western journals and, hopefully, to publish them there.[33]

Professor Samuel C. Parmar, ecumenical economist of India, presses the point that "technology is power, and that power is never neutral." He adds:

> It becomes the carrier of those systems and ideologies within which it is nurtured. For the poorer nations, too much of the present transfer of technology is a projection of the economic needs of the givers rather than a response to the needs of the receivers.[34]

Some of the Western assumed values in the application of technology include (1) individualism, the unit rather than the community; (2) private wealth and property as the incentive to effort; (3) class distinction as a symbol of financial success; (4) the middle class as means of stability; and (5) competition as a method of deciding power, wealth, and status.

Other biases that often enter into the very concern for development include an optimistic approach to enterprise, a belief in development, a strong desire to succeed, along with compassion for those in distress and who have been exploited, and not least "a bias to deal diplomatically with the facts that may not be complimentary. Understatements as well as overstatements represent biases."[35]

No one was more aware than Jawaharlal Nehru of the changed attitudes required by the effective use of modern technology. He, if anyone, was aware that technology is not value-free. In his "Strategy of

the Third Plan," he pled dramatically that India come to terms with
the valuational crisis:

> But we have to deal with age-old practices, ways of thought, ways
> of action. We have got to get out of many of these traditional ways
> of thinking, traditional ways of acting, traditional ways of produc-
> tion, traditional ways of distribution, and traditional ways of
> consumption. We have to get out of all of that into what might be
> called more modern ways of doing so. What is a society like in
> the so-called advanced countries like today? It is a scientific and
> technological society. It employs new techniques, whether it is in
> the farm, or in the factory, or in transport. The test of a country's
> advance is how far it is utilizing modern techniques. Modern
> technique is not a matter of just getting a tool and using it.
> Modern technique follows modern thinking. You can't get hold
> of a modern tool and have an ancient mind. It won't work. We
> have 400 million people in India, very fine people, very capable
> people, very intelligent people, but people who have functioned
> for ages past in certain ruts of thought and action. Take our
> peasant; it is a matter of amazement and shame to me that any
> peasant should go about today with a plough which was used in
> Vedic times. There has been no change since then. It should have
> been a museum piece; yet the fact is, it is there. It astonishes
> me.[36]

Quite recently Indira Gandhi evaluated the developmental crisis:

> As far as industrialization is concerned we have more or less
> blindly followed the West, although we have kept our cultural
> identity. But now we are wondering whether this is right for us...
> We are rather overshadowed by the dark clouds of economic
> backwardness and inequality. We have to deal with that. But we
> are very conscious that we can't confine ourselves to the material
> aspects, that we have to raise society in many other ways.[37]

Ideological values must be translated into institutional changes; and
so ways must be found to make appropriate institutional modifications
that both reflect the old and respond to revolutionizing liberation. One
of the ways in which personal rights can emerge under modernizing
conditions can be illustrated by the Tunisian law which prohibits
polygamy. The Tunisian Law of Personal Status appeals to the Qur'anic

injunction regarding the impartial treatment of co-wives and states that in the circumstances of modern society it is impossible for a husband to treat several wives impartially to their mutual satisfaction. Thus, it is regarded in law as an irrefutable or conclusive presumption that this essential precedent condition (impartial treatment of co-wives) is today incapable of fulfillment.[38] The problem in cultural development, of which the prohibition of polygamy is an example, is "the need to define the relationship imposed by the religious faith and the mundane forces that activate society."[39] Thus, it is both an ideological problem and one of institutions and practices in law. As Coulson says,

> Law, to be a living social force, must reflect the soul of its society. And the soul of present Muslim society is reflected neither in any outright secularism nor in the doctrine of any mediaeval textbooks.[40]

In the period of rapid social change that involves conflict between new and old, there is a crisis in consciousness that begets self-consciousness in persons. In this personal self-awareness there is the opportunity for the development of culture and of a sense of personal human rights as well as of social rights for classes of persons. In the crises of institutions and of authority, personal self-consciousness becomes more significant than before. Transformation of personal existence takes place. Culture becomes self-reflective. The transformation may be either slow or dramatic depending on historical circumstances.

As we bring this essay to a close, we may note the necessity and the strains attending the themes of cultural autonomy and human dignity in the ideologies of developing countries. We have noted the appeals to traditional culture, including resurgent religion, which are parts of the ideologies. When these interact with the forces of modernization as extensions of Western technology and economics, a crisis of culture occurs. Persons tend to live at two levels. On the one hand, they take on Western patterns of culture; on the other hand, they continue to practice their own, and the result may be a divided soul. There are strains in personality when man is attuned to the old and aspires to the new. But there also are strains when he is educated as part of a Western-ized elite and yet is rooted in the past. The strain may be reflected in the class structure of the new nation with the elite in control but spiritually not at home with the people. The strain may be complicated further when the governing classes are divided among those who aspire to nonindigenous modes of thought and value and those who are committed to the cultural heritage and have been educated wholly within the developing country. These strains may be noted whether the external orientation is to some form of Western democratic capitalism or to some form of Marxism, Leninism, or Mao-ism. The phenomenon of the divided soul is more acute in some developing countries than in others, but it must in any case be recognized as a significant aspect of development.

Religion, as we noted, is one of the facets of cleavage, of continuity, or of resistance for many persons in non-Western countries. The religions of Buddhism and Hinduism have a different attitude toward nature from that which has come to dominate Graeco-Roman-Christian culture. Another facet of the problem is political, for, as B. N. Y. Vaughan and others have shown, the post-colonial independence has involved politicians in the repudiation of every vestige of colonial imperialism including imported religion and education. Hence, when people want modernization and yet discard imperialism, there is a difficult sorting out of values on the agenda of new nation building.

This task brings us to the central problem of this analysis once again:

> Unless (modernization) is supported by the culture of the country it remains an artificial importation and has unfortunate social and cultural consequences. Nor can the development process be sustained unless it is rooted in the national culture. For it is only a development process, which does not destroy the cultural identity of a people and thus does not take their dignity away from them, which will not in the end prove to be a delusive mirage and produce reactions against development itself.[41]

In the words of M. M. Thomas of India, Chairman of the Central Committee of the World Council of Churches, "Radical westernization of culture may be possible for isolated individuals living in a non-western culture or for some very backward cultures, but it is not practical for a whole advanced culture."[42]

The idea which emerges from the interpenetration of traditional meanings and values and modernizing variables is cultural transformation in which development is both continuous and creative in responses from within. This means the change or development of culture without adopting another foreign culture. Modernization which is specifically human calls for and requires a cultural transformation whereby the people develop and with that development transform the total social process. This is, of course, the opposite of cultural domination from without. It means development which has continuity with the past but is not enslaved by static institutions. This continuity provides personal security and human dignity of which people are deprived when their past culture is denied and negated. What is creative in the traditional culture is transformed by contact with the new. It is rediscovered and reinterpreted. Sometimes tradition is humored while modernization is accepted.

In this idea of transformation the principles of Troeltsch's development of historical totalities is combined with the insights of anthropology and Christian humanism as in the philosophy of Kenneth Kaunda of Zambia. Vaughan's summary of the meaning of cultural transformation deserves recognition in conclusion:

> Authentic cultural transformation means the changes which occur in the way of life of a people as a result of the activation of forces dormant but already present within the culture itself. The normal cause of cultural change is a new awareness acquired by the people themselves as a result of a change in the social and economic context of their lives. They begin to see themselves differently and, as a result, organize themselves and their way of life differently. Cultural transformation takes place as a result of developments within the specifically human consciousness of people. Changes in the way of life of a people then take place as a result not of innovations and customs imported or imposed upon them from outside, but of changes in the realm of their own consciousness about themselves which produce new attitudes and modifications in ways of living.[43]

It is thus human dignity and not economic growth or technology which is the heart of true development.

NOTES

1.   Walter G. Muelder, *Moral Law in Christian Social Ethics* (Richmond: John Knox Press, 1966), pp. 31-32.

2.   Ernst Troeltsch, *Christian Thought* (London: University of London Press, 1923), pp. 23-24.

3.   Ibid., p. 29.

4.   Ibid., p. 34.

5.   Ibid., p. 51.

6.   Ibid., p. 99.

7.   Paul E. Sigmund, Jr., ed., *The Ideologies of the Developing Nations* (New York: Praeger, 1963), p. 4.

8.   Ibid., p. 37.

9.   Ibid., p. 40.

10.   Ibid., pp. 61-62.

11.   Gustavo Gutierrez, *A Theology of Liberation* (New York: Orbis Books, 1973), p. 25.

12.   Norman Miller and Roderick Aya, eds., *National Liberation: Revolution in the Third World*, "Introduction" by Eric R. Wolf (New York: Free Press, 1971), p. 1.

13.   Ibid.

14.   Ibid., p. 3.

15.   Manfred Halpern, "A Redefinition of the Revolutionary Situation," ibid., pp. 14-15.

16.   Sigmund, *Ideologies,* part 3.

17.   Mohammed Ayub Khan, "Islam in Pakistan," ibid., p. 110.

18.   Sigmund, *Ideologies*, p. 291.

19.   Ibid., p. 156.

20.   Ibid., p. 54.

21.   Ibid., p. 66.

22.   Ibid., p. 78.

23.   Ibid., p. 147.

24.   Ibid., p. 158.

25.   Kenneth D. Kaunda, *A Humanist in Africa: Letters to Colin Morris* (New York: Abingdon Press, 1966), p. 59.

26.   U Ba Swe, "The Burmese Revolution," in *Asian Drama*, ed. by Gunnar Myrdal (New York: Pantheon, 1968), I, 79.

27.   Myrdal, *Asian Drama,* I, 108.

28.   Ibid., pp. 108-109.

29.   Ibid., p. 113.

30.   Ibid., p. 112.

31.   Ibid., p. 20.

32.   Ibid., p. 21.

33.   Ibid.

34.   B. Y. N. Vaughan, *The Expectation of the Poor* (Valley Forge, Pa.: Judson Press, 1972), p. 79.

35.   Myrdal, *Asian Drama,* I, 33.

36.   Ibid., pp. 57-58n.

37.   *Christian Science Monitor* (January 7, 1974).

38.   Noel J. Coulson, "The Concept of Progress and Islamic Law," in *Religion and Progress in Modern Asia,* ed. by Robert N. Bellah (New York: Free Press, 1965), p. 88.

39.   Ibid., p. 89.

40.   Ibid., p. 90.

41.   Vaughan, *Expectation,* p. 87.

42.   M. M. Thomas, "Modernization of Traditional Societies and the Struggle for a New Cultural Ethos," *Ecumenical Review* 18 (Oct. 1966): 436.

43.   Vaughan, *Expectation*, p. 95.

The Socratic Teacher
and the Modern University

Thomas O. Buford

IT IS GENERALLY recognized that the place of the humanities in the American university is in jeopardy. Its traditionally honored goals of humanizing and liberating students are under attack. Those outside the university who believe that the primary goal of education should be technological and pre-professional training question the value of a university education which does not contribute directly and significantly to securing a good job, to making a living, and to providing trained personnel for business and industry. The university, no doubt responding to these societal demands for a technological and professionally trained citizenry, has increasingly emphasized the production of technical knowledge and scholarship. Under these demands teachers, who are traditionally held responsible for humanistic education, have devoted their energies primarily to research and publishing. Teaching has become the menial task of disseminating information and popularizing the latest educational and scientific fads. This attack on humanistic education thus becomes an attack on teaching. While societal demands are supporting the attack, the spearhead of the assault is coming from within the university itself. William Arrowsmith, in his well-known essay, "The Future of Teaching," charges that the university has disowned the purpose of education, "the molding of men," and has committed itself to the "production of knowledge."[1] The university is technocratic, professional, positivistic, scientific, in collusion with the state, and dehumanizing.[2] Arrowsmith's tactical response to this undesirable condition is to call for "Socratic *teachers*," who are "visible embodiments of the realized humanity of our aspiration, intelligence, skill, scholarship."[3] He asks,

> What ... would education be like if humanists and teachers had the courage of their traditions and dared to face their students as men in whom their studies and texts found worthy, or at least attempted, embodiments?[4]

Such teachers, he claims, have "the power to humanize others" because they know the ends to which they are living and embody in their lives what they teach. Students learn to be fully human by imitating those who are themselves fully human. Only a virtuous man, a person who has realized his humanity, can provide for the student the "profound motivation for learning, the hope of becoming a better man."[5] In short, Arrowsmith calls for universities to reinstate humanistic education by employing teachers who successfully emulate the Socratic model of the teacher. The primary purpose of this essay is to examine this conception of the teacher. Is the Socratic teacher model correct, that is, is it the model which all teachers should emulate and by which they should be judged? Before this question can be answered, however, the meaning of the Socratic teacher model must be clarified. When that has been accomplished three difficulties in the Socratic teacher model will be discussed. In conclusion, a suggestion will be made about the importance of Arrowsmith's position for the vitality of the humanities in American universities.

THE SOCRATIC MODEL OF THE TEACHER

The Platonic dialogues help in clarifying the meaning of the Socratic model of the teacher espoused by Arrowsmith. Socrates is regarded by Plato as a virtuous man and one to be listened to because he knows the end to which life ought to be lived and embodies his teachings in his own life. But what does it mean to *embody* in one's life that which he teaches? An answer to this question will provide the key necessary for clarifying the meaning of the Socratic teacher model. Two dialogues, the *Laches* and *Symposium*, are particularly helpful in understanding the meaning of the concept of embodiment of teachings exemplified in Socrates' work and life.

One of the major topics of the *Laches* is the nature of the good educational advisor. At the outset of the dialogue two Athenian elders, Lysimachus and Melesius, invite two Athenian generals, Laches and Nicias, to attend a demonstration of fighting in armor and to give advice about the education of their sons, Aristides and Thucydides. Socrates is brought into the conversation because he knows about teaching and has shown courage in battle. Soon the discussion turns to the nature of courage, for the sake of which fighting in armor would be taught. Before Laches and Nicias offer their views on courage, they and Socrates agree that the criterion by which to judge the soundness of each person's definition of courage is that his deeds match his words.[6] Socrates has been praised as a man who speaks well and whose deeds are virtuous, and it is assumed throughout the dialogue that his deeds and words match. After a long discussion it becomes obvious that Laches' and Nicias' understandings of courage fail when the standard is applied. The dialogue ends with Lysimachus' invitation to Socrates to come to his home the next morning at daybreak to continue the conversation. We are led to believe that Socrates is the best educational advisor for Lysimachus and Melesius. Though some crucial ethical and educational issues are being discussed, what is pertinent to our discussion is Plato's characterization of Socrates as the expert educational consultant. A good educational advisor is one about whom it can be said, "His deeds and words harmonize." But what are we to understand by this criterion? I submit that it is central to what is meant by a teacher embodying in his life what he teaches.

Plato develops the deeds-words criterion within the context of the discussion of the value of learning to fight in armor. Socrates and his friends agree that the question of fighting in armor cannot be settled on utilitarian grounds alone. Rather, it must be settled on the basis of the kind of soul which ought to be developed, that is, a virtuous soul, a courageous soul. At this point Socrates raises an interesting question, "Which of us is skillful in the treatment of the soul, and which of us has had good teachers?"[7] In other words, "Are we the expert advisors Lysimachus and Melesius are seeking? Do we have the needed credentials?" Regarding his own credentials, Socrates takes his characteristic ironic position that he must not be listened to since he did not have a teacher (he could not afford a Sophist) and has not learned the art of making men virtuous. He defers to Laches and Nicias to show the worth of fighting in armor. He points out that "they are far wealthier than I am, and may therefore have learnt of others, and they are older, too; so that they have had more time to make the discovery."[8] But Socrates wants them to supply their own credentials. Lysimachus encourages Laches and Nicias to answer Socrates' questions. Contrary to what would be expected, neither Laches nor Nicias answers Socrates' inquiry. Their replies to Lysimachus' encouragement to engage with Socrates in the discussion of the credentials they possess constitute a shift from the *credentials* of the expert to the *criteria* on the basis of which the expert is to be determined. In effect they establish Socrates as the one for whom they are looking. Obviously their speeches deepen the Socratic irony. But what are the criteria for determining the expert educational advisor?

From what Plato tells us about both Nicias and Laches the criterion each suggests is characteristically in agreement with his previous speech. Nicias, the intellectual soldier who believes that fighting in armor will lead to the more noble training of the general, replies approvingly to Lysimachus' encouragement (and, one suspects, in keen anticipation) that

> ... he will be continually carried round and round by (Socrates), until at last he finds that he has to give an account both of his present and past life; and when he is once entangled, Socrates will not let him go until he has completely and thoroughly sifted him.[9]

The expert educational advisor must be a man of λόγος, one who is skillful in *elenchus*; that is, he will seek to give a consistent account, to develop reasons for positions, to explore meanings, and to investigate thoroughly the topic. However, the man of λόγος is also one who knows, and in the instance of the *Laches* he would know the nature of courage. The dialogue ends on an inconclusive note because no *dramatis personae* in the *Laches* possess a knowledge of the nature of courage and can give sound educational advice. Laches, the practical soldier, who believes that fighting in armor has no practical benefit, agrees to discuss the issue with Socrates. He says,

> I am delighted beyond measure: and I compare the man and his words, and note the harmony and correspondence of them.... As to Socrates, I have no knowledge of his words, but of old, as would seem, I have had experience of his deeds; and his deeds show that free and noble sentiments are natural to him .... So

high is the opinion which I have entertained of you ever since the
day on which you were my companion in danger, and gave a proof
of your valor such as only the man of merit can give.[10]

The expert educator will be a man of 'έργον, that is, he will habitually
act virtuously. Furthermore, his deeds and words must match. Laches is
at least saying that he will not heed the advice of a man who claims to
understand the nature of courage but whose behavior is cowardly.
Hence from Nicias we learn that Socrates demands that people give an
account of their views, that they possess knowledge. From Laches we
learn that Socrates has shown courage and should be listened to to
determine if his words fit his deeds. The clear implication of this
conversation is that Socrates embodies in his life that which he teaches.
In the *Laches* the deeds-words criterion is used to distinguish the
educational advisor, whose advice should be accepted, from the pseudo-
advisor, whose advice is not trustworthy.

Additional insight into the meaning of the deeds-words criterion can
be achieved by relating it to two Socratic paradoxes: (1) virtue is
knowledge, and (2) no man intentionally does evil.[11] Socrates' answer
to Protagoras' view that people ought to seek their own interests,
particularly as regards what gives pleasure and what gives pain, is that
this will not do. Interests pull us in many directions at one time, some
in beneficial directions and some not. The issue is which ends are best.
That which is truly in our best interests is determined by insight,
knowledge.[12] For a man continually and habitually to live well he must
know what is in his own best interest.[13] Furthermore, if a man truly
knows what is best for him he will do it. This means that if one knows
what is in his best interests as distinct from what only appears to be,
then he will do it. This also means that no man intentionally does evil;
that is, he will not seek that which truly is not in his best interests. A
necessary implication of knowing the best is a desire to do the best. The
resolution of these paradoxes is not at issue here, but the meaning of
the deeds-words criterion is. It is clear that for Plato the man of *aretê* is
one who knows what is truly in his best interests and does it. The
virtuous man is one who knows the best, who acts on the basis of what
he knows, and who does this habitually.

In the light of these paradoxes we can better understand what Plato
means by deeds and words matching and by a person embodying in his
life that which he teaches. The deeds-words criterion is the standard by
which the man of *aretê* can be determined; it is also the standard by

which the good educational consultant can be determined. If the one whose deeds and words match is a man of *aretê* (virtue), and if the good educational consultant is one whose deeds and words match, then the good educational consultant is a virtuous man. This seems to be the Socratic teacher-model praised by Arrowsmith.

This analysis can be clarified by illustrating it with an event from the life of Socrates. Plato nowhere better summarizes his picture of Socrates than in the speech of Alcibiades in the closing scenes of the *Symposium*. Socrates has praised the love of the Beautiful, the True, the Good. Alcibiades, drunk with wine and incoherent in speech, adores Socrates, is afraid of him, yet knows that Socrates is right. Ironically, Socrates appears other than he is. Alcibiades asserts that Socrates "is exactly like the busts of Silenus, which are set up in the statuaries' shops, holding pipes and flutes in their mouths; and they are made to open in the middle, and have images of gods inside them."[14] Though Socrates' speeches seem foolish in stark contrast with the speeches of the sophists', "when they are opened and you obtain a fresh view of them by getting inside, first of all, you will discover that they are the only speeches with any sense in them, and secondly, that they are so divine, so rich in images of virtue."[15] Furthermore, Socrates is a man of action, courageous and calm in battle; though disinclined to drink, he can drink without becoming overcome by it. Socrates was the only man awake and sober at the end of the banquet! He mixes with men, but is never one of them. In contrast to the tyrant whose soul is pulled by every desire, who is drunk with power, and whose statements about the art of ruling are incoherent, Socrates is guided by reason and σωφροσυνή characterizes his life. Socrates is the man who, while knowing what is best and habitually acting virtuously, has integrity. He is one whose deeds and words match; he has mastered the art of living.[16] He, above all men, is worthy of emulation. Assuming that this portrayal of the Socratic teacher is an accurate interpretation of what Arrowsmith means, it is time to evaluate it.

CRITICISM OF THE SOCRATIC MODEL OF THE TEACHER

The main issue of this paper is whether the Socratic model of the teacher is the pattern necessary for a good teacher to emulate. The contention of Arrowsmith seems to be that the Socratic teacher-model, formulated as a man who embodies in life that which he teaches, whose deeds and words match, is the standard by which to distinguish a good teacher from a bad one. I want to argue that Arrowsmith is wrong.

Plato assumes that to accept the deeds-words criterion is also to accept the paradoxes. One way to attack this criterion would be to show that the paradoxes which it implies do not hold. Attacks on the Socratic paradoxes are numerous and it is not necessary to recount them here. Generally, they are developed along the following lines:[17] Consider the assertion that virtue is knowledge. Persons often know what is best but do not act virtuously. A man may be intellectually sure that an action is wrong and wish to do it nevertheless. This point also raises serious questions about the second assertion, that no man intentionally does evil. We all know the experience of intending to do the best but not doing it. Strong cases are easily found, such as knowing murder to be wrong yet committing it nevertheless. These cases are based on the assumption that a distinction can correctly be drawn between knowledge and will. We may understand the circumstances of our life but wish they were otherwise. We could even go further and say that though we understand the goals we seek to achieve, we believe we ought to achieve other goals. On this basis, then, an evil life is not necessarily one of ignorance. It could be a failure of will as well as of knowledge. If this rather traditional line of critique is correct, then Plato's paradoxes and the ethical system based on them are seriously impaired. Insofar as accepting the criterion is contingent upon accepting the truth of the paradoxes, any serious weakness of the paradoxes is by implication a serious weakness of the criterion. However, it could be argued that the deeds-words criterion is nevertheless defensible as a way of distinguishing a man of integrity from a man who has no integrity. Its cogency is not dependent on the cogency of the paradoxes. Even on this assumption the deeds-words criterion is open to another objection, an objection which is more devastating with regard to its educational implications.

According to the Socratic model of the teacher, the good teacher must have mastered the art of living. He is one who cares for the soul and can properly do this only if he first knows what is good for the soul. If he knows what is good for the soul he lives his life accordingly. What is open to question here is whether a good teacher must also be a good man, a man who has integrity, who has mastered the art of living. One can accept the separation of the two paradoxes from the deeds-words criterion and still question whether being a good man is necessary to be what most of us would call a good teacher. It is obvious that a man may have mastered the art of living, may be one who knows what is good and chooses to live his life accordingly, and yet not have mastered his discipline adequately to guide his students into a thorough understanding of that discipline. Being a good man is not sufficient for a person to be a good teacher of a discipline, a good teacher of logic, for example. Likewise, it is not the case that to be a good teacher of a discipline one must first be a good man. One can be a good teacher of logic, for example, without being a good man. Being a good man is neither necessary nor sufficient for being a good teacher of a discipline. If these observations are correct, it is difficult to determine what connection, if any, there is between being a good teacher of a discipline and a good man in the sense that a good teacher would embody his discipline in his life. It is not clear how a good logic teacher can embody logic in his life except in the most general way, in that any person who attempts to live rationally also attempts to reason soundly. However, if that is what is meant, then the logician's life would be indistinguishable from any other well-educated person's life. There is no sense in saying that the logician lived as a logician as contrasted with a historian living as a historian. The connection between the professional life of a teacher of a discipline and his personal life as a good man is tenuous at best.

But, if it were the case that it is necessary for a good teacher of a discipline to be a good man, there are further difficulties. It would mean that the good teacher would be professionally competent only if his character were exemplary. This places a moral or ethical demand on the teacher. There are at least two problems with placing such a requirement on the teacher: (1) determining the ethical ideal which is to be adopted and adhered to, and (2) determining a teacher's competence necessarily by reference to that moral idea. The first issue can be disposed of rather quickly by observing that it is obviously not clear what constitutes the good life. This issue is itself a nettle of philosophical problems extremely difficult to handle. If we demand that they be settled before we hire teachers, no teachers would be hired, and all formal education would rather quickly grind to a halt. Assuming, however, that the ethical issue has been settled, the implications of asserting that a teacher's competence must be assessed by reference to an ethical demand are far-reaching and highly undesirable. The competence of each teacher, whatever his discipline, would be open to scrutiny from the vantage point of a moral position. It would be reasonable to say that a teacher of logic is not a good teacher because he does not live according to Christian moral ideals. It has already been said that whether or not one adheres to a coherent moral position or has developed a thorough understanding of what it means to be a good man has no necessary relation to a man's competence as a teacher of logic or any other discipline. Indeed, Socrates himself would be judged to be a bad teacher if the moral ideals imposed are those of traditional Christianity. Further, such a requirement would, if imposed, halt the investigation of a free dissemination of controversial viewpoints. Involving oneself in controversy clearly outside the subject matter of his discipline may be legitimately ruled out. Such a ruling would be clearly within the spirit of the American Association of University Professors' 1940 statement on academic freedom.[18] The point is that if being a good teacher sometimes means the serious, scholarly investigation and discussion of controversial material within one's subject-matter area, and if such an investigation and discussion is inconsistent with or raises serious questions about the moral standard imposed, then the teacher's work can be stopped on the grounds of the moral standard. Indeed, if the teacher is compelled by the evidence gathered in the investigation to reject the moral standard, then the teacher by definition can no longer be a competent teacher. He does not meet the necessary conditions for being a good teacher simply because by the moral standard he is no longer a good man. Many teachers might find themselves back in the Renaissance facing the court along with Galileo or in Soviet Russia facing the people's court with Solzhenitsyn. This is tantamount to denying an essential dimension of academic freedom; imposing the moral ideal prohibits the legitimate search for knowledge and understanding and the open dissemination of knowledge. If the foregoing analysis is correct the kind of requirement Arrowsmith places on the university teacher is simply unacceptable.

CONCLUSION

Nevertheless, Arrowsmith's suggestion has a certain persuasiveness about it. No doubt a teacher can better motivate his students if he believes in what he teaches and acts on the same principles of rationality by which he expects his students to conduct themselves. Somehow the personal integrity of the teacher in the sense of deeds and words matching seems to be important for good teaching, at least good teaching in its widest sense. But if it is, we must do better than simply appeal to the Socratic model to help us understand what it means to be a good teacher. If the foregoing interpretation is correct, the Socratic model of the good teacher is not the one to follow to strengthen the humanities. I submit that the loss of humanistic education is not only the result of bad teaching but also of the kinds of institutions persons teach in and the goals of those institutions. Of this Arrowsmith is not totally unaware.[19]

Institutions do not, generally at least, outline their goals, and the ethical values they transmit are usually left undefined or, even worse, unnoticed. The result is that teachers are hired with little consideration of the quality of their lives. Universities emphasize the production of knowledge and pay little attention to the development of persons who are humane and liberal in their lives and conduct. If the only goal of the university is the "production of knowledge," then any placing of a moral requirement on the faculty seems ruled out. Arrowsmith is no doubt correct in his view that most universities have in practice accepted this as their only goal. Yet the answer to this is not to move to the opposite extreme and say that the only goal or even the primary goal of the university is the humane, liberal development of persons. Producing knowledge and vocational education are at least as important as producing good people. Rather, *both* moral education *and* discipline-oriented education are important. The problem in university education is not that they have espoused an incorrect goal. The university has failed because it has not, in addition to the goal of knowledge, committed itself to the goal of moral education. If both goals are adopted, then universities should seek persons who are not only competent in their disciplines but who are virtuous as well. The relation between knowledge within a discipline and human virtue is neither that of sufficiency nor necessity. If they are related, it is within the context of the goals of the university. There the teacher can learn and discuss with his students what he knows and understands about his discipline, about humane living, and the possible relations between them. The relation between theory and practice becomes a topic of investigation and discussion.

Until universities and colleges determine what they are trying to do, I submit that teachers will not be able to be evaluated in any other manner than by such means as the publish-or-perish criterion. If schools seeking the moral growth of students as well as the growth of knowledge would determine what ethical, humane goals they are teaching for, and if they would also accept the position that the achievement of such goals by students is effectively done by following exemplars, then these schools could legitimately demand of their teachers at least a minimal quality of life. This would enhance the possibility of the achievement of humanistic educational objectives. In this context the good teacher is one who meets two criteria: he is a rational, humane individual and he is competent in his field. Thus, if universities set humanistic as well as discipline-oriented goals and hire teachers who are committed to those goals, then humanistic education will have a new lease on life.

NOTES

1.   William Arrowsmith, "The Future of Teaching," in *Campus 1980*, ed by Alvin C. Eurich (New York: Dell, 1968), p. 117.

2   Ibid., pp. 116-133.

3.   Ibid., p. 119.

4.   Ibid., p. 121.

5.   Ibid., p. 119.

6.   *Laches*, 188-189.

7.   Ibid., 185d.

8.   Ibid., 186.

9.   Ibid., 187-188.

10.   Ibid., 188-189.

11.   *Euthydemus*, 282; *Meno*, 89.

12.   *Protagoras*, 354-358.

13.   *Meno*, 97B.

14.   *Symposium*, 215.

15.   Ibid.

16.   Ibid., 219-222.

17.   Norman Gulley, *The Philosophy of Socrates* (New York: St. Martin's Press, 1968), pp. 109-151.

18.   *American Association of University Professors Bulletin*, 61 (Sept. 1970):324-325.

19.   Cf. Arrowsmith, pp. 119-120.

Vocation Reconsidered:
Toward a Philosophy
of Postsecondary Education

Richard M. Millard

IN TWO OF THE more frequently quoted passages from *The Aims of Education* Whitehead suggests first that "education is the acquisition of the art of utilization of knowledge."[1] In the second passage he points out that "the antithesis between a technical and a liberal education is fallacious. There can be no adequate technical education which is not liberal, and no liberal education which does not impart both technique and intellectual vision."[2] Whitehead seems to be saying that in spite of identifiable differences in emphasis between what he called in *The Function of Reason*[3] the reason of Plato and the reason of Ulysses, there is an essential continuity between them and that either one divorced from the other becomes sterile. Thus, if education is in fact to be the acquisition of the art of the utilization of knowledge, it does need a focus or an aim that transcends and combines both technical and liberal education, both the reason of Plato and the reason of Ulysses in terms of the concrete individual acting, knowing, appreciating, developing, and growing in society.

In a fascinating way the Plato who is so frequently and correctly identified with the recognition of the importance of knowledge for its own sake, of contemplation of eternal ideas, was not so far from Whitehead as is sometimes supposed in his conception of the function of education. Even the philosopher-king who has grasped the eternal verities reaches this stage not only for contemplation but to return to the shadows of the cave and insure that ideas are translated into action in the just state. Plato's theory of education is an integral part of his theory of the just state and the just individual, and the emphasis throughout is upon effective realization of potentialities in complementation of each other in accordance with a practical life plan. Thus in describing justice in the *Republic* Plato says:

> Our principle that the born shoemaker should stick to his trade turns out to have been an adumbration of justice . . . but in reality justice is not a matter of external behavior, but of the inward self and of attending to all that is, in the fullest sense, a man's proper concern. The just man does not allow the several elements of his soul to usurp one another's functions; he is indeed one who sets his house in order, by self-mastery and discipline coming to be at peace with himself. . . . Only when he has . . . made himself one man instead of many, will he be ready to do whatever he may have to do.[4]

For Plato as we pointed out in *Personality and the Good*:

> The just society is that society which respects individual differences and makes possible the mutual complementation of life plans—both for the enrichment of each citizen and of society as a whole. Plato saw that an adequately formed life plan is not possible apart from societal orientation on the one hand and the objective assessment of individual capacities as available to individuals and society on the other.[5]

Plato was a firm believer in the concept of vocation as related to abilities; in fact, right vocation was so important that Plato was not willing to leave the determination up to individual inclination alone. Determination of vocation was integral to the whole educational process. Starting with primary education, the total educational process was devoted to the discovery of where abilities lie as these relate to educational accomplishments. Again, as pointed out in *Personality and the Good*, for Plato:

> Specialized education would be introduced at whatever level of educational proficiency any individual was able to benefit from it. In this way, coordination of life plan with abilities could

be assured. The famous myth of the metals, far from requiring a rigid caste system, aimed specifically at differentiation in the light of abilities.[6]

If anything, not Plato but the authors of *Personality and the Good*, while they had much to say about life plans, had far too little to say about vocation.

But what has all this to do with higher or postsecondary education in the United States today? This author, at least, would contend that it has a great deal to do with it and its problems in the current world. Higher education in the United States has undergone a rather fascinating evolution—an evolution that might well be characterized by the dual tensions of the Whiteheadian concepts of the reason of Plato and the reason of Ulysses. From its inception, and into the first half of the nineteenth century, it tended to be dominated by the classical British conception of education for gentlemen. The classical curriculum dominated, so much so that in 1828 the Yale faculty closed the Yale curriculum for all time against such modern and unscholarly intrusions as modern languages and the natural sciences. Yet even in the colonial colleges, in spite of the search for the eternal verities through classical modes, the practical could not be shut out. The early colleges were established not merely to educate gentlemen but to train clergymen, lawyers, and teachers. Regardless of their curricula their function was vocational. Insofar as a number of the colleges during the first part of the nineteenth century were founded by churches specifically with the training of clergy in mind, they could even be said to be vocationally oriented in the medieval sense.

The nineteenth century was not very far along, however, before a very different type of institution began to appear to meet a growing need, the need for teachers in the elementary and secondary schools. These institutions, the normal schools, started as public institutions by Horace Mann in Massachusetts in 1839, were designed to meet specific vocational needs. The curriculum was designed or adapted to serve these needs. Their products, first in New England and then across the country, were manning the school houses as the drive for universal and compulsory elementary and secondary education continued throughout the nineteenth century.

However, probably the single most important development in the nineteenth century in terms of the future development of higher education in this country was the passage in the midst of the Civil War of the Morrill Land-Grant Act in 1862. The Morrill Act set aside grants of land for the support or endowment of higher educational institutions to provide education in agriculture and the mechanical arts as well as liberal learning. These were to be the colleges for the sons and daughters of farmers and mechanics. The act was crucial in at least five respects: First, it expressed a national commitment to a utilitarian conception of post-high school education—a commitment that not only has not been abrogated but has been strengthened and specified in the twentieth century with increasing emphasis and federal as well as state support for occupational, technical and vocational education. Second, it served as an additional incentive to the states to develop over the next hundred years a system of major complex universities and university systems designed to meet the variety of needs of students and various communities within the states and nation. Third, although it was perhaps not fully realized at the time, it spelled the beginning of the end of any pretensions that there is a single body of knowledge that constitutes the subsistence of "higher learning" or a single standard of excellence that can be applied to all institutions, schools or programs. Fourth, it committed at least the land-grant institutions to public service as well as to instruction and research as an integral part of their total educational function. Finally, it marked the beginning of what was to become in the twentieth century something close to a national as well as state commitment to make access to postsecondary education something close to a right for any person interested and capable of benefiting from it regardless of economic or social background.

To be sure, not all of these implications became evident immediately. In fact during the last half of the nineteenth and the early years of the twentieth century many of the land-grant colleges struggled just to keep alive. Indeed, they were frequently looked down upon as "cow colleges" and not considered serious contenders by their considerably more prestigious eastern private counterparts.

The latter half of the nineteenth century witnessed the growing impact of German ideals of research and scholarship and the progressive development of graduate education. By the turn of the century, President Elliot had introduced the elective system at Harvard, and the Yale faculty resolution of 1828 was done for.

Both constitutionally and historically the responsibility for education has been state and local rather than federal. By the turn of the century most states had established public higher educational institutions. The opportunity for a high school education was extended theoretically to all children in the nineteenth century, in harmony with the Platonic pattern. The twentieth century, and particularly the last half of it, has seen post-high school educational opportunity extended to a progressively wider range of citizens. While it would not be correct even today to say that postsecondary educational opportunity is available to all citizens interested and capable of benefiting from it, this is at least a goal which is being progressively more closely approximated.

A number of factors have contributed to the approach towards this goal of equality of postsecondary educational opportunity. The first has been the growing conviction, at least until relatively recently on the part of the general public and their legislative representatives, that some form of postsecondary education for most citizens is essential in a highly complex technological society. Along with this has come the increased recognition on the part of parents and their children that postsecondary education is the key to social mobility. The states in particular have responded to such public recognition through progressive expansion of public higher and postsecondary education systems. Until close to the middle of the twentieth century private higher educational institutions dominated the higher educational scene, but by mid-century public higher educational institution enrollments began to surpass private enrollments. Currently seventy-five percent of higher educational enrollments are in public institutions.

The move towards egalitarianism and universal access received major reinforcement as a result of the G.I. Bill at the end of World War II. If any doubt remained that higher education should be for the privileged few, the impact of the G.I. Bill laid it to rest. The record of the veterans was most impressive, and even the more conservative members of faculties who grumbled about possible dilution of quality were impressed by the seriousness and determination of the returning veterans in their pursuit of education. One very important aspect of the bill which perhaps did not receive as much attention from the academic community as it should have as a portent of things to come was the fact that it did not limit postsecondary educational opportunity for veterans to traditional higher educational institutions. The benefits were available for use at proprietary institutions, technical and occupational programs, apprenticeship programs—in fact, all reasonable forms of post-high school education.

Federal concern with post-high school education in skills immediately applicable in the world of work dates, as noted, from the Morrill Act of 1862. Introduction of vocational training in secondary schools began before the turn of the century. John Dewey, among others, attempted without notable success to keep vocational education as an integral part of the regular high school curriculum. In 1915 he argued: "The democracy which proclaims equality of opportunity as its ideal requires an education in which learning and social application, ideas, practice, work and recognition of the meaning of what is done, are unified from the beginning and for all."[7]

Unfortunately the traditionalists who questioned whether vocational training should even be a part of "formal schooling" won the day. As a result, too frequently vocational education was relegated to "trade schools" for students who could not quite make it in college preparatory programs. Vocational education tended to be looked at as a second-class kind of education, and vocational educators in reaction tended to develop their own defensive orthodoxies.[8]

The continuing federal concern for expanded vocational education was expressed during World War I in the Smith-Hughes Act, during World War II in the George-Barden Act, and most strikingly in the Vocational Education Act of 1963 followed by the Amendments of 1968. In the sixties particularly, the states reinforced by the federal government developed state systems of vocational education with area vocational schools and technical institutes offering thirteenth and fourteenth-year work—some offering associate degrees.

The later 1950s through the 1960s was the greatest period of expansion of postsecondary and higher education in the history of the country. Enrollments in higher educational institutions alone jumped from 3,789,000 in 1960 to 8,581,000 in 1970, an increase of 126 percent. While most institutions expanded, the public institutions expanded at a far more rapid rate than the private ones. State expenditures for higher education rose from $4,540,000,000 in 1960 to $13,920,000,000 in 1970, an increase of 207 percent. More than 400 new campuses were created by the states bringing the total number of state institutions to 1,089.[9]

One of the most important and fascinating developments was the emergence of comprehensive community colleges. While junior colleges primarily designed to offer the first two years of college go back to the early part of the century, the comprehensive community colleges offering a wide variety of occupational as well as liberal arts courses, closely related to their local communities and in most states partially supported by local tax funds, were a new development. If the Land-Grant colleges brought diversification of opportunity on the state level, the community colleges brought diversification and utilitarian as well as liberal education to the local level on a commuting basis. These community colleges grew and continue to grow at a phenomenal rate; by the end of the decade they enrolled some 2 million students, a quarter of all students in higher educational institutions.

With the rapid expansion of the sixties the states more clearly than the institutions became aware of the necessity of effective statewide planning for higher and postsecondary education. Some order, direction, and coordination were essential if the higher and postsecondary educational needs of the states and nation were to be met, if public funds were to be expended wisely, and if the end product was to be reasonable diversification and extension of opportunity instead of the chaos of competing but essentially similar institutions.

Jencks and Reissman in *The Academic Revolution*[10] documented in some detail the net effect of the pressure of increasing enrollments on the tendency of institutions to become progressively more selective and to adopt a misguided kind of "meritocracy" as a goal. Institutions tended to be ranked not by what happened to students while in college but by how selective they were in admissions. Using the "university college" model—how many graduates went on to prestigious graduate schools—as their goal, institutions tended to become, if not more alike, at least pale copies of each other. Instead of a healthy pluralism of complementary institutions serving different purposes, the higher educational picture among senior institutions verged more on an atomism, with atoms of different sizes duplicating or attempting to duplicate each other. It was this and not state planning and coordination, as is sometimes charged, that led to the kind of homogenization that probably had more than a little to do with the student unrest of the sixties.

In part to counteract such homogenization, in part and perhaps primarily to insure orderly growth and diversification, and, as noted, in part to encourage effective use of public funds in meeting higher and postsecondary educational needs, states in the sixties rapidly developed state higher or postsecondary education coordinating or governing boards or agencies charged, among other things, with responsibility for statewide planning. While the oldest of such state agencies, The New York State Board of Regents, goes back to colonial times and fifteen other boards were in existence before 1960, by the end of the decade forty-seven states had developed such agencies. These agencies vary considerably in scope, in power, and in type of institutions under their purview. Currently some twenty agencies are governing agencies and twenty-seven are coordinating agencies. In most cases their primary concern is with public higher educational institutions, but some also have some responsibility for including private institutions in the planning process, and in a few cases they also have peripheral responsibility for proprietary institutions. If anything, the trend since 1960 has been to strengthen such agencies. In no case has a coordinating board or agency been replaced by a return to institutional laissez faire. The states seem clearly to have recognized and accepted the responsibility for developing and expanding postsecondary and higher educational opportunity by design in contrast to random unplanned growth.

During the major period of expansion the federal position in relation to postsecondary and higher education also changed radically. From 1958 (post Sputnik) until 1972 more federal legislation affecting higher and postsecondary education has been enacted than in the entire previous history of the country. Following the National Defense Education Act of 1958 came such landmark pieces of legislation as the Higher Education Facilities Act of 1963, the Vocational Education Act of 1963, the Comprehensive Higher Education Act of 1965, the Education Professions Development Act and a series of health education acts. While it could not be said that there was or is a coherent national higher education policy, the federal government did make major funds available for everything from research to a complex of student aids. Most of the federal programs were and are categorical in nature, designed to meet specific federally identified needs. Further, most but not all of the programs involved direct federal institutional relationships without direct coordination with and through the states. One thing that did appear, however, as a rather clear national policy or at least a national goal enunciated by Presidents Johnson and Nixon by the end of the decade was the principle that no student should be barred from postsecondary education by economic or social barriers.

Potentially the most far-reaching piece of federal legislation affecting higher and postsecondary education to be enacted is the recent Education Amendments of 1972 which replaced the Higher Education Act of 1965. It comes closer to defining national postsecondary educational policy than any of its predecessors. Unlike its predecessors it clearly addresses itself not merely to higher education in the traditional sense but to the range of postsecondary education, public, private and proprietary. In the new Basic Education Opportunities Grant Program it establishes the concept of entitlement of all interested and capable citizens to some form of postsecondary education. It recognizes for the first time the role of the states in comprehensive planning for post-secondary education. It provides for strengthening community college and postsecondary occupational education, and it recognizes that planning and expansion in either of these areas cannot be done in isolation but must be done by the states taking into account the range of post-secondary education. It provides for institutional support grants tied to institutional cooperation in furthering the national goal of extending postsecondary educational opportunity to economically disadvantaged students. It also recognizes and reinforces the major contribution the states are making in student aid through federal matching funds for the states. It moves, in other words, a long way toward developing an effective state-federal-institutional partnership. While much of this act has not been implemented to date due to the current Administration's unwillingness to follow through congressional mandates, the impact of the Act in terms of broadening the scope of postsecondary education policy and planning already has been widespread.

In spite of the developments of the last decade—the unprecedented expansion of higher and postsecondary education, the development of statewide planning, the infusion of federal funds, the extension of access to progressively wider groups of students, and the recognition of the range of postsecondary education—higher and postsecondary education are today faced with crises of major proportions. While the student unrest of the sixties and early seventies has abated, it has left its mark in reduced public confidence, at least in traditional higher education. Even though the unrest may have had its primary origins in social issues and national policies beyond the control or responsibility of campuses, it raised fundamental questions of relevance, direction and purpose of higher education in current society. The demands for innovation and change have become more insistent, frequently without very clear conceptions of change to what or why. Rising costs without increased productivity have complicated the picture. While all institutions have felt the growing financial pinch, the private institutions with constantly increasing tuitions have felt it most, and the question for some has become one of survival itself.

The period of continuing expansion, at least in terms of the traditional college age student population, is over. While the peak population of 18 to 21-year-olds will not be reached until the late seventies, percentages of that age group going to college, particularly among males, are dropping. From the late seventies at least until the end of the century the actual population of eighteen to twenty-one-year-olds will continue to decrease. Yet, while the enrollment pinch is already being felt in senior institutions, enrollments in proprietary schools, community colleges and vocational-technical institutes continues to increase.

In the meantime not only state governments but the federal government (see the report of the National Commission on the Financing of Postsecondary Education)[11] and private donors are insisting on greater accountability in the use of funds both public and private.

To help preserve the viability of private institutions, some thirty-six states have made public funds in some form available to private institutions. The accountability extends not only to fiscal accountability but to how effectively funds are being used to accomplish educational goals.

At the same time that prospects for increased traditional college-age students are diminishing, the interest of adults in additional forms of education, in forms of lifelong learning, are increasing. The Commission on Nontraditional Study estimates that in 1972 alone some 32.1 million adults were actually involved in additional education of some form and an additional 79.8 million expressed interest in continuing their education if opportunity were available.[12] Given tight budgets, decreasing enrollments of traditional college-age students, and the potential educational market for adults, without clear development of goals and effective planning we could in the next few years be faced with the most intense kind of interinstitutional competition for survival imaginable. The end result of such unlimited competition could be not only the Hobbesian warfare of all against all but the further eroding of public confidence and a continuing tendency of institutions to become more alike rather than more effectively diversified to meet the varieties of postsecondary educational needs.

It is in this context that we need to return to the question of goals or aims of postsecondary education. We need to find a key to effective institutional differentiation and statewide and institutional planning. Robert Nisbet in *The Degradation of Academic Dogma*[13] has suggested that the only solution to reestablishing the integrity of higher education is to reject as major goals public service and applied research and return to what he considers the goal of the medieval universities of the pure search for knowledge and its transmission. He tends to overlook the fact that given the evolution towards egalitarianism, towards making postsecondary educational opportunity progressively available to all citizens who desire and can benefit from it, we cannot return to an elitist conception of the function of higher education which by the nature of the case would exclude large numbers of students with postsecondary educational needs. Granted that the search for knowledge is central to postsecondary education, that search has many forms and many applications. Postsecondary education today is so central to the various functionings of society that it cannot withdraw into an ivory tower without undermining itself and weakening society immeasurably. Second, he overlooks the fact that the medieval universities were not all that "pure." Their aim was vocational and the aim of their students was social mobility, as restricted as that mobility was.

What we need to identify is the kind of aim or goal that will avoid the Scylla of institutional atomism on the one hand and the Charybdis of organicism on the other. It should be a goal in the light of which functional differentiation could take place at the same time that one preserves sufficient institutional autonomy or leeway to preserve integrity in meeting specific institutional goals. It needs to be the kind of goal which insures complementation of efforts rather than conflict and yet recognizes the inherent differences between complex universities and proprietary vocational schools, but which does so in such a way as to create no second-class citizens or institutions and links the community of postsecondary educational institutions together in serving citizen, state and national interests. It should be the kind of goal which gives not just a clue but a direction to planning on institutional, statewide and national levels and at the same time gives focus to instruction, research and public service. Finally, it should be a goal that recognizes individual differences in interests, abilities and development among potential students of all ages as persons.

It seems to me that the clue to such a goal does lie in the quotations from Plato, Whitehead, and *Personality and the Good* with which we started. From this viewpoint, the fundamental aim of education is vocation conceived of in the broadest sense as involvement in and preparation for life work, life plan, life style, even "calling" in the older theological sense. This means taking Whitehead seriously in his insistence that the question of education is not just a question of the acquisition of knowledge but also of the art of utilization of knowledge. It means that with Plato we should recognize that education should be adapted to a variety of needs and abilities and should be the instrument through which individuals discover what their needs, abilities, and interests are. By putting vocation, or involvement in and preparation for vocation, back as the critical aim of education a number of things begin to fall into perspective, and some of the artificial distinctions and dichotomies begin to disappear.

To begin with, to recognize that the central aim of education is vocation suggests equal involvement in vocational or occupational education whether one chooses the life of a sociologist or an accountant, a lawyer or an auto mechanic, a doctor, a nurse or an inhalation therapist, an engineer or an electronics technician, a stockbroker or a secretary, a philosopher or a building contractor. It does not invalidate other aims of education such as social development, personal enlightenment, exploration of the realms of knowledge, even search for identity, but it does give them focus and direction. It recognizes the organic relations of vocations to each other in society, and it does away with invidious comparisons, such as the pseudo-elitism that separates blue-collar workers from white-collar workers, the scholar or the research scientist from the business man, professionals from technicians, and recognizes that all are or should be engaged in finding the most effective way to utilize and develop abilities in a changing society for mutual advantage.

The individual vocation so conceived makes concrete the principle of the most inclusive end with its emphasis upon life plan, provides a continuing yet flexible context for what Dr. Bertocci calls orchestrating the symphony of values, and through the society of vocations and their mutual yet shifting complementation provides the social context for harmonizing the principles of individualism and altruism. It should be clear that vocation in this sense is not static but developing, even changing, with new experiential content and shifting social context. It embodies the constantly expanding, ever retreating ideal of the principle of the best possible. Again, it includes life work as one component; but life style, life plan, and what might be described as life attitude are integral to it. It calls, in Plato's words, for "one who sets his house in order, by self-mastery and discipline coming to be at peace with himself. ... Only when he has ... made himself one man instead of many, will he be ready to do whatever he may have to do."[14]

Utilizing then the concept of vocation, the art of the utilization of knowledge means that education is a lifelong concern and "college age" is not and should not be considered eighteen to twenty-one years of age or any other single set of years. Lifelong learning in the light of changing circumstances should be the essential characteristic of education. Even the divisions between secondary and postsecondary education are at best arbitrary if not artificial. Articulation of the various levels and types of education to assure continuity becomes even more critical than frequently realized. We should accept as normal, even as fundamental, the desirability of dropping in and stopping out, of the rhythm of alternation between education and other areas of experience.

As far as the educational system is concerned, recognition of vocation or career as central does away with the invidious comparisons between and among institutions and programs. As the author has pointed out elsewhere:

> It calls for the kind of diversified educational system which will in fact provide the range of opportunities commensurate with human interests and needs and societal demands. It means that the full range of education from kindergarten through graduate school and continuing education is not a babysitting operation, or a dodge to keep people off the streets or the labor market, but is concerned with the vital business of societal renewal and development.[15]

To this should be added individual renewal and development as essential to societal renewal and development.

Such a concept of education not only fits in with the egalitarian and utilitarian evolution of postsecondary education in this country but reinforces the national goals of increased access and choice for all persons who can benefit from postsecondary education. Further, it is a thoroughly pluralistic concept that calls in turn for the recognition of a series of pluralisms and of an organic relation among them.

The first pluralism is the pluralism of vocations, their legitimacies and the societal and manpower needs for them ranging from cosmetologists and data processors to auto mechanics, sanitary engineers, research scholars, biologists, Old English scholars and clergymen.

The second pluralism is the pluralism and diversity of individuals with their interests, abilities, and backgrounds. To make vocation the central aim of education does not mean forcing individuals into particular stations and their duties, but rather opening up the process of discovery in developing abilities, interests, and concerns and helping individuals to structure these in such a way that vocation capitalizes on these, actualizes them, and is not something imposed on individuals from without. If opportunity is to be more than a shibboleth, doors must be open to the kinds of vocational educational opportunities commensurate with individual interests, needs, and backgrounds. Availability of effective counseling throughout the educational process becomes crucial.

The third pluralism is the pluralism of institutions, programs, and agencies essential to the real diversity necessary to meet human, societal and occupational needs. The time seems clearly past, if it ever existed, when any one institution or program can be all things to all people. The plurality of educational opportunities today cannot and should not be limited to traditional schools or higher educational institutions but extended to business, industry, communities, political structures and social agencies.

The fourth pluralism is the pluralism of the fields of knowledge and their relevance for the range of careers conceived of as life styles or life plans, not just as jobs. The aim again is to open doors, not close them. "In the context of 'vocation' the arts and sciences may be as integral to the life of the dental technician as the knowledge of mechanics may be to the budding philosopher."[16]

The fifth pluralism is a genuine pluralism of standards related to program and institutional excellence. The kind of egalitarianism, of extension of opportunity, of emphasis upon vocation we are concerned with does not involve abandonment of standards or their dilution. It clearly involves recognition of a concept of standards not unrelated to the Aristotelian concept of the *entelechy*, that is, that the standards for different programs and institutions must be related to particular programs and their aims. One can and should demand excellence in all education, but the criterion of excellence is not the "university college" or any other single model. The standard of excellence must be indigenous to the program: to expect a community college to be a research university is not only nonsense but extraordinarily dangerous nonsense. Somehow the community college is looked down upon because it is not a research university; such differentiation or definition of excellences applies to the different programs in the community college as well. To judge a faculty in auto mechanics on the basis of credentials devised for mathematics serves neither mathematics, auto mechanics, students, nor society. To carry the matter one step further, for all institutions, programs, and systems involved in vocational or career education in this broad sense, this points to the urgent need for achievement standards related to differential functions and purposes rather than pseudo-quantitative measures of the forms of the process. No institution should be judged by whom it admits or how many it eliminates but by what it does to and for students when they are there—how well, in other words, it succeeds in opening doors.

Finally, the concept of vocation as the central aim of education and the various pluralisms involved, including the pluralism of standards, also calls for the recognition of the essential importance of comprehensive planning and real rather than token interinstitutional cooperation and complementation. Such planning, particularly on the statewide level, should involve all types of institutions and should be designed to insure their real plurality and diversity. Without such planning pluralism, as already noted, too easily becomes an atomism and the old internecine warfare of institutions and systems of institutions is too easily reinstituted. Further, such planning cannot be simply the sum of individual institutional plans. If we are to avoid needless duplication, if we are to insure effective diversification, if we are to approximate meeting the various needs of students of all ages and the manpower needs of society, the state has an obligation to support and reinforce effective comprehensive planning for the range of education. But to be effective such planning must be done with the cooperation and full involvement of the systems, institutions and agencies concerned. On such cooperation may well depend the future development, the institutional integrity, and the very functional autonomy and leeway necessary for experimentation within systems, institutions, and programs themselves for the years ahead.

If, as this author believes, adequate and diversified education is the essential condition of a free and democratic society, and if such a society is an organic pluralism of persons in mutual interaction but with different interests, abilities, and potentialities, then the return to vocation as the central aim of education—the vocations not of every man but of each person in interaction with others—may well be the minimum condition of our survival as a free society.

NOTES

1. A. N. Whitehead, *The Aims of Education* (London: Williams and Norgate, 1932), p. 6.
2. Ibid., p. 74.
3. A. N. Whitehead, *The Function of Reason* (Boston: Beacon Hill Press, 1958), p. 37ff.
4. Plato, *Republic* IV, 443, trans. by F. M. Cornford (London: Oxford University Press, 1945), pp. 141-142.
5. Peter A. Bertocci and Richard M. Millard, *Personality and the Good* (New York: David McKay, 1963), p. 559.
6. Ibid., pp. 559-560.
7. John Dewey, *Schools for Tomorrow* (New York: Alfred A. Knopf, 1915), p. 143.
8. Cf. Louis W. Bender, *Articulation of Secondary and Postsecondary Occupational Education Programs* (Columbus, Ohio: ERIC Clearinghouse on Vocational and Technical Education, 1973), pp. 8-15.

9. Clark Kerr, "The Future of State Government–Higher Education Relationships," in *The Changing Face of Higher Education*, Proceedings of the 22nd Legislative Conference (Atlanta: Southern Regional Education Board, 1973), p. 33.

10. Christopher Jencks and David Reissman, *The Academic Revolution* (New York: Doubleday, 1968).

11 *Financing Postsecondary Education in the United States* (Washington, D.C.: National Commission on the Financing of Postsecondary Education, 1973).

12. Commission on Nontraditional Study, *Diversity by Design* (San Francisco: Jossey-Bass, 1973), pp. 16-17.

13. Robert Nisbet, *The Degradation of Academic Dogma* (New York: Basic Books, 1971); see pp. 24-47.

14. Plato, loc. cit.

15. R. M. Millard, *Vocation: Central Aim of Education* (Iowa City, Iowa: American College Testing Program, 1973), p. 5.

16. Ibid.

Bibliography
of Peter Anthony Bertocci

BOOKS

The Empirical Argument for God in Late British Thought. Cambridge, Mass.: Harvard University Press, 1938. Reprint. New York: Kraus Reprints, 1970.

The Human Venture in Sex, Love and Marriage. New York: Association Press, 1949.

Introduction to the Philosophy of Religion. Englewood Cliffs, N.J.: Prentice-Hall, 1951.

Free Will, Responsibility and Grace. New York: Abingdon Press, 1957.

Person and Reality by Edgar S. Brightman. Edited with Jannette E. Newhall and Robert S. Brightman. New York: Ronald Press, 1958.

Religion as Creative Insecurity. New York: Association Press, 1958. Reprint. Westport, Conn.: Greenwood Press, 1973.

Why Believe in God? New York: Association Press, 1963.

Personality and The Good: Psychological and Ethical Perspectives. With Richard M. Millard. New York: David McKay, 1963.

Sex, Love, and the Person. New York: Nelson, 1971.

The Person God Is. London: Allen & Unwin, 1970.

Is God For Real? New York: Sheed and Ward, 1971.

Mid-Twentieth Century American Philosophy: Personal Statements (editor). New York: Humanities Press, 1973.

ARTICLES

1936

"The Authority of Ethical Ideals." *Journal of Philosophy* 33 (May 1936):269-274.

1937

"We Send Them to College—To Be Confused." *Journal of Higher Education* 8 (Oct. 1937):343-350.

1938

"An Empirical Critique of the Moral Argument for God." *Journal of Religion* 18 (July 1938):275-288.

"The Perplexing Faith of a Moralist." *Review of Religion* 3 (Nov. 1938):38-51.

"Is Wieman Empirical Enough?" *The Personalist* 19 (Winter 1938): 56-67.

1939

"Comments and Criticism: Concerning Empirical Philosophy." *Journal of Philosophy* 36 (1939):263-269.

"Tennant's Critique of Religious Experience." *Religion in Life* 8 (1939):248-259.

1940

"A Critique of G. W. Allport's Theory of Motivation." *Psychological Review* 47 (1940):501-532. Later appeared in *Understanding Human Motivation,* edited by C. L. Stacey and M. F. DeMartino, pp. 82-105. Cleveland: Howard Allen, Inc., 1958. Appearing in the same volume: "Motivation in Personality: Reply to Peter A. Bertocci," by Gordon W. Allport, pp. 105-120.

"Sentiments and Attitudes." *Journal of Social Psychology* 11 (May 1940):245-257.

1941

"The Focus of Religious Education." *Religion in Life* 10 (1941): 54-63.

1942

"The Man Neglected by Science and Education." *Crozer Quarterly* 19 (1942):209-217.

"A Critique of Professor Cantril's Theory of Motivation." *Psychological Review* 49 (July 1942):365-385.

"The Personal and Social Roots of Democracy." *The Personalist* 23 (Summer 1942):253-266.

1943

"Macintosh's Theory of Natural Knowledge." *Journal of Religion* 23 (July 1943):164-172.

1944

"The Crucible of Religion and the Pastoral Function." *Crozer Quarterly* 21 (1944):25-29.

"An Analysis of Macintosh's Theory of Religious Knowledge." *Journal of Religion* 24 (Jan. 1944):42-55.

"Faith and Reason: The Implications of Dr. Ferre's View." *Review of Religion* 8 (May 1944):359-369.

"The Moral Outlook of the Adolescent in War Time." *Mental Hygiene* 28 (July 1944):353-367.

1945

"The Psychological Self, the Ego, and Personality." *Psychological Review* 52 (1945):91-99. Also appeared in *Understanding Human Motivation,* edited by C. L. Stacey and M. F. DeMartino, pp. 174-183. Cleveland: Howard Allen, 1958. Later appeared in *The Self in Growth, Teaching and Learning,* edited by Donald E. Hamachek. Englewood Cliffs, N.J.: Prentice-Hall, 1965.

"A Reinterpretation of Moral Obligation." *Philosophy and Phenomenological Research* 6 (Dec. 1945):270-282.

In *An Encyclopedia of Religion,* edited by Vergilius Ferm. Paterson, N.J.: Littlefield, Adams & Co., 1945. The following articles:
    "Attributes of God," p. 45.
    "Bruno, Giordano," p. 90.
    "Conservation of Value," p. 198.
    "Creation," p. 207.
    "Creationism," p. 207.
    "Datum," p. 217.
    "Immanence," p. 359.
    "Immediacy," pp. 359-360.
    "Leibniz, Gottfried Wilhelm," p. 439.
    "Lotze, Rudolf Herman," p. 453.
    "Martineau, James," p. 473.
    "Monadism or monadology," p. 502.
    "Panpsychism," p. 557.
    "Pringle-Pattison, Andrew Seth," pp. 609-610.
    "Realism, moral," p. 636.
    "Religious datum," p. 647.
    "Santayana, George," p. 688.
    "Sorley, William Ritchie," p. 727.
    "Taylor, Alfred Edward," p. 762.
    "Temporality of God," p. 772.
    "Tennant, Frederick Robert," p. 772.
    "Ward, James," p. 818.

1946

"Personality." In *Encyclopedia of Psychology,* edited by P. L. Harriman, pp. 455-477. New York: Philosophical Library, 1946.

"The Logic of Naturalistic Arguments Against Theistic Hypotheses." Abstract. *Journal of Philosophy* 43 (1946):71.

"On Relevance in Philosophical Teaching." *Journal of Higher Education* 17 (Feb. 1946):82-86.

"William James' Psychology of Will: An Evaluation." *Philosophical Forum* 4 (1946):2-13.

1947

"The Logic of Naturalistic Arguments Against Theistic Hypotheses." *Philosophical Review* 56 (1947):82-87.

1948

"A Sixth Conception of Christian Strategy." *Christendom* 13 (No. 1, 1948):45-55, 57-58.

"Problems of Philosophy." In *College Reading and Religion*, pp. 28-79. New Haven: Yale University Press, 1948.

1949

"Spiritual Summons of Marriage." *National Parent-Teacher* 43 (Feb. 1949):30-32.

1950

"Brightman's View of the Self, the Person, and the Body." *Philosophical Forum* 8 (1950):21-28.

1952

"Fullbright Scholar in Italy." *Boston University Graduate Journal* 1 (1952):57-59.

"Ramsey's *Basic Christian Ethics*: A Critique." *Crozer Quarterly* 29 (Jan. 1952):24-38.

1953

"Toward a Christian View of Sex Education." *Pastoral Psychology* 4 (Feb. 1953):47-54. Later appeared as a chapter in *Sex and Religion Today,* edited by Simon Doninger. New York: Association Press, 1954.

"Edgar Sheffield Brightman, 1884-1953." *Bostonia* 26 (July 1953): 15-17.

"Edgar Sheffield Brightman." *The Personalist* 34 (Oct. 1953):358-360.

Facing the Facts about Sex. Booklet. New York: Association Press, 1953.

1954

"The Nature of Cognition." *Review of Metaphysics* 8 (1954):49-60.

"Edgar Sheffield Brightman, Through His Students' Eyes." With M. Alicia Corea. *Philosophical Forum* 12 (1954):53-67.

"Edgar Sheffield Brightman." *Philosophical Forum* 12 (1954):92-94.

"Religious Diversity and American Education." *School and Society* 80 (August 21, 1954):55-56.

"Gordon W. Allport's *The Nature of Prejudice* and the Problem of Choice." *Pastoral Psychology* 5 (Nov. 1954):31-37.

1955

"The Juncture Between Creative Arts and Creative Science." *Main Currents in Modern Thought* 11 (Jan. 1955):51. (Later reproduced in *The Braille Star Theosophist* (Jan., Feb., 1957).

"Philosophy as Wisdom." *Boston University Graduate Journal* 4 (Sept. 1955):5-7.

"Bases for Developing Religious Community." In *Crucial Issues in Education,* edited by Henry J. Ehlers, pp. 124-130. New York: Holt, 1955.

1956

"Is God a Fool?" *Motive* 4 (Jan. 1956):7-8, 27-29.

"Marriage Demands Maturity." *Christian Action* 11 (Jan., Feb., March 1956):1-5.

"A Vacuum in Educational Theory." *School and Society* 82 (Feb. 18, 1956):59-61. Later appeared in *Boston University Graduate Journal* (April 1956), and in translation, with some changes, in the Greek journal, *Deltion.*

"Unless Educators Be Philosophers, and Philosophers Be Educators . . ." *Harvard Educational Review* 26 (Spring 1956):158-161.

"What Makes a Philosophy Christian? A Liberal Speaks." *Christian Scholar* 39 (June 1956):102-112.

"Credo for CP." (Letter.) *Contemporary Psychology* 1 (July 1956): 222.

"The Person as the Key Metaphysical Principle." *Philosophy and Phenomenological Research* 17 (Dec. 1956):158-161.

1957

"Is an Existentialist Christian Approach to Sex Adequate?" *Pastoral Psychology* 8 (March 1957):15-27.

"Comment on 'What Can Philosophy of Religion Accomplish?' by Horace L. Friess." *Review of Religion* 21 (March 1957):145-155.

"Can the Goodness of God Be Empirically Grounded?" *Journal of Bible and Religion* 25 (April 1957):99-105.

"Free Will, Responsibility and Grace." *Faculty Forum* (May 1957):1-2.

"Croce's Aesthetics in Context." *The Personalist* 38 (Summer 1957): 248-259.

"Is a Humanistic Grounding of Democracy Adequate?" *Religion in Life* 26 (Autumn 1957):550-559.

"What It Means to Be Human—And a College Student." In *The Responsible Student.* Booklet. Nashville: Methodist Student Movement, 1957.

1958

"Does the Concept of Christian Love Add Anything to Moral Philosophy?" *Journal of Religion* 38 (Jan. 1958):1-11.

"Toward a Clarification of the Christian Doctrine of Grace and the Moral Life." *Journal of Religion* 38 (April 1958):85-94.

"The Goodness of God and Two Conceptions of Value Objectivity." *Journal of Bible and Religion* 26 (July 1958):232-240.

"Philosophy and the Philosophy of Education." With Richard M. Millard. *Journal of Education* 141 (Oct. 1958):7-13.

1959

"The Person, Obligation and Value." *The Personalist* 40 (Spring 1959): 141-151.

"What Makes a Christian Home." *Christian Century* 76 (May 7, 1959): 544-546.

"Personalism versus Naturalism." A Reply to an Address by Henry N. Wieman. Mimeographed. May, 1959.

1960

Education and the Vision of Excellence. University Lecture, delivered on March 23, 1960. Booklet. Boston: Boston University Press, 1960.

"Borden Parker Bowne: Philosophical Theologian and Personalist." *Religion in Life* 29 (Autumn 1960):587-591.

"The Renaissance of Bowne: A Symposium." With Richard M. Millard, John H. Lavely, and Walter Muelder. *Bostonia* 34 (Fall 1960):23-27.

1961

"The Moral Structure of the Person." *Review of Metaphysics* 14 (March 1961):369-388.

"Edgar Sheffield Brightman." *Bostonia* 35 (Summer 1961):28.

"Tagore." *Religion in Life* 30 (Autumn 1961):555-561.

1962

"In Defense of Metaphysical Creation." *Philosophical Forum* 19 (May 1962):3-15.

"A New Area of Concentration for Women?" *Boston University Graduate Journal* 10 (June 1962):143-150.

"A Temporalistic View of Mind." In *Theories of Mind,* edited by Gordon M. Schere, pp. 398-421. New York: Free Press, 1962.

"God: Creator and Redeemer." *Workers with Youth* 15 (Aug. 1962): 2-5.

"The Logic of Creationism, Advaita, and Visistadvaita: A Critique." In *Essays in Philosophy,* edited by C. T. K. Chari for presentation to Dr. T. M. P. Mahadevan, pp. 26-42. Madras: Ganesh & Co., 1962.

"Three Visions of Perfection and Human Freedom." *Psychologia* 5 (1962):59-67.

"The 'Self' in Recent Psychology of Personality." (Abstract.) *Journal of Philosophy* 59 (1962):685.

1963

"Of Pattern and Purpose." *Christian Century* 80 (Jan. 9, 1963):50.

"Edgar S. Brightman—Ten Years Later." *Philosophical Forum* 20 (May 1963):3-10.

"The Person, the Ego, and Personality in the Light of Recent Psychology." In *The Problem of Man,* vol. 3, pp. 43-58. Memorias del XIII Congresso Internacional de Filosofia. Mexico City: Universidad Nacional Autónoma de México, 1963.

"Mind." In *The Encyclopedia of Mental Health,* edited by Albert Deutsch, vol. 4, pp. 1231-1234. New York: Franklin Watts, 1963.

"Personalism: Borden Parker Bowne." In *Masterpieces of Christian Literature,* edited by Frank N. Magill, vol. 2, pp. 851-856. New York: Salem Press, 1963.

1964

"Extramarital Sex and the Pill." *Christian Century* 81 (Feb. 26, 1964): 267-270.

"The 'Self' in Recent Psychology of Personality: A Philosophical Critique." *Philosophical Forum* 21 (June 1964):19-31.

"Toward a Metaphysics of Creation." *Review of Metaphysics* 17 (1964):493-510.

"Foundations of Personalistic Psychology." In *Scientific Psychology,* edited by Benjamin B. Wolman and Ernest Nagel, pp. 293-316. New York: Basic Books, 1964.

"Interrogations." Questions asked of Brand Blanshard, Martin Buber, Charles Hartshorne, and Paul Tillich. In *Philosophical Interrogations,* edited by Sydney and Beatrice Rome. New York: Holt, Rinehart, and Winston, 1964.

1965

"Is There a *System* of Human Rights?" In *Proceedings of the Twenty-First Annual Meeting of the Philosophy of Education Society* (April 11-14, 1965), edited by Maxine Greene, pp. 53-68. Lawrence, Kansas: Ernest Bayles, 1965.

"Change and Creation: Reply to Dr. Frazier." *Philosophical Forum* 22 (May 1965):79-81.

"Values and Ethical Principles: Comment on Professor Reck's Review of *Personality and the Good.*" With Richard M. Millard. *Philosophical Forum* 22 (1965):82-86.

"Reply to Elmer Lear's Review of *Personality and the Good.*" With R. Millard. *Studies in Philosophy and Education* 4 (Spring 1965):62-65.

"Existential Phenomenology and Psychoanalysis." *Review of Meta physics* 28 (June 1965):629-646.

"An Impasse in Philosophical Theology." *International Philosophical Quarterly* 5 (Sept. 1965):379-396.

1966

"Free Will, the Creativity of God, and Order." In *Current Philosophical Issues,* edited by Frederick C. Dommeyer, pp. 213-235. Springfield, Ill.: Charles C. Thomas, 1966.

"The Co-responsive Community." In *The Knowledge Explosion,* edited by Francis Sweeney, pp. 49-60. The Centennial Colloquium at Boston College. New York: Farrar, Straus, and Giroux, 1966.

1967

"The Freedom to Be Free!" *Faculty Forum* 42 (Nov. 1967):1-3.

"The Cosmological Argument—Revisited and Revised." *Proceedings of The American Catholic Philosophical Association* 41 (March, 1967): 33-43.

"George Holmes Howison." In *The Encyclopedia of Philosophy,* edited by Paul Edwards, vol. 4, pp. 66. New York: Macmillan and Free Press, 1967.

"Borden Parker Bowne." In *The Encyclopedia of Philosophy,* edited by Paul Edwards, vol. 1, pp. 356-357. New York: Macmillan and Free Press, 1967. Also, "Borden Parker Bowne." *Enciclopedia Filosofica* (Turin).

1968

"Descartes and Marcel on the Person and His Body: A Critique." In *Proceedings of the Aristotelian Society,* n.s. vol. 68, pp. 207-226. London: Harrison & Sons, 1968.

1969

"Free Will, Creativity of God, and Order." In *East-West Studies on the Problem of the Self,* edited by P. T. Raju and Alburey Castell, pp. 44-60. The Hague: Martinus Nijhoff, 1969.

"The Person and His Body: A Critique of Existentialist Responses to Descartes." In *Cartesian Essays: A Collection of Critical Studies,* edited by Bernd Magnus and James B. Wilbur, pp. 116-144. The Hague: Martinus Nijhoff, 1969.

"The Person God Is." In *Talk of God,* edited by G. N. A. Vesey. Royal Institute of Philosophy Lectures, vol. 2, 1967/68, pp. 185-206. London: Macmillan, 1969.

"The Responsible University." *Comment* (distributed by the Boston University Christian Movement).

1970

"Susanne K. Langer's Theory of Feeling and Mind." *Review of Metaphysics* 23 (March 1970):527-551.

"The Perspective of a Teleological Personalist." In *Contemporary American Philosophy,* edited by John E. Smith, pp. 248-272. New York: Humanities Press, 1970.

"Creation in Religion." In *Dictionary of the History of Ideas,* edited by Philip P. Wiener, vol. 1, pp. 571-577. New York: Charles Scribners' Sons, 1970.

1971

"The Scholar, The Liberal Ideal, and Freedom." *Journal of Social Philosophy* 2 (Oct. 1971):13-17.

"Psychological Interpretations of Religious Experience." In *Research on Religious Developments*, edited by Merton P. Strommen, pp. 3-41. New York: Hawthorn Books, 1971.

"The Partners That Cannot Be Divorced: Psychology and Philosophy." *Psychologia* 14 (1971):148-152.

1972

"In Memoriam: Harold C. Case." Delivered at Marsh Chapel, Boston University, March, 1972.

"Hartshorne on Personal Identity: A Personalistic Critique." *Process Studies* 2 (Fall 1972):216-221.

1973

"Dynamic Interpersonalism and Personalistic Philosophy." In *Dynamic Interpersonalism for Ministry,* Essays in Honor of Paul E. Johnson, edited by Orlo Strunk. Nashville: Abingdon Press, 1973.

John Lukacs, *The Passing of the Modern Age, Philosophy Forum* 13 (1973):111-124.

"Man: Responsible Agent, Not Reactor!" Review article on Isidor Chein, *Science of Behavior and The Image of Man. Contemporary Psychology* 18 (July 1973):307-310.

"Is the Thomistic Bridge Strong Enough?" A reply to E. L. Mascall's "The Gulf in Modern Philosophy: Is Thomism the Bridge?" presented October 24, 1973 to the Boston Institute in the Philosophy of Religion and Philosophical Theology, Boston University.

1974

"A Life Good to Live: A Psycho-Ethical Perspective." *Military Chaplains' Review,* Winter, 1974, pp. 47-66.

"Creative Insecurity: A Style of Being-Becoming." *Humanitas* (Pittsburgh) 10 (May 1974):127-139.

Forthcoming Publications:

"Does Blanshard Escape Epistemic Dualism?" In *The Philosophy of Brand Blanshard,* vol. 16 of The Library of Living Philosophers, edited by Paul A. Schilpp. La Salle, Ill.: Open Court.

"Love and Reality in E. A. Burtt's Philosophy: A Personalistic Critique." To appear in *Idealistic Studies,* Sept. 1975.

Reviews

1941

W. Köhler, *The Place of Value in a World of Fact. Journal of Social Psychology* 13 (Feb. 1941):243-251.

Edgar S. Brightman, *A Philosophy of Religion. Review of Religion* 5 (1941):223-234.

1943

Edgar S. Brightman, ed., *Personalism in Theology. Journal of Bible and Religion* 11 (1943):174-175.

R. Kröner, *The Primacy of Faith. Crozer Quarterly* 20 (1943):355-356.

1944

L. Berman, *Behind the Universe. Crozer Quarterly* 21 (1944):181.

F. Künkel, *In Search of Maturity. Journal of Bible and Religion* 12 (1944):124-125.

1945

E. W. Lyman, *Religion and the Issues of Life. Crozer Quarterly* 22 (1945):84-85.

J. G. Johnson, *Highroads of the Universe. Religion in Life* 14 (Spring 1945):305-306.

1946

B. Blanshard, C. J. Ducasse, C. W. Hendel, A. E. Murphy, M. C. Otto, *Philosophy in American Education, Its Tasks and Opportunities. Harvard Educational Review* 16 (Spring 1946):116-127.

P. E. Johnson, *Psychology of Religion. Journal of Bible and Religion* 12 (1946):122-123.

A. P. McMahon, *Preface to an American Philosophy of Art. Philosophical Forum* 4 (Spring 1946):37-38.

R. Klibansky, *The Continuity of the Platonic Tradition During the Middle Ages. Philosophical Forum* 4 (1946):41-42.

W. A. Orton, *The Liberal Tradition. Religion in Life* 15 (Summer 1946): 453-454.

1947

R. T. Flewelling, *The Things that Matter Most. Journal of Bible and Religion* 15 (1947):107-108.

M. C. Nahm, *Aesthetic Experience and Its Presuppositions. Philosophical Forum* 5 (Spring 1947):43-44.

1948

J. C. Bennett, *Christian Ethics and Social Policy. Journal of Bible and Religion* 16 (Jan. 1948):56-57.

Book Notice of A. Gesell and F. Ilg, *The Child from Five to Ten.* *Journal of Bible and Religion* 16 (Jan. 1948):71.

B. E. Meland, *Seeds of Redemption. Journal of Bible and Religion* 16 (April 1948):120-121.

B. S. P. Morgan, *Skeptics Search for God. Journal of Bible and Religion* 16 (April 1948):125.

W. M. Allen, *The Realm of Personality. Journal of Bible and Religion* 16 (April 1948):56-57.

H. W. Schneider, *A History of American Philosophy,* and J. L. Blau, ed., *American Philosophic Addresses. Philosophical Forum* 16 (1948):28-29.

J. Maritain, *The Person and the Common Good. Journal of Bible and Religion* 16 (Oct. 1948):223.

R. Tsanoff, *Ethics. Journal of Bible and Religion* 16 (1948):224.

1949

C. Frankel, *The Faith of Reason. Crozer Quarterly* 26 (1949):70-71.

H. A. Reinhold, ed., *The Soul Afire. Journal of Bible and Religion* 17 (1949):152-153.

Jean-Paul Sartre, *The Emotions and the Psychology of Imagination. Philosophical Forum* 7 (1949):45-46.

1950

Book Notice of O. Karrer, ed., *St. Francis of Assisi. Journal of Bible and Religion* 19 (1950):106.

V. Ferm, *What Can We Believe? Philosophy and Phenomenological Research* 11 (June 1950):597-598.

D. L. Evans, *A Free Man's Faith. Philosophy and Phenomenological Research* 11 (Sept. 1950):124-125.

H. M. Kallen, *The Education of Free Men. Harvard Educational Review* 20 (Fall 1950):285-302.

J. Haroutunian, *Lust for Power. Crozer Quarterly* 27 (1950):255-257.

1951

H. A. Bosley, *A Firm Faith for Today. Crozer Quarterly* 28 (1951):168-169.

"Child's *Morals and Education:* A Review." *Harvard Educational Review* 21 (Fall 1951):203-219.

L. Harold DeWolf, *The Religious Revolt Against Reason. Review of Religion* 15 (1951):200-203.

1952

J. D. B. Hawkins, *The Essentials of Theism. The Journal of Bible and Religion* 20 (Jan. 1952):111-112.

A. W. Calhoun, *The Cultural Concept of Christianity. Crozer Quarterly* 29 (1952):70-71.

1953

A. C. Garnett, *The Moral Nature of Man. Journal of Bible and Religion* 21 (Jan. 1953):111-112.

1954

"Is Widgery's Conception of Philosophy of Religion Adequate?" Review article of A. G. Widgery, *What Is Religion? Journal of Bible and Religion* 22 (Jan. 1954):32-37.

R. Niebuhr, *Christian Realism and Political Problems. Religion in Life* 23 (Spring 1954):299-302.

H. C. Lindgren, *Effective Leadership in Human Relations. Pastoral Psychology* 5 (Dec. 1954):59-60.

1956

N. Micklem, *Fundamental Questions. Journal of Bible and Religion* 24 (Jan. 1956):58-61.

A. Stiernotte, *God and Space-Time. Philosophical Review* 65 (Jan. 1956):124-127.

W. G. Cole, *Sex in Christianity and Psychoanalysis. Contemporary Psychology* 1 (June 1956):181.

George F. Thomas, *Christian Ethics and Moral Philosophy. The Journal of Bible and Religion* 24 (July 1956):222-223.

D. S. Robinson, *Crucial Issues in Philosophy. Encounter* 17 (Summer 1956):298.

1957

J. A. Hutchison, *Faith, Reason, and Experience. Journal of Bible and Religion* 25 (Jan. 1957):51-52.

W. Hamilton, *The Christian Man. Journal of Bible and Religion* 25 (April 1957):164-165.

D. Jenkins, *Believing in God. Journal of Bible and Religion* 25 (April 1957):165-166.

1958

D. E. Trueblood, *Philosophy of Religion. Journal of Bible and Religion* 26 (Jan. 1958):60-63.

W. H. Clark, *The Psychology of Religion. Religion in Life* 28 (Winter 1958-59):129-130.

M. Buber, *Pointing the Way. Journal of Bible and Religion* 26 (July 1958):244-246.

1959

H. N. Wieman, *Man's Ultimate Commitment. Philosophical Forum* 16 (1958-59): 60-63.

N. O. Brown, *Life Against Death: The Psychoanalytical Meaning of History. Christian Century* 76 (June 24, 1959):750-751.

Seward Hiltner, *The Christian Shepherd—Some Aspects of Pastoral Care. The Christian Century* 76 (Oct. 14, 1959):1187.

J. MacMurray, *The Self as Agent. Journal of Philosophy* 56 (1959): 419-424.

1960

C. A. Campbell, *On Self-hood and Godhood. Journal of Philosophy* 57 (March 17, 1960):188-195.

Phillip Hallie, *Maine de Biran, Reformer of Empiricism. Philosophical Forum* 17 (1959-60):71-72.

A. W. Burks, ed., *Collected Papers of Charles Sanders Peirce*, vols. 7 and 8. *The Philosophical Forum* 17 (1959-60):86-87.

1962

K. Burke, *The Rhetoric of Religion: Studies in Logology. Christian Century* 79 (Feb. 21, 1962):232-233.

J. MacMurray, *Persons in Relation. Journal of Philosophy* 59 (1962): 785-792.

1963

John Edwin Smith, *Reason and God: Encounters of Philosophy and Religion. Christian Century* 80 (Jan. 9, 1963):50.

Harry and Bonaro Overstreet, *The Iron Curtain.* (Appeared in several current magazines in June, 1963.)

E. Mounier, *Be Not Afraid. The Christian Century* 80 (August 21, 1963):1031-1032.

1964

R. Menninger with M. Mayman and P. Pruyser, *The Vital Balance: The Life Process in Mental Health and Illness. Christian Century* 81 (March 18, 1964):367-368.

R. Zavalloni, *Self-Determination: The Psychology of Personal Freedom.* (Translation of *La Liberta Personale*, Virgilio Biasiol and Carroll Tageson). *Contemporary Psychology* 9 (April 1964):166, 168.

M. Heidegger, *Being and Time. Interpretation* 18 (July 1964):369-372.

1965

Paul Weiss, *The God We Seek. Philosophical Forum* 22 (May 1965): 91-94.

Abraham Maslow, *Religions, Values, and Peak Experiences. Contemporary Psychology* 10 (Oct. 1965):449-451.

1966

P. F. D'Arcy and E. C. Kennedy, *The Genius of the Apostolate: Personal Growth in the Candidate, the Seminarian and the Priest. Contemporary Psychology* 11 (June 1966):316.

W. W. Meissner, S. J., *Group Dynamics in the Religious Life. Contemporary Psychology* 11 (June 1966):316.

1967

Jesse A. Mann and Gerald F. Kreyche, general editors, *Reflections on Man: Readings in Philosophical Psychology from Classical Philosophy to Existentialism*. *Contemporary Psychology* 12 (April 1967):234.

1968

"Values at Stake." Review of *The Sexual Wilderness: The Contemporary Upheaval in Male-Female Relationships,* by Vance Packard. *The Boston Globe,* Fall Book Review Supplement, Sept. 22, 1968, p. 3.

C. Winckelemans de Clety, *The World of Persons. Religious Studies* 4 (Oct. 1968):165-167.

Frederick J. Streng, *Emptiness: A Study in Religious Meaning. Religious Studies* 4 (Oct. 1968):168-169.

Frederick Olafson, *Principles and Persons: An Ethical Interpretation of Existentialism. Philosophy* 44 (Jan. 1969):79-80.

Ralph Harper, *Human Love: Existential and Mystical. Philosophy* 44 (April 1969):167-168.

Rupert E. Davies, ed., *We Believe in God. Religious Studies* 4 (April 1969):292-294.

Abraham Amsel, *Judiasm and Psychology. Contemporary Psychology* 14 (Nov. 1969):612.

"Challenge to 'Matter of Fact' Thinking." Review of William A. Sadler Jr., *Existence and Love: A New Approach in Existential Phenomenology. The Boston Globe,* Christmas Book Review Section, Sunday, Dec. 7, 1969, p. 2.

1970

Joseph Havens, ed., *Psychology of Religion—A Contemporary Dialogue. Contemporary Psychology* 15 (Feb. 1970):104, 106.

E. Mansell Pattison, ed., *Clinical Psychiatry and Religion. Contemporary Psychology* 15 (Feb. 1970):157.

Thomas A. Langford, *In Search of Foundations: English Theology, 1900-1920. Interpretation* 24 (Oct. 1970):533-534.

Giorgio Zunini, *Man and His Religion: Aspects of Religious Psychology. Contemporary Psychology* 15 (Dec. 1970):806.

1971

Peter Homans, *Theology after Freud: An Interpretive Inquiry. Contemporary Psychology* 16 (March 1971):184.

T. M. Robinson, *Plato's Psychology. Contemporary Psychology* 16 (May 1971):332.

Terrance Penelhum, *Survival and Disembodied Existence. Contemporary Psychology* 16 (June 1971):411.

Paul Besanceney, *Interfaith Marriages: Who and Why. Contemporary Psychology* 16 (Nov. 1971):737.

William Bier, ed., *Conscience: Its Freedom and Limitations* (The Pastoral Psychology Series, No. 6). *Contemporary Psychology* 16 (Nov. 1971):738.

John A. Hammes, *Humanistic Psychology: A Christian Interpretation. Contemporary Psychology* 16 (Nov. 1971):739-740.

John N. Kotre, *The View from the Border: A Social-Psychological Study of Current Catholicism. Contemporary Psychology* 16 (Nov. 1971):740.

1972

C. M. Beck, B. S. Crittenden, and E. V. Sullivan, eds., *Moral Education: Interdisciplinary Approaches. Contemporary Psychology* 17 (Oct. 1972):561.

Robert H. Thouless, *An Introduction to the Psychology of Religion. Contemporary Psychology* 17 (Oct. 1972):563-564.

J. Preston Cole, *The Problematic Self in Kierkegaard and Freud. Contemporary Psychology* 17 (June 1972):357-358.

1973

"On Human Sexuality." Review of *The Goals of Human Sexuality,* by Irving Singer. *The Boston Globe,* Books Section, Sunday, May 6, 1973, p. 81.

Ernest Becker, *The Birth and Death of Meaning: An Interdisciplinary Perspective on the Problem of Man. Contemporary Psychology* 18 (June 1973):296.

R. Van Over, *Unfinished Man. Contemporary Psychology* 18 (July 1973):348-349.

S. M. A. Malik, *The Conquest of Cosmophobia. Contemporary Psychology* 18 (1973):393.

A. Rodin, ed., *Death and Presence: The Psychology of Death and the After-Life. Contemporary Psychology* 18 (Aug. 1973):394.

Philip M. Helfaer, *The Psychology of Religious Doubt. Contemporary Psychology* 18 (Dec. 1973):680-681.

1974

Fred Richards and Anne Cohen Richards, *Homonovus: The New Man. Contemporary Psychology* 19 (Jan. 1974):58.

L. B. Brown, *Psychology and Religion. Contemporary Psychology* 19 (April 1974):332.

BIBLIOGRAPHER'S ACKNOWLEDGMENT

The encouragement and helpfulness of Dr. Alan M. Cohn of Morris Library, Southern Illinois University, is greatly appreciated. He is a master sleuth in bibliographic research and without his assistance many entries would have been incomplete.

John Howie
May 1, 1974

Index

★ *OF RELATED INTEREST* ★

STUDIES IN PERSONALISM:
Selected Writings of Edgar Sheffield Brightman
ROBERT N. BECK and *WARREN E. STEINKRAUS*, Editors
ISBN: 0-89007-010-5

★ *Additional titles from the "GOD SERIES"* ★

SPIRITUAL PRACTICES:
Memorial Edition with Reminiscences by His Friends
By *SWAMI AKHILANANDA*
ISBN: 0-89007-001-6

HINDU VIEW OF CHRIST
By *SWAMI AKHILANANDA*
INTRODUCTION by *WALTER G. MUELDER*
ISBN: 0-89007-009-1

GOD OF ALL:
Sri Ramakrishna's Approach to Religious Plurality
By *CLAUDE ALAN STARK*
ISBN: 0-89007-000-8

GOD IN AFRICA:
Conceptions of God in African Traditional Religion and Christianity
By *MALCOLM J. McVEIGH*
ISBN: 0-89007-003-2

GOD AS MOTHER:
A Feminine Theology in India
By *CHEEVER MACKENZIE BROWN*
FOREWORD by *DANIEL H. H. INGALLS*
ISBN: 0-89007-004-0

THE PROPHET'S DIPLOMACY:
The Art of Negotiation as Conceived and Developed
by the Prophet of Islam
By *AFZAL IQBAL*
ISBN: 0-89007-006-7

THE CUP OF JAMSHID:
A Collection of Original Ghazal Poetry Translated from the Urdu
by the Author. Contains "An Introduction to Ghazal,"
Notes and Glossary
By *MUHAMMAD DAUD RAHBAR*
ISBN: 0-89007-002-4

BEAUTY UNKNOWN:
Twenty-Seven Psychic Drawings of Spirit Beings with Their
Messages for Our Planet
Through *DAPHNE & NELSON*
ISBN: 0-89007-007-5

CLAUDE STARK & CO.
PUBLISHERS, BOX 431, WEST DENNIS
CAPE COD, MASSACHUSETTS 02670 U.S.A.